THE MARKET ECONOMY AND CHRISTIAN ETHICS

Peter Sedgwick explores the relation of a theology of justice to that of human identity in the context of the market economy, and engages with critics of capitalism and the market. He examines three aspects of the market economy: firstly, how does it shape personal identity, through consumption and the experience of paid employment in relation to the work ethic? Secondly, what impact does the global economy have on local cultures? Finally, as manufacturing changes out of all recognition through the impact of technology and global competition, what is the effect in terms of poverty? Drawing on the response of the Catholic Church, both in the United States and in papal encyclicals, to the market economy from 1985 to 1991, Sedgwick argues that its involvement deserves to be better known. Moreover, he recommends that the churches remain part of the debate in reforming and humanising the market economy.

PETER H. SEDGWICK is Assistant Secretary, Board for Social Responsibility of the Church of England. He was formerly lecturer in theology at Hull and Birmingham Universities and was a Member of the Church of England's Industrial Committee from 1985 to 1996. Revd Dr Peter Sedgwick is the author of *The Enterprise Culture* (SPCK, 1992) and co-editor of *The Weight of Glory* (T. & T. Clark, 1991).

NEW STUDIES IN CHRISTIAN ETHICS

General editor
Robin Gill

Editorial board
Stephen R. L. Clark, Stanley Hauerwas and Robin W. Lovin

Christian ethics has increasingly assumed a central place within academic theology. At the same time the growing power and ambiguity of modern science and the rising dissatisfaction within the social sciences about claims to value-neutrality have prompted renewed interest in ethics within the secular academic world. There is, therefore, a need for studies in Christian ethics which, as well as being concerned with the relevance of Christian ethics to the present-day secular debate, are well informed about parallel discussions in recent philosophy, science or social science. New Studies in Christian Ethics aims to provide books that do this at the highest intellectual level and demonstrate that Christian ethics can make a distinctive contribution to this debate – either in moral substance or in terms of underlying moral justifications.

Other titles published in the series

THE MARKET ECONOMY
AND CHRISTIAN ETHICS

PETER H. SEDGWICK

CAMBRIDGE
UNIVERSITY PRESS

PUBLISHED BY THE PRESS SYNDICATE OF THE UNIVERSITY OF CAMBRIDGE
The Pitt Building, Trumpington Street, Cambridge, United Kingdom

CAMBRIDGE UNIVERSITY PRESS
The Edinburgh Building, Cambridge, CB2 2RU, UK http://www.cup.cam.ac.uk
40 West 20th Street, New York, NY 10011–11, USA http://www.cup.org
10 Stamford Road, Oakleigh, Melbourne 3166, Australia

© Cambridge University Press 1999

First published 1999

Printed in the United Kingdom at the University Press, Cambridge

Typeset in 10/12 ½pt Baskerville [CE]

A catalogue record for this book is available from the British Library

Library of Congress cataloguing in publication data

Sedgwick, P. H. (Peter Humphrey), 1948–
The Market Economy and Christian Ethics / Peter H. Sedgwick.
p. cm. (New Studies in Christian Ethics)
Includes bibliographical references.
ISBN 0 521 47048 x (hardback)
1. Capitalism – Religious aspects – Christianity. 2. Capitalism – Moral and ethical
aspects. 3. Christian ethics – Anglican authors.
I. Title. II. Series.
BR115.C3S43 1999
261.8'5 – dc21 98–53577 CIP

ISBN 0 521 47048 x hardback

Contents

General editor's preface

This book is the fourteenth in the series New Studies in Christian Ethics. Like Michael Northcott's book in the series, *The Environment and Christian Ethics*, the book is concerned with one of the macro issues facing the new millennium, namely the now dominant world culture of the market economy. Again, like other books in the series, a central concern here is to engage centrally with the secular moral debate at the highest possible intellectual level and, secondly, to demonstrate that Christian ethics can make a distinctive contribution to this debate, either in moral substance or in terms of underlying moral justifications.

Peter Sedgwick is unusually well placed to offer a critical, theological guide to the culture of the market economy. His role within the Church of England's Board for Social Responsibility, along with his previous work as a lecturer at Birmingham and Hull Universities, has given him an exceptionally wide range of contacts and resources in social economics. He has combined sustained scholarship and teaching in Christian ethics with the practical work of the Board. In the process, he has been an important contributor to theological studies following the Church of England report *Faith in the City*, a key contributor to the more recent report *Unemployment and the Future of Work*, and the author of the well-received book *The Enterprise Culture* (1992).

His focus here is upon the cultural and ethical implications of market economics in the modern world. He is particularly concerned with the way personal identity is shaped today by consumerism, by fast-changing patterns of work, and by the powerful forces of globalization. Especially after the collapse of

Communism, market economics has become a dominant force
in the world. Many theologians tend to regard it with enormous
suspicion and often denounce it as inherently opposed to
Christian ethics. They remain deeply critical of the effects of
market economics in the modern world – effects such as
insatiable greed and consumerism, personal and international
debt, and an ever-widening gap between rich and poor individuals and nations. For them, Christian faith offers a sharply
opposing vision. Peter Sedgwick is certainly sensitive to this
viewpoint, but he argues here that theologians are in danger of
claiming too much. He points out that theologians, like others
in the modern world, enjoy the benefits of the market world
even while they denounce its egregious effects. For him, Christian faith does not offer a complete alternative to secular
economics, although it can and should alert us to some of its
moral weaknesses.

Peter Sedgwick argues at length that Christian ethics can
offer a renewed sense of vocation and service even within the
market world. Work and leisure, within this world, can properly
be understood in theological terms as creation and recreation.
Well aware of the dangers of market economics, he is also
concerned that we should notice and then transform its benefits. I hope that others will learn from his careful argument as
much as I have myself.

ROBIN GILL

Acknowledgements

This book has been a long time in writing. It was begun in 1991, when the collapse of the Soviet Union and the Social Justice Commission set up by the late John Smith MP made talk of a 'middle way' between socialism and capitalism seem a possible option after the demise of state socialism. It seems a very different world at the end of the decade. Two groups have been a source of inspiration and encouragement during this period, when it seemed as if this book would never be finished. One has been the Industrial Mission Association. In particular, my many conversations with Revd Dr Peter Stubley have been both a source of insight and an encouragement to persevere. His teaching at Hull University on the MA course Theological Understanding of Industrial Society, which I ran for six years, remains fresh in my memory. Other fruitful conversations were with Revd Chris Percy and Revd Dave Rogers at Hull, Revd Chris Beales in Newcastle, Canon Mostyn Davies in Peterborough and the Essex Industrial Chaplains team. The other source of much good debate, sometimes vigorous but always helpful, was the membership of the Industrial Committee of the Church of England Board for Social Responsibility. Canon Dr John Atherton read through a first draft, and Mr Andrew Britton gave freely of his time as an economist. When I joined the staff of the Board for Social Responsibility, I worked alongside Revd Andrew Davey, Mrs Ruth Badger and Mr David Skidmore, finding their work in related fields illuminating and very supportive. Two trips to the German Evangelical Church in Hanover and an ecumenical dialogue in Brussels (especially the conversation with Tilman Winkler) showed how other churches were wrestling with the same issues. Dr Margie Tolstoy was an excellent colleague on these trips. Finally, Revd Peter Skov-Jacobsen in Copenhagen discussed with me the issue of social identity and the market. His insights were very helpful.

Others have also given generously of their help. Dr Al McFadyen and Professor Dan Hardy discussed early drafts, and their perceptive comments enabled me to see the centrality of the question of human identity. The sabbatical at the Center for Theological Inquiry, Princeton, enabled a first draft to be written in 1991. I am grateful for much hospitality, and the encouragement of Dan Hardy, the Director. Dr Nick Adams guided me through the intricacies of Jürgen Habermas. Revd Patrick Cotton debated the question of education in a market-driven culture. Revd Colin Hart invited me to try out my ideas in chapter 1 at Nottingham Theological Society and I am grateful for this. Other conversations with Revd Ken Leech, Dr Alan Suggate, Professor Richard Roberts and Revd Malcolm Brown helped me see how a theology of the market might develop. I spent a fascinating afternoon with The Very Revd Peter Baelz on the thought of Philip Oppenheimer discussed in chapter 2. There are three debts which I should especially mention. One is to the Board for Social Responsibility and the Central Board of Finance, for study-leave to finish this project. Secondly I would like to thank my secretary Mrs Barbara Johnson for her patience in deciphering my hand-writing over several years and Mrs Debbie Cunnigham, Mrs Margaret Rees and Mrs Ana King for typing the text against the odds. Thirdly, there is the gratitude of love. The encouragement of my parents, and of my wife Revd Jan Gould, has been more than simply an enabling presence. They have believed in this project when I have not, and it is as much due to them as to anyone that this book has been finished. How can you express that sort of gratitude?

Introduction

In this introduction, the central thesis of the book is laid out. This is that the market world has created the modern society in which our lives are lived, whether as citizens of a European democracy or of an Asian, newly emerging nation. The focus in this book is overwhelmingly on Europe, and it explores the relation of a theology of justice to that of human identity in this market world. It is not, therefore, a work of business ethics, nor one simply of Christian social ethics in its ultimate questioning. It is shaped by the tradition of Anglican social ethics in England, within which I write and continue to work: the tradition of Hooker, Coleridge, Lux Mundi, Temple, Preston and Atherton. The concern of the book, however, is with human nature and the question of justice, or, as it is called by theologians, theological anthropology and ethics. The paradox is simple to state, but difficult to resolve. As our society becomes more industrialized, market driven and pluralist, human identity becomes more problematic. The resolution of human identity is made, for those who have the freedom to choose, through their self-expression in employment, consumption and the human relations which sustain them. Less and less is it made through religious faith, or the implications which flow from that faith, such as the Protestant Work Ethic. However, it is not clear that paid employment, or consumption, can provide the satisfactory definition of that identity which is sought. Ironically, the very restlessness of employment and consumption is the reason why such activity is both so attractive and so illusory at the same time. Equally, the ethical standards which should govern such employment, or consumption, become unclear.

I

This book is not an attack on the overindulgent world of the conspicuous consumer, nor a description of the inherently alienating world of modern capitalism. Both these descriptions may be true, and indeed the prophetic Christian voice may well contrast the world of religious faith, waiting for the coming of its Lord, with the frenetic activity of shopping at Christmas: it is a familiar, and justified, theme of the Christian preacher across the years. Nevertheless, such a move would set the theologian over-against the question of human identity as it is posed at the end of the twentieth century.

The argument begins with the work of Jürgen Habermas, who has set out with impressive clarity two facets of modernity. One is the increasing dominance of an instrumental way of thinking, which is a type of rationality which excludes social values and the nature of justice. The second facet is the pervasive interplay of capitalism in economic life, and bureaucracy in social life, which together dominate contemporary culture with their pattern of thought (rationality) and values. In a phrase which will be explained later, there is a 'colonization of the lifeworld' all the more powerful because it is often taken for granted. In this world, discussion of social value, or the understanding of human flourishing, becomes difficult and even problematic. It is the great merit of Habermas' thought that he has laid out his argument with such force that it becomes a way into the question of human identity and social justice and the market world. Nevertheless, Habermas is not the answer to the discussion of modernity and late capitalism for the theologian. There are a series of assumptions which he makes about the nature of language, tradition, society and moral value which set him outside the Christian tradition, as much as his enduring refusal to admit the reality of religious language as having any validity. Habermas, therefore, both illustrates the conceptual argument which a Christian theologian must address ('what does it mean to speak of human identity and justice in a world dominated by this colonization of our culture by the power of capitalism and bureaucracy?') and yet leaves a set of issues for further argument.

The book is not confined to the question of the theological

interest of the analysis posed by Habermas. Instead, a series of four chapters explores different aspects of the resolution of human identity and the nature of distributive justice. There are two chapters, following the initial one on Habermas, on consumption and work. It is here that the central issues of human identity and justice are considered, as the demise of the Protestant Work Ethic is described. In part, the argument is historical, so that the place of aesthetics and the Romantic Movement can be shown in the transformation of a work ethic into an ethic of consumption. This is the predominant thesis of the book, and it encompasses the views of T. Veblen at the start of the twentieth century on conspicuous consumption. It is still the case, however, that paid employment (colloquially, if inaccurately, called work) provides a great source of meaning and self-identity, even if it no longer stands within the framework of the Protestant Work Ethic. In particular, the studies of Robert Lane, the American social psychologist, in his book *The Market Experience*, show how persuasive the nature of paid employment still is to human identity. Whether this employment is sufficient, what its relationship is to human society and the wider set of social bonds which constitute our identity, and whether such activity at work renders a transcendent relationship irrelevant are all questions which must be explored.

The nature of paid employment, and of consumption, is set within the framework of the global market-place. Again this has an impact on human identity, both from the dimension of the market and from the scope of globalization. Nicholas Boyle's recent study of western European culture and globalization is aptly called *Who are we Now?* In part, the question of the market is a question of social justice, and this has been well discussed by many theologians in the social ethics tradition within which I write. In recent years, David Jenkins, Ronald Preston, John Atherton and (from the Scottish Reformed tradition) Duncan Forrester have all probed the justice of the market. Indeed, as market relationships spread further and further in the last decade of the twentieth century into education, welfare, penal policy and health care, there seemed no end to the remit of the market. This gives us our clue, for the question then becomes not simply whether the market is just, but how it frames the question of human identity. Can there be a 'theory of public co-operation'? This is the sub-heading of an important study by Jonathan Boswell entitled *Community and the Economy*. Given that human identity must be related to the nature of community, what form of community is possible in a market system?

Equally, the question of globalization raises acute questions of the rootedness of human identity under the advancing power of global capitalism. Both Boyle and John Gray, in his recent brilliant polemic against globalization *False Dawn*, believe that the western European tradition of social democracy and culture will be swept away by the tide of globalization. In a related, but different, perspective, the English Anglican bishop and theologian Peter Selby argues that only a theology of Christ's universal sovereignty over all that enslaves us will enable us to resist the ever-growing power of financial debt, both domestically and globally. Here issues of justice press hard.

Consumption, paid employment, the relationships of trading in the market and the global economy are the four elements which define human identity today in the market world. Two relate to what we do (consuming and working), while the latter pair place this activity in the context of the global market. These four chapters take up the conceptual questions posed by Habermas in the opening chapter and examine them in a multifaceted way, partly historical, sociological, economic and, of course, theological. Through all of this the nature of human identity, as consumer, worker and global citizen, is subject to scrutiny. In brief, the question is 'who are we now?'

This leaves open what the response of the Christian churches might be, in terms of justice and human identity. As much of my recent employment has been within the churches, as they seek to respond to social change and to discern some patterns in the often frequently bewildering pattern of events, it is only natural that the final chapter should examine the adequacy of contemporary church documents on the issues of work, unemployment, consumption and the global market. In a sense, this final chapter mirrors the opening one in which Habermas' thought was set out so that the conceptual issue could become clear. The opening and concluding chapters frame the four chapters as they discuss consumption and employment in a global market. (This framework is in part inspired by the unpublished Ph.D. written a decade ago by Philip West on Habermas and a theology of work, although the argument and conclusions are developed in a very different way.) Once again, it is not simply the nature of social justice which is important in the examination of Roman Catholic, Anglican and German Lutheran thought. It is the possibility of a viable set of social relationships, which can both nourish human identity and yet recognize the reality of holding together a market economy and a theory of justice that is at issue. This task has not proved easy for the churches, and the temptation to fall into theological rhetoric or detailed policy options is very apparent. Nevertheless, it is also the case that the last few years have seen the beginning of an understanding of what it means to be a human being, both worker and consumer, at the end of the twentieth century. The implications of this understanding, of course, go into the fields both of social justice and of mission. Nothing shows this more clearly than the writings of the Industrial Mission in England at its beginning in the 1940s when compared with its self-description now. The task of relating the Christian faith to the world of the shopping-mall, and the hi-tech industrial and service sector, within the constraints of a global market-driven culture, is one that can only be begun in this book. It overlaps very clearly with work on gender and sexuality in this same series, and with our attitude to the environment which encompasses all our actions. It is, however, a discrete area, and one in which there have been continual shifts in social awareness since this book was begun at the beginning of this decade. It would require a much more detailed study to trace the ramifications of a study of human identity for business ethics and the regulation of the global market. Equally, the churches will continue their dialogue with government and economic institutions on the public-policy implications of their Christian faith at the end of this century. I am encouraged that this work is being undertaken by many colleagues, as the social and economic forces which shape our lives change ever more fundamentally. This study stands back from that debate and seeks to discern the outline of human personhood in our contemporary society, which is the often dimly discerned reality shaped by the forces of the market for good or ill. Whether there can be a resolution of the question of human identity, as it is expressed in the global market, in terms of the Christian faith is perhaps the most difficult question of all. It is clear that for many theologians – Düchrow, Gorringe, and, I suspect, Selby – the choice is either/or. While we have no choice about living in this market world, it is for them a dehumanizing world which takes away the choice of the poor so that they have doubly no choice: no choice but to live in it, and no choice but to be oppressed by it. Even for the rest of us, global capitalism is often seen as an idol to be resisted by the power of the Gospel. I leave the resolution of this dichotomy between human identity in the global market-place and Christian faith to the end of the argument. It is a question to be worked through stage by stage, neither denying the fundamental injustices in the market nor reducing the entire argument into a consideration of this point. Justice certainly demands a reformulation of the global market, but (as Raymond Plant argued a few years ago in his Gore Memorial Lecture) the churches cannot simply walk away from the market because it is unjust. If they proclaim their own theory of human nature, in narrative form, then one must ask how this relates to others who participate in political discourse and the market.

Holding together questions of justice and human identity is never easy. The reason for doing so is that it is, it seems to me, too simple to criticize the market in terms of justice without seeing how human beings are themselves shaped by those forces of work and consumption, and find their identity by participating in those activities. It is not as though there is a neutral standpoint from which to stand in our critique of the market: we are shaped by the forces which we criticize. Duncan Forrester, in his recent book, has explored in a very helpful way the manner in which theories of justice have become fragmented and only provide glimpses of a whole truth. In a similar, but more descriptive and historical, way, I would point to the way in which we work, shop and consume as part of the enormous fragmentation of human identity in the late twentieth century. Like Forrester, I believe that we must seek to fashion an identity, however fragmented, which is demonstrably Christian out of the experience of contemporary life, so that a theory of justice which holds up the flourishing of human identity under God may be still possible.

This leads, in conclusion, to some reflections on theological method. There can be a tendency to exalt this to too great a preoccupation of theologians: John Atherton's criticism of *Putting Theology to Work* in his review in *Crucible* makes exactly this charge. Nevertheless, while recognizing this point, it is important to be clear about the theological method which has been adopted. The book begins, as said above, with the philosophical analysis offered by Habermas, but this is then subjected to a theological critique from Bonhoeffer and Hardy. Similarly, in the chapters on consumption and work, the method employed is to trace the development of contemporary reflection through both the historical evolution of intellectual ideas and the analysis of social psychology. The chapter on consumption follows more of a historical approach, while that on work is primarily based on social psychology. In each case, the work of contemporary theologians is then correlated with this analysis, but it is not the intention that a theological statement should serve as a theological 'transformation' of the initial presentation. This is the position taken by M. Douglas Meeks, who, in his fascinating book *God the Economist*, in some ways approximates to this study. In both, there is a study of the market, work and consumption, although Meeks has also an extensive and very interesting section on property, while mine concentrates more on global capitalism. (Perhaps this merely reflects the fact that Meeks published his book in 1989, a decade ago, before talk of globalization was commonplace.) In both, there is a concern for social justice and a theological account of work, consumption and the market – in other words, of the economy. However, Meeks develops his theology out of a fully developed Trinitarian and biblical account of the nature of the Christian God and of the early Christian community.

Therefore, it is part of his intention that a Trinitarian theology (largely developed from Jürgen Moltmann) and a sociology of the New Testament should deepen the challenge of the Christian tradition to modern economic thought, the structure of the western economy and the pattern of daily living in ways that are inspired by, but, ultimately, go beyond, Latin American liberation theology. They go further than this liberation theology in three respects. First, there is a highly articulated doctrine of the Trinity which sees the divine 'economy' as not only liberator but creator and sustainer. Secondly, the exposition of scripture is indebted to much work in the 1980s and 1990s on the sociology of the New Testament. This avoids the rather crude literalism of some biblical work in liberation theology, although more recently this has begun to change. Thirdly, and most importantly, Meeks is concerned to discover how the entire western political economy fits together and is legitimated in its dimensions of property, work and consumption. This is far more sophisticated an attempt than a straightforward analysis of economic, social and political oppression. Since Meeks is interested in a critique of the legitimation of the economy, economic thought and daily life, he therefore offers a brief, but very suggestive, sketch of the meaning of property, work and consumption.

In so far as Meeks is concerned, in the meaning of each of these dimensions of the economy there is a helpful correlation of social ethics, concerned with theories of justice, and Christian anthropology, or sociology, concerned with the nature of personal identity and society. This goes in a different direction from the writing of Ronald Preston and John Atherton, which is primarily concerned with the proper ordering of economic life. Preston's careful analysis of Christian social thought in the last two centuries, and indeed of earlier periods as well, has enabled him to present an unparalleled account of the modern economy. As a trained economist, as well as a theologian, Preston has presented a sustained description of the tasks which a Christian critique of the contemporary economy must accomplish. This rich combination of past theological ethics, contemporary economic thought with economic activity and

current Christian reflection on society has made Preston un-
iquely equipped to analyse and expound Christian social
thought. John Atherton has built on the work of Preston (he was
taught by Preston) in describing how the development of the
contemporary global economy goes beyond some of Preston's
careful, and cautious, acceptance of the market system. Neither
theologian is primarily concerned with the meaning of work,
consumption or the market: they take them as they are, and
correlate the best secular analysis of them with the Christian
tradition following the method of middle axioms. This allows
their work to be inductive, arguing from contemporary experience and social realities, while arriving at a clear set of principles for a Christian social ethic in the economy. J. Philip
Wogaman, an American Methodist, has followed a similar path
in the United States. It is also the usual pattern of working of
the Board for Social Responsibility of the Church of England,
as well as other Protestant denominations in England, such as
the Methodist and United Reformed Churches, and the (now
defunct) British Council of Churches.

My own method combines elements of Meeks with those of
Preston/Atherton. The historical analysis of why consumption matters so much in modern western society; the
meaning of work; how human identity is fashioned in the
global economy – all this serves to create a theological
account of the human being as consumer, worker and participant in modern society. To this extent, I am sympathetic to
Meeks, and those who have written like him, such as Volf or
Biggar – all from the Protestant Reformed stable. Equally, I
would want to hold together an account of social justice with
a theology of society, finding the justification for a theological
ethics in an account of why theologically things may be said
to be the way they are. This leads into a social ethics which
is more in dialogue with systematic theology than Preston is:
I would be far more cautious in giving his criticisms of
Trinitarian thought in relation to social ethics. However, the
failure of Meeks appears to be that he refuses to accept the
genuine dialogue of secular reality with theological thought.
At several points, Atherton applies the term 'pre-modern' not

so much to Meeks' own thought, but to the theological ethics which he prefers. I find this criticism compelling. Atherton writes of

the perennial temptation for theologians to return to pre-modern understandings, and the confusion it generates over the relationship between economics and market economies. So when Meeks promotes the superiority of a household economy over contemporary market systems . . . then we are faced with failures to understand contexts and changes.[1]

There are two further implications of this critique. One is that the nature of social ethics must always recognize the complexity and interwoven nature (indeed, the *oikonemia*) of contemporary economies. Forming ethical judgements must be a patient task, which cannot simply deduce principles from the Christian tradition. Here, the strength of the Preston/Atherton/Board for Social Responsibility tradition has been proved in many reports. Indeed, theologians like Duncan Forrester in Scotland show that this approach, while rejecting middle axioms, can also be correlated with the Reformed tradition, as several reports from the Church of Scotland argue very well. The end result is an approach which may not adopt detailed policy changes (although the *Unemployment* report of the British Churches did this in 1997), but does seek to produce concrete changes in economic behaviour. So this book will also wish to look for different strategies which could be adopted on work, consumption and the market.

The final difference from Meeks is that the theological style is far more inductive, where the nature of a Christian understanding of the human agent as worker or consumer emerges out of dialogue with secular, and contemporary, thought. Biblical material is certainly important, but there is no attempt to narrate a biblical '*meta-narrative*' over against secular thought. The reason for this is well put by Raymond Plant, who is an English political philosopher, Labour peer and an Anglican. He argued in the Gore lecture in Westminster Abbey (analysed in depth in the chapter on the market) that there were profound problems of social engagement with the evangelical, counter-cultural approach. There are also problems of revelation and the contemporary expression of Christianity. Plant made his point forcefully:

My worry about this latter (Hauerwas/evangelical) approach is that it is frankly disingenuous. It urges the Church to be the church to live and witness by its own doctrines and that of course is admirable, but equally it does not want to engage in that kind of democratic collaboration with other bodies which will help to secure the kind of democratic society with the protection of the rights of individuals and groups which has to be in place for the Church to be free to witness to its own truth. This approach trades on the fact of a common good of liberal democracy which secures a rightful role for the church without being prepared to engage with others in the constant task of justifying the moral claims of democracy, social justice, virtue based liberty and restrictions of the claimed morally free zone of the market which seems central to the churches own possibility of witness.[2]

The issue of revelation turns on how the Christian faith is seen to relate to its biblical expression and the nature of tradition. It is the question of isomorphism. If, in a theory of language, words, thoughts and things match each other in a parallel one-to-one way, and therefore isomorphically, then the correlation between verbal signs, mental concepts and objects is a stable one: there are self-same meanings, flourishing in a subsistent medium.

What was experienced, and the language in which it was expressed, were well-matched.[3]

Implicit in such a view was the belief that both what was perceived, and the language used, are placed in a state of universal conditions which ultimately depended on God. Such awareness of universality died in the nineteenth century, where science, history and culture all celebrated the constant process of change, and the inability in any simple way to find 'their grounds in God'. One response by theologians is to claim that religious faith is exempt from such a development. God's activity establishes in the knower by the Trinitarian activity of revelation a 'time-neutral, unitary method – which provides isomorphism of words/symbols and states of affairs in the world'.[4] Another alternative is to accept that there can be an involvement of God in history which accepts the reality of change, development and contemporary experience which is different from the past. So, while the biblical account of God's nature and activity remains paradigmatic for any Christian account of truth, there are different ways of referring to the activity of God. One way moves to symbols and models, with an overall philosophy of history or cosmology, thus jettisoning the Trinitarian language about God. A different approach sees language and experience as deriving from an attention to reality, which means that both experience and language can move beyond the cultural forms and expressions of any one period.

For this reason, there can be a continuity and universality in history and its language which can be revalidated by present experience . . . Those who find this continuity find in it a true language which meets present-day experience and gives it the form which it needs. This is, they find, a living tradition in which one lives from and with God, much like a memory from which one derives an identity.[5]

Within this tradition, key events can be narrated, and lived out, so that there can be an 'economy' of history. The task of theology is to establish how that economy works 'in terms of the agency of God and human beings.' It is not as simple as finding a pattern of events in human history, grounding it in God's action and being, and seeing it in terms of divine revelation. Such a view sees language as merely instrumental: find out what is going on in society or in science, believe in God, and express this going on in religious language.

Instead, his identity and creative and redemptive activity occur through his participation in our language and culture. And God actively confers himself in establishing and reestablishing our language and truth as we communicate with each other. The result is the possibility of a richer and more dynamic language and truth from God and amongst us than traditonal theories of isomorphic language . . . can allow.[6]

Such an understanding of revelation will see the theological appreciation of history, events, situations and persons as redemptive. It discerns how they are, what prevents them from being more fully themselves, and attempts to see how they might fulfil their potential. Theology only engages in this task with other disciplines, and seeks to find the presence of God within culture and language itself. The crucial point, to which this book will return continuously, is how human beings are related one to another, and how social groups cohere. Within the nature of those relationships, theology claims to discern glimpses of the presence of God, but, as the relationships changes from person to person, and group to group, something of the dynamic of God's redemptive love is shown most fully. Four aspects of particular relationships, which all interconnect, are studied here: work, consumption, the market and globalization. Two issues run persistently through these relationships, which are the nature of our identity and that of justice. What is just work, and what identity is found in vocation? What identity is conferred in the act of consumption, and how can consumption be regulated in terms of debt and fair transactions (the issue of commutative justice)? Can there be a community which is the basis of human identity within a market society, and, again, how should the market be regulated? Lastly, how can local and global identities coexist in a global market without uniform homogeneity squashing local differences in culture, and how are the rights of the poor preserved and vindicated?

'The constant task of justifying the moral claims of . . . social justice' is a splendid way of describing the collaborative task of the church, and its language of theology, in the fragmented and pluralist global market which our life on earth has now been transformed into. This collaboration takes place with secular bodies and secular disciplines, and there can be no other way of acting. Nevertheless ,in and through this collaboration, theology seeks to discern the presence of God in dynamic and liberating ways which are faithful to his being and action shown in revelation, yet also recognize the complexity and ever-deepening nature of that action which sustains all life in relationship and being. That is so even of the world of the market economy.

CHAPTER I

Modernity, the market and human identity

The question of human identity as being at the heart of modernity is one posed a century ago by Max Weber. Weber studied the Protestant Work Ethic as the fundamental force which shaped large portions of European civilization, and eventually spread world-wide through the expansion of European imperial power. Out of this power came the identity of the European industrial worker, who creates the self-alienating world of modern consciousness. This is a seamless argument, but we will pick it up, not chronologically, but in terms of a thematic approach, following the approach set out in the Introduction. The question of the Protestant Work Ethic, and its survival in the present day, is taken up in chapter 3, and the transformation of this ethic into an ethic of consumerism is argued historically in chapter 2. In chapter 1, a philosophical overview of the marketing identity and rationality is given. Those who would prefer to move into the substantive issues of consumerism and work can begin this study at chapter 2, ignoring the philosophical argument. Nevertheless, the philosophical grounding encapsulates the entire book.

What is important at this point is to notice how central Weber's formulation of the Protestant Work Ethic is to Jürgen Habermas, who is the pre-eminent German philosopher of social relations at the present time. This is because Habermas uses Weber's theory as a way into the question of human identity. However, Habermas believed that Weber's understanding of the growth of human identity within the market is fundamentally a mistake. Theologically it is worth beginning at this point, becuase it can be argued that the abyss in the middle of human society is that of identity. Kant's overemphasis on rationality and human choice, expressed through the good will, undermines the nature of identity. All that remains in a Kantian understanding of human identity is the correct moral choice, made in terms of rational decision-making, and implemented through human action governed by the will. Identity becomes a matter of moral choice. The nature of the person, as a being with a moral character, becomes abstracted into the moral individual who stands alongside his neighbours in a fragmented universe.

It was this challenge which drove both Max Weber, and the critics of Weber found in the Frankfurt School, into their historical account of why Kant's philosophy had come to be accepted. Weber traced the demise of magic and myth to the gradual dominance of the Protestant ethic, which then became secularized by Kant. Although Kant retained a place for religion, the effect on religious faith was to subject it to a severe form of rationalization. Weber's account of the Protestant ethic gave the first systematic account of rationalization in western culture. In turn, Weber's own views were themselves criticized at length by the Frankfurt School of sociology in the inter-war years of the 1920s and 1930s, especially by Max Horkheimer and Theodor Adorno. Their pessimism about western civilization built on the work of Max Weber, arguing that the full development of capitalism was inherently alienating, and rationalized human identity out of existence.

Habermas sets out to confront this traditon of Weber and the Frankfurt School, but to offer a far more positive reading of modern civilization. In so doing, he rewrites the tradition which Weber had constructed of the origin of western rationalization, and the demise of human identity. Habermas' theory is highly complex, in its own right, and here only a few aspects will be selected. In particular Habermas confronts the issues of human identity, the fragmentation of modernity and the nature of justice. Human identity and the achievement of justice are questions which are resolved through communicative competence. Identity is given as a human being by being a person who communicates. Justice is defined as the process by which this communication is carried on. In brief, if there is no over-arching narrative, there can be good 'networking'. The import-ance of Habermas, as will be shown, is that he sets this within the most sustained discussion of capitalism and bureaucracy in contemporary philosophy.

How did Habermas rewrite the account which Weber gives of the problematic status of human identity in a rationalized world?

MODERNITY AND THE PROTESTANT WORK ETHIC

Habermas' argument that modernity is a development to be welcomed is not one which earlier theorists in the Frankfurt School would have accepted. Horkeimer and Adorno were deeply critical of modernity in *The Dialectic of Enlightenment*. Habermas believes that modernity is beneficial, but the price has been the alienation of human beings. Their consciousness becomes morally and psychologically damaged. The costs of modernization are the loss of freedom in an increasingly bureaucratized society, and the loss of meaning in a world far beyond the enchantments of the pre-modern world.

Habermas spends some time outlining why he finds Weber's view both the basis from which he starts, and ultimately unsatisfactory.[1] First, Weber relates the end of a magical or mythical world-view to the rise of the world religions (Chris-tianity, Judaism, Hinduism, Buddhism and Islam). All these religions have a coherent world view, where they explain the cosmos as a meaningful whole. The great world religions are, for Weber, the forces which brought the modern era to world civilization. Suffering can be explained, and an ethical and spiritual framework guides the individual in ways that will enable her to find (or sometimes earn) salvation in that suf-fering.[2] As this religious rationalization became accepted world-wide, in different religions forms, so the West came to organize the economy and administration in terms of purposive, formal rationality. By this is meant a planned, intentional organization of work and society on rational lines. Work no longer is a response to the demands of hunger or shelter: it is organized, and profit is consciously sought after. This social rationalization was linked to the universal rationalization of the world religions through the ascetic nature of European Protestantism. Religion becomes in Protestantism a force for disciplinary work and labour. Ascetism spread out of medieval monasticism into the organization of the whole of society on rational and methodical lines through the impact of Calvin and his Reformed theology. Capitalism begins its ascendancy.

At the same time, Weber linked the rationalization of religious beliefs and the social–economic rationalization of the sixteenth century, with a third form of rationalization. As the first two processes get underway, so the values within society and culture become rationalized. The modern world 'is composed of a number of distinct provinces of activity, each having its own inherent dignity and its own immanent norms'.[3] Each sphere has its own inner logic, with great conflict between them. Fraternity, aesthetic worth and economic efficiency are all values which are in conflict. For Weber, this leads to the loss of harmony and meaning in the modern world. There was the world of religious beliefs, which, by 1900 when Weber wrote, had become a highly secular cosmology and epistemology, thanks to Kant's philosophical impact. There was the claim of political and social cohesion, expressed at the time as fraternity or class consciousness. Finally, there was the scientific and technological revolution of the eighteenth and nineteenth centuries, resulting in very rapid industrialization.

Habermas finds much of this a necessary starting-point for his own analysis of modernity, and yet he wants to reconceptualize it. He examines the change in consciousness brought about by the rise in the world religions. Instead of emphasizing the connection between religion, moral standards and the emergence of the Protestant ethic, he examines the change in cognitive structures within religious world views. Contemplative theorizing comes from Greek cosmology in the West, and eventually creates modern experimental science. Habermas is fascinated by the revival of Aristotlean thought in medieval philosophy and theology, which created Thomism. This was then secularized by Baconian induction in England, and the growth of scientific empiricism in such scientists as Isaac Newton. This is analysed in terms of the shift from a consciousness focused on itself in a magical, or mythical, world (a 'sociocentric' consciousness) to one which has no centre. Pre-Thomist religious thought in the West was, for Habermas, immersed in a magical world of religious forces, where the universe expressed divine anger or blessing through sickness or prosperity. After the lengthy evolution of thought from Aquinas, through Bacon and Newton, to the post-Kantian secular world, Habermas finds a fragmented human identity which thinks and feels in different ways about cosmology, society, the self and the economy. The centre has disappeared. This decentred consciousness or identity does however recognize that there are sharp divisions between the natural, social and subjective worlds. Within each of these there are validity claims which differ in their arguments. The reflexive capacity of agents leads to new forms of rationalization. For each they can consider different interpretations of what is the case (the natural world), what is legitimate (the social world), and what is authentic self-expression (the subjective world). So for Habermas modernity is not simply about cultural rationalization and the emergence of the Protestant work ethic. Modernity is complex, and is more than the acquiring of formal rationality, in which one learns how to enact science and technology. It is about the multi-dimensional enhancement of learning (we will return to this with Lane's study of cognitive complexity in chapter 3). It is above all about a fragmented human identity. As Habermas says, the emphasis on science and technology has 'led to an uncritical self interpretation of the modern world that is fixated on knowing and mastering external nature'.[4]

Habermas distinguishes three different cultural value spheres, which are science and technology, morality and law, and art and literature, based on the three worlds of the natural, the social and the self. This claim would be disputed by theologians, as being too simple a division of culture, but nevertheless Habermas does attempt to understand the importance of aesthetics in understanding modernity. Hence the rise of modern science and modern art stand as significant for modernity as the Protestant Work Ethic. Even in ethics itself, the establishment of formal processes in modern law must be taken alongside the ethical preconditions of bourgeoise capitalism. It is Habermas' contention that, to understand the crisis in human identity, the fragmentation of society and the disordered forms in which one group attempts to speak to another, one must understand not just the work ethic and the decline in religious faith, but also the growth of modern art and music. So, for Habermas, the purposive rationalization of science, technology and capitalism 'is only one possible way of developing of that broader potential . . . which is made available with the culture of modernity'.[5] Modernity therefore represents an enormous unfolding of possibilities for humanity. In each situation there are alternative possibilities of what is the case, what is legitimate and what is authentic self-expression. This dissolves any concept of self-evident human flourishing (as in the American Declaration of Independence, which runs: 'We hold these truths to be self-evident') into a position which must be defended rationally through communicative rationality. By this Habermas refers to a mode of arguing which includes the other in such a way that the formal principles of Kantian ethics are broadened to include dialogue and respect for others. What it means to be a human being, with an identity which is not fragmented, is answered by an appeal to ways of arguing with one another. It is also the case that these 'specialized forms of argumentation'[6] which make up the modern world, are institutionalized as well. The threefold system of validity claims is therefore the basis for three forms of argumentation, and results in three different institutional spheres. It is worth quoting Habermas at some length here:

Along this line we find (a) the establishment of a scientific enterprise in which empirical-scientific problems can be dealt with according to internal truth standards, independently of theological doctrines and separately from basic moral-practical questions; (b) the institutionalization of an artistic enterprise in which the production of art is gradually set loose from cultic-ecclesiastical and courtly – patronal bonds, and the reception of works of art by an art-enjoying public of readers, spectators and listeners is mediated through professionalised

aesthetic criticism, and finally (c) the professional intellectual treatment of questions of ethics, political theory and jurisprudence in
schools of law, in the legal system and in the legal public sphere.[7]

Habermas therefore argues that the changes brought by
modernity go far beyond Weber's understanding of the conflict
of values in the modern world. He perceives the modern
consciousness as decentred, recognizing clear boundaries
between nature, society and self, with different forms of argument (or systems of validity claims) in each. Each of these
spheres is itself institutionalized, and in each there are alternative possibilities of arguing what might be true, in the
complexity of the meaning of that term. It is because of this
understanding of consciousness that Habermas differs from
Weber in his understanding of capitalism and market forces.
For Weber, the rationalization brought about by the world
religions need not have caused social rationalization, and only
did so through the rise of the Protestant ethic. But, once this
event had happened, social rationalization spread through
society by means of purposive–rational action. Indeed, the two
became identified as one force. For Habermas, the critical issue
is not the Protestant ethic but the growth of self-critical rationality in different ways. Certainly social rationalization would
occur, but it must be seen through the perspective of cultural
rationalization. By this Habermas means that the crucial issue
is not the spread of the Protestant Work Ethic to the economy
and society, as Weber had claimed, but the gradual emergence
of changes in art, music, literature (culture) and the increasing
professionalization of such areas as medicine, the law, accoun-
tancy etc. These two changes reinforce each other. The significance of this is that purposive–rational action, or strategic
rationality, is not the only means of organizing society. It is here
that Habermas responds to Weber's analysis of the loss of
meaning and freedom in the modern world. First, he accepts
that there will be differentiated spheres of meaning in modernity, but the individual can recognize this, so long as there is a
common, universal structure of consciousness in each of these
spheres.[8] Secondly, the experience of loss of meaning is a
challenge to reorder society in some other way than purposive

rationality. The scientific world, and scientific way of thinking, in an instrumental manner, is no longer normative. Thirdly, it makes Habermas hostile to any talk of 'essential humanity' or invariant forms of human flourishing. What matters is that new possibilities of social relationships are explored.

We are now in a position to move to the second aspect of Habermas' thought which is significant, namely, the relationship of modernity and capitalism. At this point, Habermas introduces the concept of the 'lifeworld'. The 'lifeworld' is what nourishes human identity. As this world becomes dominated by money and social power it becomes weaker. So, too, does human identity.

THE COLONIZATION OF THE LIFEWORLD

The lifeworld is constituted by unproblematic, diffuse background convictions. It stores the work of past generations. Since Habermas has so emphasized the lack of importance of tradition in society, and the necessity of society reaching agreement through consensus and communicative action if it is to act at all, there is a possibility that society could ground to a halt, as it considers every option. This ignores the substantial work by philosophers such as Gadamer who have argued persuasively that human understanding is based on tradition as it encounters new experiences. Indeed, right at the very beginning of this exposition of Habermas' complex and careful argument, there must be some dissent by a theologian. Theology in the western Christian tradition has always given a high place to the tradition of the church. Instead, Habermas appeals to the weight of understanding that is stored in society. It is not legitimated by tradition, but is instead an implicit rationality: a 'conservative counterweight to the risk of disagreement that arises with every actual process of reaching an understanding'.[9]

This lifeworld has basic structures of consciousness, and pervades every aspect of thought. Less and less is there a traditional reservoir of beliefs which we accept 'immune from criticism'. We live in a rationalized world, and we assess new experiences in terms of these background convictions. Ha-

bermas rejects the authority of norms and values whose sources
are not amenable to rational justification, but accepts that in
place of 'opaque sources of authority' there can be implicitly
known rationalizations which pervade our thought. It is important to note that, for Habermas (as, of course, for Kant and
Weber), the justification of a belief, value or command in terms
of its purely religious authority is no longer acceptable. 'The
Bible/Pope/Spirit says' is a pre-modern way of thinking, which
is rightly meaningless to contemporary human beings. Always
we must explain in terms others can understand, accept and
justify why we think, act and feel the way we do. Communication is the answer for Habermas to the issue of both identity
and social fragmentation. If pressed, we could give a reasoned
justification of why we act the way we do, or at least some
people could do this on our behalf. The lifeworld pervades
culture, society and personality. Habermas writes:

In relation to culture and society the structural differentiation indicates an increasing uncoupling of world views from institutions; in
relation to personality and society, an expansion of the available space
for the generation of interpersonal relations; and in relation to culture
and personality, it indicates that the renewal of traditions is ever more
strongly dependent on individuals' readiness for critique and capacity
for innovation. The end point of these evolutionary trends is: for
culture, a condition allowing for the continual revision of traditions
which have become hardened and reflexive; for society, a condition
allowing for the depending of legitimate orders on formal procedures
for the . . . justification of norms; and for personality, a condition
allowing for the continually self-steered stabilization of a highly
abstract ego-identity.'[10]

This is such a critical passage of Habermas' understanding of
how society becomes rationalized, and only then is affected by
the working of capitalism and the market, that it is worth
exploring the meaning of the text. Habermas contends that the
beliefs and values predominant in each social group are no
longer shaped to a decisive extent by the institutions which
individuals may belong to. Neither the state, nor large employers such as the multinationals or a broadcasting company,
still less the church, or a political party, mould the outlook

which individuals have. Habermas will later argue that the mass media certainly affect beliefs and values, but his crucial point is that they no longer spring from the experience of being part of an institution. So traditions become much looser, there is much more discussion of their origin, validity and future existence, and they can become changed. In Habermas' words, traditions are 'unhardened and reflexive'.[11] Once again we see the hostility of Habermas to the role of tradition, but what Habermas is seeking is an understanding of social change and the transformation of beliefs and values. Society also changes, as social roles becomes much freer. This has been especially true of relationships between men and women, and between the generations. The possibilities of change become greater, and there is an 'expansion of the available space' in which people can express who they are. Norms as such must be justified by argument, and the social structures which do exist, such as the family ('legitimate orders') or educational institutions, depend on arguments for their continuing relevance to society. It is noticeable that this claim says nothing about the truth of these norms and the norms are agnostic about the understanding of the good. Habermas puts this in a highly abstract way, speaking of 'a condition allowing for the dependency of legitimate orders on formal procedures for the . . . justification of norms'[12] but his meaning is clear. As a social philosopher and critic, Habermas believes that personalities only exist in this rationalized, modern world by achieving their own ego-identity which must be continually maintained by oneself. This appears to be rather an exaggeration. It is true that there is far less support for personal identity in the fluid, atomized world of the modern city, but it is not clear that the stabilization is quite as precarious as Habermas implies. Part of the problem is that Habermas places individuals in the position where they are always struggling to renew traditions by engaging in a critique of them, and seeking innovative ways forward. This leads to a vision of the intellectual ever debating the issues of social existence in a manner necessarily removed from any acceptance of continuity or stability. Individuals must always take up an attitude of examination, discussion and seeking consensus ('communicative action') on the entire claims made within society. Only so is the lifeworld passed on. Hence Habermas both accepts that the lifeworld is made up of unproblematic, background convictions and that its transmission to new generations and different parts of the world can only be through the challenge of communicative action. In conclusion, Habermas sees the lifeworld as being highly rationalized; by which he means that society no longer develops through the force of tradition or uncritical thought, but that an explanation or justification, in principle, could be given by an expert in that particular area; secondly, it is therefore differentiated into culture, society and personality, concepts which are clearly related but not to be reduced to one another as might be possible through reductionist arguments in a pre modern culture; thirdly, it can only be passed on ('reproduced') through argument and challenge (the 'performative attitude' of 'communicative action'). Society continually seeks to reproduce its knowledge, while groups seek a more integrated form of solidarity or integration. Habermas is thinking here of the slow process of new towns achieving an identity, or firms a corporate culture. Individuals also seek greater socialization and self-awareness as a 'responsible actor'. One final aspect of this reproduction is that each factor in the lifeworld, of culture, society and personality, affects each other. Thus, for example, the individual personality will be affected by cultural reproduction through educational and behavioural goals; by social integration through social memberships; and by socialization through achieving personal identity.

Habermas bases his understanding of personal identity from the work of Lawrence Kohlberg on moral reasoning. The ethics of the ideal speech situation is related to Kohlberg's study of the stages of moral argument. This is not, as such, an understanding of human nature, as Forrester has made clear. The fluidity of personal identity is precisely the result of living in a highly sophisticated industrial society, and sets any theory of human nature at risk. What there is instead is an empirical account of the development of moral consciousness in young people, which Kohlberg claimed was a reasonably universal account of human development.

I – Preconventional Level. Here the child responds to punishments and rewards or the physical power of the person who commands.

1. The Punishment and Obedience Orientation: here it is the consequences of actions rather than any idea of the meaning or value of these consequences that determines moral behaviour.
2. The Instrumental Relativist Orientation: right action is what satisfies one's own needs, or occasionally the needs of others. Simple ideas of fairness and reciprocity are present, but 'human relations are viewed like those of the market place'.

II – Conventional Level. Here the stress is on loyalty to the group, family or nation, and conformity to the standards of the group.

3. The 'Good-boy-nice-girl' Orientation: good behaviour is what pleases others, and there is a tendency to conform to stereotypes.
4. Law and Order Orientation: here authority, fixed rules and maintaining the social order are the most important emphases.

III – Post-conventional, Autonomous or Principled Level. Here there is an effort to discover and follow moral principles which have a general validity and are not simply based on the norms of one's group.

5. Social Contract Legalistic Orientation: there is a tendency to stress rights and to base moral action on a properly achieved social consensus.
6. Universal Ethical Principle Orientation: conscience decides what is right in the light of universal ethical principles like the Golden Rule or the Kantian categorical imperative, which are freely chosen and reflect logical comprehensiveness, universality and consistency.

Kohlberg believed that the majority of adults remained at stage four. About 20 per cent reached stage five, and only between 5 and 10 per cent reached stage six. What happens to this argument in the hands of Habermas is that these stages become stages of social development.

Forrester is cautious about the unexamined value assumptions of Kohlberg's work, important though it undoubtedly is. Indeed Carol Gilligan, who was an assistant of Kohlberg, challenged him in the most authoritative study of psychological theory yet written from a feminist viewpoint. This study was entitled *In a Different Voice: Psychological Theory and Women's Development.* She points out that, both Piaget and Kohlberg primarily study young boys. Indeed, she argues that whereas Piaget made some reference to girls, Kohlberg ignores them. What is directly relevant about Gilligan's criticism, and bears heavily on the discussion of society in this chapter, is that she argues that Habermas believes that women have a different way of construing the relationship of private and family life to the public realm. Habermas, in Gilligan's view, is mistakenly persuaded by Kohlberg into a whole set of beliefs about women. For Kohlberg, women remain at stage three of his sequence. Morality is seen in interpersonal terms at this stage, and goodness is equated as helping and pleasing others. Goodness is lived out by mature women whose lives are primarily centred on the home. Gilligan believes that this is research primarily on male subjects, with women as an afterthought. Since the research reflects male experience, it leads, not surprisingly, to male conclusions. Women are best, in this theory, in the home and in private, and are less adequate in the public sphere. Women, for Kohlberg, must become like men to survive in the public realm. However, this division between public and private reflects the division between system and lifeworld discussed in this section.

The alternative picture presented by Gilligan is that justice in the public realm and feelings in the private belong together. There is a dual impoverishment. On the one hand, justice is separated from an ethic of care. On the other, injustices in family life are not addressed. Gilligan writes on the need to combine justice and care:

Through the tension between the universality of rights and the particularity of responsibility, between the abstract concept of justice and fairness and the more contextual understanding of care in relationships, these ethics keep one another alive and inform each other at crucial points. In this sense, the concept of morality sustains a dialectical tension between justice and care, aspiring always toward the ideal of a world more caring and just.[13]

After this discussion of personal identity and psychological development, which is related to moral thought, it is time to return to the discussion of the lifeworld, and in particular to the threat which is posed to it. As we have seen in the first part of this chapter, Weber believed that rationalization posed a threat to the harmonious development of moral values in the modern world. Habermas disagrees with Weber's understanding of rationality, and also denies that rationality poses a threat. Nevertheless, like Weber, and unlike Veblen who is discussed in chapter 2, Habermas believes that modern civilization is threatened. This is because the lifeworld is corrupted in a unique way. The threat is not from rationalization. Habermas, as shown above, welcomes the growth of a rationalized lifeworld. However, the lifeworld (or civilization) is corrupted by the system of bureaucracy, found in the state, and finance. 'System' here is a term which must be explained. The ways of thinking, acting and feeling which are appropriate to the worlds of the economy and of administration form a system which gradually pervades and dominates the lifeworld. The family is part of that lifeworld, and it is gradually dominated as well. The phrase Habermas uses is 'colonization'. However, it is clear that, for Habermas, as for Piaget and Kohlberg, the family inhibits moral development after a certain stage. Habermas looks for a universalizing justice which is impersonal, at home in structures, and is impartial. He does not see that the family can be a place where justice is learnt. The family should not be dominated by economic systems, but it is not an end in itself either. Instead, it remains as a place for loyalty, conventional behaviour, and pleasing others in Habermas' view. Feminists criticize him in two ways. On the one hand, they feel that the family should be a place where relationships are just, and that

justice is seen to be important. On the other, feminists argue
that Habermas is insufficiently aware of injustice in the family.
The critique is profound. There is a need to critique the division
between the public realm and the domestic.

Habermas' argument ultimately resolves itself into one point,
which he repeatedly emphasizes. There are not different types
of action, but a continual reproduction of the lifeworld through
different principles of 'sociation'. Sociation involves socialization, the social integration of groups and cultural reproduction.
A rationalized society or lifeworld reproduces itself in a different
way from the traditional, pre-modern societies where our
beliefs and values were born. Two factors make for conflict and
suffering. First, Habermas believes that there is insufficient
challenge to prevailing structures which dominate the lifeworld
and that existing ideologies, social integration and socialization
carry on in an uncritical way. Habermas therefore distinguishes
a 'normative consensus' (where society accepts the existence of
existing patterns of belief or action) from a 'communicatively
achieved consensus' (where each individual is respected, their
views discussed, and the resources of the rationalized lifeworld
employed). Secondly, and this will occupy us in the remainder
of this section, there is the 'colonization' of the lifeworld by
money and power. Habermas is thus the quintessential moder-
nist. If one offered a justification of, say, marriage from a
Roman Catholic standpoint, he would reject it as traditional
and uncritical. However, if one justified marriage (or divorce) in
terms of the demands of the modern economy, he would reject
that as domination by the economic system.

Habermas welcomes the enhanced possibility of social reproduction which modern consciousness and a rationalized lifeworld bring. These are in brief a greater awareness of meaning
and greater freedom of action, self-expression and beliefs. This
is the modern, self-aware human identity in a secular world. It
is these aspects of modernity which Habermas values, and in an
ironic twist precisely these aspects which modernity also threatens. For capitalism and bureaucratic administration are the
means by which society reproduces itself not only symbolically,
but materially. The irony is that capitalism and bureaucracy

depend on social rationality for their very existence, as shown in the first part of this chapter. Once again, Habermas does not simply define individual, or even collective, actions, but analyses capitalism and bureaucracy through systems theory. Therefore, the issue lies at the juxtaposition of social–cultural reproduction and 'sociation' on the one hand, and systems theory on the other. Capitalism is an ever-growing advance in terms of systems theory, with its use of strategic rationality as discussed in the first section.[14]

At the core of Habermas' thinking on capitalism are two beliefs. First, modern societies are much more prone to instability and changes of direction than traditional ones. This is true not only of societies but of individual identities, as argued above. Perhaps Habermas is reflecting on the massive dislocation which the Weimar Republic, Nazism and the Third Reich caused in Germany from 1920 to 1945. Secondly, however, the media of money and power can increasingly work to stabilize society in a manner unrelated to (Habermas' word is 'uncoupled' from) the lifeworld. The media of money and power develop in a manner that suits their needs. The needs of human identity, groups and culture are barely considered (if at all). Neither culture, social groups nor personal identity need affect the power of money and bureaucracy, as they operate in an ever more powerful manner through strategic rationality in a global context. Hence the reproduction of society ('sociation') in a purely material sense goes on unchecked. Not only is it unchecked, it also threatens the meaning and freedom which the lifeworld offers as it seeks to reproduce society in the opportunities, but also the unstable risks, of modernity. Habermas' greatest fear is, therefore, that society will become culturally impoverished and unable to challenge the dominance of capitalism, relapsing into a modern barbarism devoid of meaning. Tradition is lost, as traditional societies and their consciousness are left behind, but modernity also fails to deliver its promise. How does Habermas justify these fears, in a global perspective which is now the context of the future of our social life? The questions of human identity and of social justice are paramount for Habermas.

Habermas is aware that Marx attempted an answer a century earlier. There are three shortcomings in Marx, which flow from each other. First, he overemphasized the role of class conflict in employer/employee relationships, centring on labour power, capital and income. There are also several other factors which must be taken into account, which Marx ignored. First, within the economic system, there is the role of the consumer, much emphasized by English social ethicists such as R. H. Preston.[15] Secondly, there is the administrative system, where the private sphere of the employee and consumer gives way to the public sphere. In this arena, individuals become clients of the Welfare State, paying taxes and receiving the benefits of organization, sometimes literally in the form of welfare benefits! They also thirdly become citizens, offering loyalty in return for political decisions. The complex of relationships is thus far more sophisticated than Marx allowed, and can be demonstrated in the form of a diagram.[16]

Private	Employee	Gives Labour Power (**P**) Receives Income (**M**)	Economic
Sphere	Consumer	Gives Demand (**M**) Receives Goods (**P**)	System
Public	Client	Gives Taxes (**M**) Receives Benefits (**P**)	Administrative
Sphere	Citizen	Gives Loyalty (**P**) Receives Decisions (**P**)	System

P refers to power, **M** refers to money.

The second problem in Marx's thought is that of the future. For, if Marx ignored most of the relations replicated in this diagram, he also failed to realize that in a modern, rationalized society there was no possibility of ending the high degree of structural differentiation even if capitalism was abolished. Marx denied that the divisions within work need exist in a communist society. This is fantasy for Habermas. Thirdly, Marx failed to understand how capitalism must be seen in relation to the complex differentiation of everyday life. Capitalism affects modern societies in different ways, depending on how differentiated they are. As Habermas says, class conflict in Marx is always seen as the destruction of 'a nostalgically conjured, often romanticized past of premodern forms of life'.

Marx is, in his ultimate standpoint, a conservative, looking to the past. So Marx is regarded by Habermas as laying the groundwork over a century ago for analysing the relationship of capitalism and society. Yet it is excessively, and unhelpfully, focused on class relationships within the employer/employee context of industrial life, and it takes as its norm an ideal of a traditional, pre-modern world which was passing away, even as he wrote. Although Habermas does not make the comparison, for a theologian the parallels with the social conservatism of Martin Luther is striking. Luther offered a revolutionary re-appraisal of vocation in daily life (German: *Beruft*) which respected the autonomy of the ordinary Christian apart from the church, yet he still thought of daily life in unchanging, medieval terms.[17]

Habermas speaks of a 'colonization' of the life world by economic and administrative systems. He thus believes that strategic rationality increasingly dominates the thinking of individuals and groups as employee, client and citizen. Habermas sees that advanced capitalist societies are increasingly threatened with a loss of meaning or value, seeking to find a justification for their own morality. It is in the spheres of social life in which knowledge is passed on, social norms are formed between groups and individuals, and responsible people are formed that the problem lies. Capitalism offers rewards to individuals through their roles as private consumer and public client of the Welfare State. However, human identity and social cohesion are weakened by the power of the market.

Habermas speaks of the loss of meaning and of freedom as the issues which concern him here. Capitalism operates in a fragmented universe of consciousness, for, although more and more information is shared, it cannot be put together in a proper way. He believes that rationalization has stripped away the power of metaphysical or religious ideas ('religion as the

opium of the people' in Marx's well-known phrase), so that
human beings now live in a 'definitely disenchanted culture' in
which such beliefs (or ideologies) no longer can sustain their
power to convince. Although many people still believe them, in
the long term he sees a culture which is not integrated by
metaphysical and religious beliefs. This is something which he
welcomes. However, these ideologies are replaced by an equivalent force, which is the splitting off of expert cultures. Metaphysical beliefs worked positively by providing an interpretive
understanding of social life, even if they were pre-modern and
invalid beliefs. Today there is a negative function, as fragmented consciousness is unable to make use of the culture of
modernity. What does Habermas refer to? He does not give
many instances, but White (as a commentator on *The Theory of
Communicative Action*) suggests the complexity of science and
technology; the removal of art from everyday comprehension;
and the professionalization of legal matters, or the use of
'experts' to decide a growing number of situations. White
regrets the failure of Habermas to sketch out more fully the
problems which are given by this analysis. There are two
questions which remain acute. First, there is a failure to take
further the claim that insulated, expert cultures and fragmented
consciousness are 'functional' for advanced capitalism. What
social processes promote these two phenomena, and how are
they interrelated? What is the role of experts within the class
structure, and how do they see the question of social ethics in
giving an order to the activities of large corporations or
government? We will return to this theme later, but it is noticeable that Habermas identifies the issue without taking it much
further.[18]

There is also the question of where this discussion leaves
Habermas' earlier, and substantial, work *Legitimation Crisis*.[19]
This study, translated into English in 1975, shaped a great deal
of reflection on industrial society. Habermas changed his mind
dramatically in the 1980s, but the argument of the original work
is still worth spelling out. Classical bourgeois ideology was seen
as being distorted by the inexorable pressures of advanced
capitalism. As this ideology gradually fell apart, and capitalism

failed to replace it with a new ideology, Habermas foresaw a massive crisis in legitimizing capitalism. There would then be a contrast between the values of communicative action, which spoke of open discussion, democracy and social inclusion, and the structured society of advanced capitalism, with its commitment to ever greater production and wealth. He now feels that such a development is rendered unlikely, due to the way in which expert cultures exist apart from society, leading to greater fragmentation of social thought.

Legitimation Crisis failed to see that even if disequilibrium in the workings of capitalism and politics is related to the workings of the lifeworld, yet the two can continue to interact indefinitely. Where Habermas has developed his thought is in analysing what sort of problems can now arise. This is best described in terms of a diagram (see below). It describes both how the lifeworld reproduces itself structurally, but also how capitalism and the state cause the social disintegration which is so much a feature of contemporary discussion.[20]

	Culture	Society	Personality
Cultural Reproduction	Valid Knowledge	Legitimation	Educational Goals
Social Integration	Obligations	Legitimately Ordered Relationships	Social Memberships
Socialization	Interpretative Accomplishments	Motivation	Personal Identity

The theory works through the three aspects of the lifeworld, which are culture, society and personality. These are what structure the lifeworld, and give it its shapes. However, each one of these interacts with each other. This is not a static process, for the lifeworld is continually reproducing itself: what Habermas calls symbolic reproduction or sociation. As culture interacts with itself, and produces new ideas, theories and knowledge, by the process of cultural reproduction, there arises the fruit of communicative action, which is interpretative patterns of thought secured by debate and consensus. This is 'valid knowledge'. Likewise, the cultural values of a society, interacting with the ongoing process of social integration, create new obligations, and, as they relate to personal self-expression (socialization), they become literary, artistic and intellectual accomplishments: the writer, artist or philosopher. This is Interpretative Accomplishments. So, too, society in relation to cultural reproduction gives rise to new justifications of political and social theory, such as modern, participative democracy, clearly seen in election campaigns. The relationship of society and social integration creates the ordering of society in terms of law and order, group behaviour and roles. This is legitimation in the second column. In terms of socialization, society installs in individuals the acceptance of morality, and conformity to norms. Finally, there is the question of the individual personality. Cultural reproduction gives the individual educational goals, where the person can form herself in behavioural terms which will influence her growth, and thus end up becoming one of the persons embodied in the accomplishments already outlined. The interaction of culture and socialization produces interpretative accomplishments, such as in the artist. The interaction of cultural reproduction and personality gives the person the educational goals whereby these interpretative accomplishments are created. The person also lives out the social roles of orderly behaviour, by joining social groups, and forming social memberships. Lastly, the socialization of the individual achieves in the personality a strong identity, with the capability for interaction.

This is Habermas' ideal society, where communicative action flourishes. There are no neuroses, but persons with strong identities, integrated into groups, strongly motivated, and living out their educational goals in terms of the interpretation of culture. Culture flourishes, creating new forms of knowledge, legitimating society and giving individuals obligations, while there is an ever-greater expression of cultural life. Lastly society is ordered in terms of obligations (as moral values in society), roles and memberships, its direction and goals, instilling in the individual a strong sense of motivation to conform to social norms.

It is worth spelling this out in some detail, because Habermas believes that here is an answer to the imperious demands of strategic rationality. Strategic rationality assumes that individual agents are egoistic, and act out of self-interested motivation. The maximization of utility is all that matters, whether it be wealth, power or happiness. However Habermas claims that, in his model of communicative rationality, the questions of how persons are to co-operate and reach understanding becomes resolved.

Habermas thus contrasts the domain of strategic rationality, or instrumentalism, with that of communicative rationality. It is time that a discussion of strategic and communicative rationality is now given. We therefore turn for a moment aside from the main argument on lifeworld and system to a brief discussion of epistemological issues. In a striking quote, Stephen White sums up why for him contemporary political theory has failed to resolve the dilemma of human relationships:

> the position most rational choice theorists seem, at least tacitly, to adhere to is one which takes the systematic expansion of strategic rationality to be a beneficial process which clears the necessary cognitive and social ground for an ever greater degree of individual freedom and welfare coming to fruition in the modern democratic state.[21]

White sees strategic rationality as the dominant political culture of our day. It occurs both in economic and political ideology. The problem lies in its failure to envisage the cost of modernization, and the way in which traditional, normative societies are eclipsed by strategic rationality, leaving a question as to the ultimate purposes of that society.

Such a question was first raised by Max Weber at the beginning of this century.[22] As the twentieth century comes to its end, the dominance of strategic rationality in the form of market capitalism and management theory becomes ever more dominant.[23] It is therefore important that an alternative to a strategic rationality is set out. In this section, Habermas' understanding of rationality will be contrasted with strategic rationality. Following from this, his concept of discourse ethics and communicative action will present a different way of formulating moral questions. Habermas has a strong commitment to reaching a consensus, although there are theological questions to be asked about this.

There has been a continuing debate among theologians, especially in North America and Germany, about the significance of critical theory, which is the tradition Habermas represents, for theology. Critical theory has worked on the basis of unmasking idolatry. The market is seen as one such idol. If this is so, then it is not possible to place theology directly against the market world, and to ask how theology will respond. Instead, the response must be mediated through the analysis of critical theorists who have conceptualized the market in a way which theologians cannot ignore.

We turn, then, to a definition of strategic rationality, and its place in economic and political theory, before moving on to the concept of communicative action (or rationality). Action as strategic rationality is seen as intentional, self-interested behaviour carried out by individuals and social groups. Such behaviour regards others as the objects of possible manipulation, and therefore can be said to view them in an 'objective' manner. Rationality is conceptualized as instrumental, whereby actions are carried out in as efficient a manner as possible so that particular goals may be realized. Such rationality says nothing about how goals are decided, or what they might be. Concepts such as 'the good' are discounted.

Rational choice theorists can predict how individuals will act, if they act rationally.[24] This is formal, predictive theory. It therefore declines to endorse any particular moral position, not even that of rationality. It merely states what can be predicted if people act rationally in the way described above. Nevertheless, it is often the case that such a theory falls back on the assumption that rational agents are egoistic, and act out of self-interested motivation. In the formal language of moral philosophy, they maximize their own (or their group's) utility, seeking the greatest amount of the value which is preferred, whether that be wealth, power or some more experiential value, such as happiness. The reason why this theory proposes this is because self-interested motivation appears to explain a greater degree of collective behaviour than any other assumption. Nevertheless, rational choice theory is left with the classic problems of economic and political theory. How are collective arrangements made possible, so that conflict is not the only dimension in economic or political life? If one then tries to explain co-operation, is one inevitably forced to resort to a moral sense of rationality?

It is not simply that one can argue that individuals and groups do co-operate, thus placing benevolence (or altruism) alongside self-interest as a motivational force. There is the more difficult and widely discussed problem as to why a rational agent should participate in co-operative behaviour when it is not clear whether the benefits of the action are greater than the costs of participation. There are two aspects to this issue:

1. It is never clear before one acts co-operatively whether the benefits will outweigh the cost of acting.[25]
2. It may be that the benefits of co-operation arise even if one had not acted at all.

Thus the 'free rider' problem becomes a familiar question of contemporary political and economic discussion, such as in providing training within companies over against poaching trained staff.

Rational choice theorists have thus widened their theory to include psychological incentives, although this results in a complex model which combines contextual rationality with strategic rationality. Norms, beliefs, values, traditions, customs and incentives are all relevant. An alternative theory is suggested by Peter Winch. Contextual rationality describes actions as being rational because they fit in with the existing beliefs, norms and values of a particular culture. One example is that of capital punishment. It was seen as a rational action in eighteenth-century England as the legal punishment for stealing a sheep. Jurists developed arguments to defend this, and it was enshrined in English law. Later commentators, such as Bagehot a century afterwards, found it incredible that such actions had been thought justifiable. Contextual rationality would not point to objective moral values of human behaviour, as Bagehot did, but would explain actions as being rational within the beliefs of that culture. Habermas' concern is that this theory of contextual rationality both undermines the universality of moral judgements and ignores issues of power, and changes in social structures. Thus, the most that contextual rationality can do is to justify an action or institution by drawing connections between that action/institution and the social context of beliefs and norms. An appeal to higher principles instead of traditional norms has no higher power of moral rationalization. Appealing to abstract universalizable principles as a privileged way of rationalizing actions is simply one possible strategy of creating a hierarchy of justification.

Habermas also justifies the strategic – rational perspective, by showing it offers a description of social change in terms of shifting power interests. It explains collective beliefs and norms in terms of the power which these beliefs legitimate. Therefore it is possible to conceptualize the processes of social change, studying the ways in which traditional norms break down under the pressure of conflicting interests or systemic changes in social structures. Contextual rationality denies that an appeal to higher principles is valid, or argues that it is no more than a particular philosophical position. Contextual rationality finds it equally hard to explain social changes, yet at the same time strategic rationality does not offer much help in comprehending the meaning of social change. As more and more areas of social life are brought under the sway of strategic rationality, the pursuit of corporate and individual self-interest becomes paramount, in place of norm-guided actions. Strategic rationality might explain why religious beliefs (e.g., the divine right of kings) legitimate power, give way under social challenge (the English Civil War) and are replaced. But it is hard to give an overall meaning to this process, except as socio-historical change. The market and liberal democracy now rule where once the king ruled. That is the only 'meaning' that there can be.

Strategic rationality is at the heart of the discussion of the market. Habermas wishes to mediate between strategic and contextual rationality. He wishes to establish a basis for social co-operation, which as shown above, is a weakness of strategic rationality. Many theologians would be critical of the ability of this mediation to be successful, since the basis for co-operation must spring out of the society itself. Habermas also wishes to determine the future direction of social change, allowing for the pressure of corporate interests. Yet he does not simply wish to produce a contextual or historical account of society.

Habermas offers the social ethicist a way through these dilemmas. In his theory of communicative action, he seeks an alternative pattern. As Stephen White puts it,

the central problem of Habermas' thought has been how to demonstrate that an exclusively instrumental or strategic understanding of rationality is somehow inadequate and that therefore the historical process of increasing Weberian rationalization of the world represents a threat to the full potential of human beings to bring reason to bear on the problems of their social and political existence.[26]

Communicative action allows the theorist to overcome the dominance of an instrumental way of thinking.

In communicative action, Habermas sets out to widen the scope of rationality. In communicative action speakers always raise three validity claims which are the claims to truth, legitimacy and authenticity. Communicative action wishes to create understanding between persons and groups without coercion. Habermas writes:

Finally the concept of communicative action refers to the interaction of at least two subjects capable of speech and action who establish interpersonal relations (whether by verbal or by extra-verbal means). The actors seek to reach an understanding about the action situation and their plans of action in order to co-ordinate their actions by way of agreement. [27]

If a speaker can convince his/her speakers that these claims are rational, and worthy of recognition, then a consensus on further action and speech can develop. Utterances are only rational if they raise criticizable validity claims, which are fallible and can be judged objectively. Verbs in language can be constative (raising truth claims); regulative (raising claims of normalivity/legitimacy); or expressive (raising claims of personal truthfulness). Once again, theologians have argued that language is more complex than this, and this neat classification is too simple. Nevertheless, Habermas argues that all three fall within the realm of communicative action. Therefore Habermas sees every discussion of social ethics, and personal authenticity, as leading to an ongoing dialogue. Communicative rationality thus engages with strategic and contextual rationality, along with the representation of subjectivity, but seeks to reflect all three worlds in a manner which allows the possibility of agreement.

The relevance of Habermas' discussion of communicative rationality to the world of the market is in the question of justice. Habermas feels that Rawls' theory of justice does not provide an impartial account of what constitutes goals for society. There is an individualist bias in his account of the market, and in his rationalizing of interests. Any attempt for Habermas to determine universal norms of justice will run into problems. He will only accept universal procedures, and has nothing on the application of moral rules. It is noticeable that procedures are separate from application. He uncouples justification of moral arguments from their application, whereas application and procedures (or beliefs) are united in Christian theology. Habermas thus makes a distinction with which Christian social ethics must wrestle, and to which we will return. Justice for him is defined as universally valid procedural criteria, appropriate to judging the justness of proposed norms. A theologian would wish to argue for the importance of the need to persuade others what norms might be discovered from the resources of the Christian tradition. Habermas argues that what justice demands is another matter altogether, which is determinate norms for guiding action. Yet these cannot be legitimately decided in advance of an actual situation. Nevertheless, Habermas does reject the problem raised in the discussion of strategic rationality, where the inability of people to find reasons for co-operating was a crucial weakness of this theory. Every agent who proposes a norm must be ready to apply it to him/herself and to others. Not to accept this is to pass into irrationality, yet language itself has a structure of intersubjectivity, from which one can derive an obligation to provide justification for one's actions. Once again a theologian would argue that the importance of language is that it is embodied in human action. Habermas had a sustained debate with Gadamer on the nature of language. Habermas does not accept the validity of tradition, for understanding language and social action. Gadamer emphasises the horizon which we move towards, as we project a meaning forward in our lives. Such a horizon of meaning encounters an object in life which resists that meaning. As a result new ways of thinking are developed which can take account of the new object. Moltmann refined Gadamer's theory into a theology of hope which allowed for tradition but also emphasized the Christian dimension of hope and new life which is found in the Christian revelation. Ultimately, Habermas is dependent on his understanding of social and cultural existence for the conceptual necessity which underpins his analysis.

Gadamer feels that enlightenment rationalism is destructive of a fully comprehensive understanding of truth. Truth is transmitted as wisdom, which allows for a genuine dialogue between those with different expectations. Tradition which is healthy and life giving transmits this wisdom. Within this tradition there can be a listening to each other, where an encounter between others can take place. Wisdom is deeper than knowledge, and reinterprets events as life giving encounters. A transformation of persons can take place. Habermas stands outside this understanding. He sees no validity for tradition, nor for a personal encounter which is transformative. All that remains is the correct process, or procedures, in which human beings meet each other in open communication. This is certainly dialogue, but it is neither transformative of self-understanding nor does it draw on the validity of tradition. Finally there is no substantive account of human identity in this account. As we shall see in the third part of this chapter, this leads to drastic consequences when discussing religious language and symbols. Habermas simply closes down the debate at this point, and does not admit of any religious reference at all.

There are a number of implications for a discussion of justice and the market. Is it possible to proceed on the basis of a denial of a substantive concept of needs, wherein the core values of a culture simply structure our needs? Habermas argues that any theory (such as that of Rawls) which incorporates any substantive set of needs, violates the requirement of reciprocity in a communicative ethic by excluding some potential voices. As White puts it: 'the universalization of a post-conventionally interpreted principle of reciprocity can be saved only if it is disconnected from the 'monological' conceptualization it has received in the formalist tradition from Kant to Rawls.'[28] Habermas admits that it can be difficult for individuals to take up such an abstract ethic although he argues that collective identity must underpin ego identity, where identity is defined as 'the symbolic structure which allows a personality system to secure continuity and consistency'.[29]

A second question is whether the distinction between 'instrumental' (or 'strategic') rationality and communicative rationality really holds. John Thompson argues that it does not, since all instrumental action follows some norms. Equally, he argues that virtually all examples of social action involve strategic elements as well. There is some truth in this criticism, although Habermas argues that there are no pure instances of instrumental or communicative action, but rather that it is the way in which human actions are finally rationalizable which matters. It is also the case that communicative action does contain purposive ends. This raises the question as to whether the concept of communicative action applies to the process of reaching agreement, or to the actions that follow from this process, or both. Habermas replies that it is the second or third option which concerns him, thus accepting the complexity of the term.[30]

Nevertheless, Habermas does offer both a recognition of the theoretical issues at stake in any discussion of justice and the market, and a sophisticated (he would use Kohlberg's term 'post-conventional') attempt to resolve them. It is important to begin with epistemological issues, since epistemology also is a central concept in the discussion of modernity and capitalism (or the 'colonization of the lifeworld') which now follows. Without a concentration on the correct methodology, the debate is flawed from the start.

After this digression into epistemological issues, we now move back into a discussion of personal identity. We have examined what is meant by the lifeworld, and some understanding of Habermas' use of the concept of the system. There has also been a discussion of strategic rationality. However, we are not yet finished with Habermas' careful delineation of communicative action and the lifeworld. Until now we have expounded Habermas' theory, and contrasted it with strategic rationality. What we must now turn our attention to is the pathology induced by the interaction of capitalism and bureaucracy with the lifeworld. This goes beyond the limitations of strategic rationality, with its functionalism and instrumental use of the person as a means to an end. Habermas now unfolds the pathology of the lifeworld. He does not feel that society will break down, as he predicted in *Legitimation Crisis*. Instead, he fears that the pressures of social change becomes too great for society, and it suffers massive social alienation. The anguished discussions about morality, youth alienation and personal insecurity are part of the social cost of an increasingly rationalized and competitive existence. In brief, the question of social justice overlaps with the nature of human identity. This is the fundamental argument of this chapter:[31]

In *Legitimation Crisis*, Habermas argued that the state would take a wider role in managing the economy, thus filling the necessary roles in demand management which advanced capitalism requires. This was the role which successive British governments pursued until the Thatcher government abandoned this belief in 1979 for supply-side economics. Habermas' earlier work believed that the expansion of the state would politicize greater and greater areas of life. As strategic rationality in any case weakened the power of traditional beliefs and values, and, as less reliance was made on the classic liberal theories of the nineteenth and early twentieth centuries about the value of education for its own sake, the representative value of democracy and the belief in social reform, so social conflict became more difficult to contain. Habermas' early belief was that before social conflict grew too great there would be less legitimation of the state (see Number 4 in the diagram below), and the possibility of a reordering of society would engage intellectuals and political activists.

	Culture	Society	Person
Cultural Reproduction	**1** Loss of Meaning	**4** Less Legitimation	**7** Educational Crisis
Social Integration	**2** Insecure Collective Identity	**5** Anomie	**8** Alienation
Socialization	**3** Breakdown of Cultural Traditions	**6** Less Motivation	**9** Psychological Neurosis

This has not happened however, and in the 1980s Habermas spent much time reflecting on the failure of his hopes of the 1960s and early 1970s. He came to believe that society was passing through a prolonged period of insecure collective identity (Number 2) and deep alienation of young people from society (Number 8). There are no strong obligations any longer to the core values of a collective society, which in his ideal of communicative action (and, indeed, in part in the past) is how culture and social integration interact. Once these obligations disappear, which were provided formerly by tradition and then by the nineteenth/twentieth-century beliefs in social reform and liberalism, there is a deep sense of insecurity. The collective identity is gravely weakened, quite apart from the fractures provided by social mobility, globalization and rapid social change. At the same time, there are massive alterations in the perception of social memberships: people experience a much less strong sense of collective identity. Habermas argues that these developments do not come about by chance. They result from the twin dependencies of consumer identity on consumption and clients on the welfare state. There is a repeated redefinition of social values in a consumer society, driven by the forces of advanced capitalism. This is discussed in depth in chapter 2. The final outcome of this process is that people are much less sure of what values bind them together, what is possible in terms of social membership, and what would be any alternative to the existing economic, political and social arrangements. The idea of social solidarity necessary to achieve change is very difficult to achieve, except perhaps in highly localized areas or on particular and very specific topics. One thinks of community organizing in areas of deprivation, but not of national movements against poverty. Equally there are national protests against the export of live animals in intensive farming, but not wider political movements which are ecological. Political, economic or social protest is either very local or highly specific. White summarizes Habermas' growing realization that large-scale change appears increasingly unlikely. 'Alienation, disintegration of collective identity and cultural impoverishment or loss of meaning are lifeworld pathologies which help to hinder the emergence of critical consciousness and action.'[32]

J. K. Galbraith has argued that contemporary society meets the needs of the majority of its members in providing affluence and social mobility. Nevertheless, there is a largely unseen degree of poverty and social exclusion for a significant, and increasing, minority. Habermas, like Galbraith, writes about social values. There is a growth in particular attitudes and values within society. He writes that 'the scope of tolerance for merely instrumental attitudes, indifference and cynicism is expanded'.

Individual commitment to personal well-being grew in the last decade, although the rise of communitarian attitudes provides some evidence that the trend is not all one way. Nevertheless, the increase in social attitudes which are indifferent to poverty, and which wish for greater social control of those who feel no stake in society and resort to criminal behaviour, is a feature of contemporary society. There is also a pervasive cynicism about politics, the standards of politicians and the fairness of the economic and political system at all to reward those who seek participation. Again, there is some contrary evidence that the limits of social acceptance of corruption are being reached. Yet, at the same time, the growth of the black economy, and the large number of fraud scandals in the City of London in the late 1980s and early 1990s, show the remorseless disintegration of previously accepted moral standards in financial and economic affairs. Whether this trend can be reversed is one of the key questions for Habermas' analysis.

If the first of Habermas' social forces is that of consumption, then the second aspect of his thought is the growing complexity of the Welfare State, which is the case both in his own country of Germany and in Britain. Habermas uses the term 'juridificatio', or in German '*Verechtlichung*'. It refers to the legal complexity of welfare regulations, and the effect it has on recipients who become clients of the state and must accept the regulations which accompany the benefits. Again there is the phenomenon of increasing social control, with hostility towards those who are held to abuse the system. This leads back to the problems of the internalization of moral values, and social obligations. One aspect of the debate in the 1980s in Britain and the United States was a focus on those who were no longer economically active, and were held to lack the motivation to work (Section 6, in Habermas' diagram above), thus becoming an 'underclass'. This was associated with the work of Charles Murray. Yet, even where there was a desire to increase social rights, the new expansion of law led (as the politician and social analyst Frank Field pointed out) to an invasion of personal freedom. The extension of law redefines the relationship of client and the administrative state, leading to further dependency and the redefinition of life. This leads Habermas to believe that a whole series of situations in modern life where values and social membership were once deeply important now have been transformed. The treatment of physical and mental health, the question of old age, and of crises such as unemployment and long-term disability, are no longer challenges to society for inclusion of its weaker members within its parameters. Nor are the values of care and compassion necessarily to be drawn from the reservoir of social obligations and motivations which once were the case. It is not that there is no caring, but that it is separated from the social bonds and values which should sustain it. The issue of the expertise of professionals (doctors, social workers) in the field of care, together with the necessity of administration, leads to the redefinition of 'limit' areas of life. In part, this leads to the well-known phenomenon of political and social apathy. It is difficult to engage citizens in co-operative action, since they have become clients. It is also the case that legal complexity reduces daily situations to pre-defined situations. Given the structural differentiation anyway of the lifeworld, in a manner not foreseen by Weber, wherein judgements about knowledge, social norms and personal expression are less and less related one to another, and also given the fragmented consciousness of a social elite which does not engage with the majority of society, the analysis Habermas offers is one which leads to the oft-discussed phenomenon of privatization, or privatized morality. What is important is that this privatization of morality (much commented on by church leaders such as Archbishop Carey and Jonathan Sachs, the Chief Rabbi), is also part of the process by which individual identities are weakened.

Habermas does not oppose law as such. He distinguishes between 'regulative' and 'constitutive' aspects of law. Regulative rules in philosophical discourse regulate pre-existing activity, such as health and safety regulation at work, or environmental issues. Constitutive rules define what is meant by an activity, such as a game of rugby with its rules, or the accepted rules for musical composition. Habermas believes that contemporary social behaviour is constituted by law, although economic behaviour is regulated by it. The distinction is crucial to his social analysis. Regulative justifications respect ethical norms, and modify actions, thus attaching themselves to pre-existing institutions. 'They give a binding state-sanctioned form to spheres of action which are already informally constituted.'[33]

Such laws are familiar in criminal law, or in constitutional affirmations of human rights, such as the European Court of

Human Rights. However, most welfare regulations on the receipt of benefits, especially in a vexed matter such as workfare where the recipient has to work in return for benefits, constitute new spheres of the lifeworld. Habermas also distinguishes between two different kinds of justification of law. Regulative law is embedded in the institutions of daily life, accepts (on the whole) the moral norms and values, and therefore can be defended on grounds of social coherence and legitimacy. It is part of the way in which society defends its core values, and ensures their survival, either against forms of attack (criminal law) or by a positive articulation (human rights legislation). They are therefore, in principle, capable of comprehension by the average citizen, and the defence of their necessity can be carried on in society. Constitutive law is enacted by administrative elites, and is defended on economic grounds or consistency with past decisions. It becomes a procedural legitimation. It is hard to understand except for the social elite which administers it.

Habermas fears that consumption and dependence on the Welfare State (juridification) work together. The private life of the consumer is presented with sexual relationships, leisure and culture as part of a commodified, economic system. Life becomes packaged into what one can consume, as aspects of a life style which is available for a price. Lifeworld becomes life style. At the same time, the client within the welfare state is also subject to a loss of freedom. There is a deep feeling of unease, and pessimism, in Habermas' understanding of modernity. What has been gained by the rationalization of the lifeworld, with the replacement of tradition by reason and open-ended discourse is being lost by the pathologies of capitalism and administrative control. Above all Habermas is concerned that the epistemological understanding which is possible in society is being ended. Strategic rationality returns to define not only the world of work and politics, but also the personal self-understanding of the subject. White comments that, for Habermas, 'even one's sense of self and development as a human being increasingly become targets of commodification, as we are presented with new and more extensive pre-selected packages of behavioural, psychological and sexual scripts'.[34] Human identity becomes pre-packed and defined by consumption, as chapter 2 will outline. The value of Habermas' thought is that it offers an all-embracing theory which sets the parameters of any discussion of the market. Modern culture, or modernity, is deeply affected by capitalism in its advanced, global form, and it is in these terms that any discussion of the market world might get under way.

Nevertheless, there are profound criticisms which can be made of Habermas' understanding of the market. In part, this is because he published *Legitimation Crisis* at a time in the early 1970s when many commentators expected a fusion of Communist-style state economies and western capitalism. The entrepreneurial emphasis of the late 1980s was completely ignored. Here Habermas was no different from many other analysts. Secondly, there are specific problems which one can find in his analysis. Habermas' theory is therefore useful as a way of opening up issues of identity and justice in modern capitalist societies, but his detailed investigations can be questioned.

In the third, and final, section of this opening chapter, the implications for theology of Habermas' theory will be discussed. Before we do this, however, a brief account of the criticisms will be given. One such critic is the English political theorist David Held. He has argued that a stable society can coexist with the loss of a sense of the worthiness of a political order. The broad mass of people accept a political and economic order because they are financially rewarded by it, and see no other alternative. Held believes that talk of any legitimation crisis is naive. It seems that Habermas has increasingly come to accept that Held is correct. Workers may feel quite detached from the attitudes of the managers and social elites above them, and feel no attachment to the existing distribution of wealth, but there is no likelihood at all of any social or political action on the basis of this detachment.[35]

Secondly, the new political movements of anti-nuclear, pacifist and ecological groups, which Habermas set so much store by in the early 1980s, also seem to be much weaker today. There is still great opposition to particular state activities, such as road building or the construction of a nuclear power plant. There is also a generalized, and deep, concern about the environmental crisis. Nevertheless, the failure of the Green movement to form a serious alternative, even in Germany, to existing political parties is very striking. The collapse of the communist states in Eastern Europe, and the reduction in the arms race, has also taken much of the steam out of the campaign for nuclear disarmament. Habermas felt that these movements arose in response to the growth of the military industrial complex, and the denial of the public right to decide the future of shared, non-renewable resources. He contrasted corporate indifference to the common good with the new political movements. In these movements Habermas saw a protest against all the features of capitalism and bureaucracy which he feared: 'the dependence of buyer–seller and employee–employer relationships, as well as the political dependence, passivity and privatism fostered by client–civil servant and elector–office-holder relationships'.[36]

These movements are concerned with what Habermas calls the 'grammar of the lifeworld' in terms of the quality of life, conditions for self-realization, and the extension of democratic participation in all aspects of life. Little of this survived the decade in which such movements were born. Indeed, Habermas himself opposed the political organization of the Greens into a mass party, fearing that mass parties can pervert political integrity. Ingram puts the point well, referring to the spin doctors of contemporary politics: 'The manipulative use of power takes on the eerie, surrealistic aspect of a postmodern nightmare in which traditional values are packaged in high-tech images and moral ideas are invested with the charismatic charm of "tinseltown" histrionics – "the waste dump of the refuse of civilization . . . dressed in plastic", as Habermas refers to it.' However it is not at all clear what Habermas offers instead. Local, informal, grass-roots groups can play a role specific to their locality. It is difficult to see them moving much beyond that.[37] In chapter 2 we shall refer to Giddens' discussion of personal identity and protest movements.

Habermas however does leave us in this respect with the

importance of communication. Daniel Hallin applies the perspective of critical theory to the American news media. He applauds the concern with dialogue which leads Habermas to focus on the character of public debate and the fate of the public sphere. Dialogue is a cardinal feature of communicative action, and the tendency of the mass media to treat the individual citizen as a consumer even in political matters is something which Habermas deeply regrets.[38] In a similar vein, Habermas describes the vogue for participatory architecture as 'nostalgia for de . . . differentiated forms of existence . . . linked to the cult of the vernacular and to reverence for the banal'.[39]

The third criticism of Habermas does not concern his account of the legitimation crisis, or of new political movements. It is the most fundamental critique of all, which is his account of the market. Criticism, predictably, comes from two directions. On the one hand, there is the orthodox Marxist critique that Habermas has never really understood the economic determinism and class struggle which Marx has enabled us to see in all social life. The American theorist Tony Smith would be a good example of this. On the other hand, there are many contemporary economists who feel that Habermas has failed to come to terms with the resurgence of neo classical economics and the growing sway of the market. This would be the case not only in the economy, but in health and education.

Smith will not accept a market society in any form. He also denies Habermas' belief that advanced capitalism will be able to sustain itself. He writes that 'Habermas may be accused of confusing the buying-off of the most organized sectors of the working class with the pacification of class struggle as a whole.'[40] It is the world outside the industrialized West, the disorganized poor, women and ethnic minorities who have suffered. The vision of uninterrupted growth in capitalist economies is only a dream. Smith denies that Habermas' separation of economic and political subsystems from the life-world can be sustained. Once growth falters in capitalism, then there will be a conflict between revenue spent on social compensation and expenditure necessary for the furthering of capital accumulation. Smith has a bleak view of capitalism: 'throughout the developed capitalist world the state institutes austerity measures, provides tax breaks to the wealthy, encourages wage cutbacks for workers, reduces social services and oversees a restructuring of the labour process in the interests of capital'.[41]

Contemporary economics has been dominated by Keynesian – neo-classical controversies. The Keynesian proposition that discretionary government policy can be used to stabilize the economy is rejected by the new classical critique of macroeconomics. The new classical approach reinstates rational economic behaviour. Keynesian economics argues that markets do not clear because prices fail to adjust sufficiently fast. It goes on to argue that economic agents do not fully optimize their behaviour. The theoretical problem which is paramount in Keynesian economics is to explain the presumption that slow price adjustment means that markets fail to clear.

The discussion of this by Levacic and Rebmann puts the point clearly.

> The existence of non-market – clearing and quantity – rationing means that there are potential exchanges between economic agents which would be mutually advantageous at prices different from the ruling ones. The failure of price adjustment to bring about these potentially advantageous exchanges imply that economic agents are not optimising. Keynesian economics is therefore based on two interrelated presumptions that agents do not fully optimize and hence, that markets fail to clear.[42]

The new classical approach has different assumptions. It claims that economic agents optimise, that markets clear, and that expectations are formed rationally. There is also an important difference about the supply side of the economy, from those found in Keynesian models. Keynesian economics argues that when the market does not clear aggregate supply depends on the level of effective demand. In the new classical approach, supply depends on relative prices and not on quantity.

There has been much discussion in recent years of markets, efficiency and public interest. If the new classical approach is correct, anticipated changes in aggregate demand will have no effect on output and employment. Unanticipated changes in aggregate demand will have an effect for a while, but only for as long as people do not realize what has happened. In time they will realize, and wages and prices will be corrected.

Habermas has not engaged in discussion with the new classical economics. It is not clear whether his views would take him to an attempt to have limited government intervention in the market, or whether he believes that economic rationality can be superseded. It would appear that he accepts the self-steering account of the economy, as it interacts with the life-world, but that there can be limited intervention by government for environmental reasons. However the development of supply-side economics, which reduces the power of unions and attacks the role of government in prices and incomes policies, makes the role of government more difficult.

THEOLOGY, IDENTITY AND JUSTICE

In this final section, the theological significance of Habermas must be taken up. He is a thinker who has inspired a number of theologians in very different ways. His dependence on the Frankfurt School makes Habermas attractive to those who wish to continue the dialogue with Marxism, and there are several theological studies on critical theory and neo-Marxism. Most prominent in England is the Roman Catholic theologian Charles Davis, whose essays on social theory use Habermas extensively.[43] However, my concern is not with the Marxist derivation of Habermas' theory, although I will refer to Davis in passing. Nor is my interest primarily with Habermas' use of language. There is an examination of this by Al McFadyen in his study of personhood, and the question of the validity of truth claims is an important part of Habermas' philosophy.[44] We shall return to the concept of the 'ideal speech situation' before we leave Habermas' philosophy. However, the chief focus must first be on the coherence of social structures and the nature of 'public' theology. Secondly there is the issue of human identity in a market-driven world. What can theology say to this? Thirdly there is the nature of justice. Does Habermas assist the theologian in the search for a more adequate expression of justice?

There have been many rejections of the public realm in modern philosophy. Richard Rorty accepts that a public realm is necessary for any modern society, but it can only be defended on historical grounds. Equality and liberty are necessary attributes of the citizens of a democracy, but the rationality necessary to defend these values is a working fiction. Some theologians have also displayed a scepticism about the public realm, except as the environment for alternative communities. Trying to unite modernity and Christianity is seen as a mistaken strategy. Such a correlation is improper because it is either foundationalist, or idealist. In the former, it incorrectly assumes the existence of shared moral values, and, in the later, it expresses a neo-Romantic belief in the self which is improperly concerned with the 'essential self' or with aesthetics. On this reading, the search for a Christian identity, or theological anthropology which is one of the concerns of this book, is a mistaken strategy. The cult of experience will not serve theologians in dealing with the public realm. A defence could be that a Christian anthropology is not concerned with personal experience, but with interpreting contemporary culture. However, the criticism of this position, which is my own strategy in this book, is that it becomes simply a sociological study. Theology is therefore advised to withdraw to a concern with its own proper role, which is the narratives, virtues and practices of the community it serves. Thus the idea of a public realm is abandoned, as is the concept of a common rationality.[45]

An alternative approach to the public realm is that of political theology, and of some forms of feminist or liberal theology. The former took up the Marxist understanding of alienation, and correlated it with the apocalyptic and eschatological language of theology. These symbols, especially in the typology of 'the powers' which govern social change are used to explore how it is that our society has become so damaged. Political theologians in Europe and North America sometimes reduced the concept of the public realm to an apocalyptic battleground, where the logic of advanced capitalism (often allied to Fascism, the military–industrial complex or the security state, as in the work of the German theologian Ulrich Düchrow) could only be defeated by an alliance of forces which saw the conception of the common good as an examples of bourgeoisie ideology. Such an analysis drew on the work of the Frankfurt School, especially in Marcuse's work in North America.[46]

Liberation and feminist/womanist theologians use the experience of those who have been oppressed by society. Their experience has been marginalized by the dominant groups. The symbol of liberation ignores the pluralism of the public realm, and does not doubt the reality of society. Racism, sexism and other forms of oppression are there to be challenged, but there is often no analysis of what structural relationships might be preferable. Otherwise such liberation theologians could exist as a permanent form of counter-culture to a dominant technical rationality.[47] The theological argument can now be reviewed. Habermas provides the theologian with a philosophical account of contemporary social structures, authority and state power. Within these structures as they exist in tension with the cultural reality of the lifeworld, there is a profound understanding both of the individual's identity and of the nature of justice, both expressed through the concept of 'communicative competence'. Justice is achieved through communicative action, hence the title of his great study of contemporary social philosophy is *The Theory of Communicative Action*. There are profound problems for the theologian in Habermas' understanding of language, tradition and moral value, but, nevertheless, it is an immense achievement. The theological response is problematic. As outlined above, theology in recent years has increasingly preferred to outline the narratives of its own community, or else to adapt a liberationalist/political approach which tackles the 'principalities and powers'.

What if one wished to adopt a different strategy? One of the most perceptive approaches in recent years has been that of Duncan Forrester, whose work on justice has explored the fragmentation expressed in contemporary political philosophy, but nevertheless argued for a vision for a Christian political theology. This will be equally fragmented, but nevertheless engages with the public realm. As Forrester himself says in his recent work *Christian Justice and Public Policy*,

In earlier chapters I have argued that it is right to see justice as the first virtue of social institutions, but that ideas like fairness are too narrow to fulfil what is legitimately expected of justice. Justice is essential for a healthy social life; it is what binds people together in community, recognizing a nexus of mutual obligations and responsibilities for one another. An acceptable degree of justice is necessary if people are to live together in harmony; a sense of systematic injustice leads to suspicion, hostility and, ultimately, divisive conduct.[48]

In this chapter I will seek to describe a response to Habermas, which in many ways will follow a similar pattern to Forrester, although the theologians whom I will predominantly engage with are Dan Hardy and Dietrich Bonhreffer.

The great virtue of Forrester's theology is that he takes social institutions seriously. In his book, he examines the question of imprisonment and punishment in the prison system, as well as the issue of poverty and welfare benefits. Forrester accepts neither the foundationalist approach nor that of self-expression. In other words, he takes very seriously the breakdown in moral value, exploring the failure to achieve shared consensus in our society in a chapter entitled 'Nobody knows what Justice is'. At the same time, he dissents from any exploration of purely personal experience. Partly this is because the personal love at the heart of personal relationships, and experience, ignores the centrality of justice as a theological norm. Here, Forrester follows Reinhold Niebuhr, and also his brother Richard, who was sceptical of the idealization of personal relationships.[49] Forrester does not explore the challenge to personal identity given in some theology which denies that there is an 'essential self'. What is deeply interesting is that Forrester has a great deal of sympathy with the alternative approach outlined above, which is concerned with its distinctively Christian narratives, virtues and practices. He refers to it approvingly on several occasions, but denies that it is necessary to choose between a public theology and the theology of the Christian community.[50] He pursues an approach which listens to the voices of the liberation or political theologian, and feminist writers. Forrester writes:

Liberation theology, despite many premature obituaries, is very much alive. But it has surely learnt the danger of tying theology too closely and unambiguously to one particular form of ideology, theory or social analysis. It is now beginning to recognize the need for a variety of dialogue partners in the task of proclaiming good news to the poor, and speaking for the dumb, and from the beginning it has recognized the central importance of serious critical theological work in the service of the poor and of justice.[51]

Forrester shows, like Linda Woodhead's writings which offer a feminist perspective on love and justice, that it is possible to unite political theology and the public realm.

The challenge presented by Habermas is, as we have seen above, to establish an understanding of identity and social justice in the face of a depersonalized social world. He denies that positivism as a secular philosophy will help. Positivism relegates ethical theory to emotivism, which is the expression of human feelings and emotions in ethical language. 'Good' means that I like this object, action or person. Habermas argues that language is not simply an expression of emotion, but the medium of all understanding and communication. It can transcend its context. It challenges others with a claim to its validity, exploring what a true identity and justice might be, even if this is not in terms of content but of process. Justice becomes the just achieving of dialogue, and identity is the stabilizing of the ego or self by a continuous dialogue with other persons.

This initial discussion leads into the three aspects of Habermas' theory which need to be resolved within a theological understanding of the economic and bureaucratic system, when discussing the public nature of theology. First, there is the nature of social structures, especially as they relate to God. Secondly, there is the question of human identity in a market world. Thirdly, there is the issue of the nature of justice. We turn, first, to the nature of social structures. The two theologians who will be studied are Bonhoeffer and Hardy. The argument turns on whether social structures can afford the individual a basis for personal identity, and whether social justice can be articulated within these structures.

Social structures, as Bonhoeffer pointed out, are not central to the New Testament. The term 'state' or ordered community includes the rulers and the ruled. The 'polis' (or state) as a term is derived from the concept of the state, and refers to the social community ordered harmoniously in its affairs by political authority. However, this term is only used in the New Testament in a future sense. It is eschatological, referring to the future city of God, the new Jerusalem or the heavenly society. When this occurs, the governing authority will be directly given by God.[52]

There is no earthly 'polis' which can be discerned by New Testament writers. Faithful to this New Testament vision, Bonhoeffer repudiates the attempt to relate the idea of polis to that of government. In the New Testament the concept of exousia, or government, takes its place. 'Government' refers to power, and can be found in family relations or in politics. In Bonhoeffer's words, 'Government is divinely ordained authority to exercise worldly dominion by divine right. Government is deputyship for God on earth . . . Government does not proceed from society, but it orders society from above.'[53] Bonhoeffer turns his back on the idea of the state as fulfilling natural society, as some political theory had argued. In particular, he disagrees with the Aristotelian and Thomist understanding of the state, where human nature is the foundation of civil society, which in turn underpins the theory of the state. He is equally critical of the Hegelian transformation of the state, whereby the state originates the very being or existence of culture, economy and community.

Bonhoeffer therefore separates social relations, or the life-world (it is not a term which he uses) from government. The task of *exousia*, of government, is to maintain 'created things in their proper order, but it cannot engender life; it is not creative.'[54] Instead it governs the institutions of marriage and labour, which he calls mandates. These exist before the Fall, as part of the divine intention for the world. Even as we know them now, they exist as divine institutions. They originate in God, and this must be acknowledged by government. The range of activities covered by these concepts is large, for the mandate for marriage includes the education of children in obedience to Christ, and the mandate for labour includes culture, science and art. Government is not creative. It merely rules what has its own creativity and spontaneity: that which forms the divinely given mandates. Only the mandates, which make up society, are creative.

Like Habermas, Bonhoeffer believes that the significance of government is 'regulative and not constitutive'. The orders of civil society are only supervised by government. Bonhoeffer would no doubt have felt that Habermas' analysis of the life-world only bears out his warning:[55] 'If it [government] asserts its authority beyond the limits of its assigned task it will in the long run forfeit its genuine authority over these fields.' Labour has its mandate, or divinely imposed task, from God. This task is 'a making of new things on the basis of the creation by God'.[56] Although it is a task performed under discipline, involving effort and hard work, nevertheless it creates the objects and values which glorify God in agriculture, the economy, science and art. It is therefore a deeply creative activity, and includes all that will be considered in the next two chapters on consumption and work.

What Bonhoeffer cannot do is to elaborate this understanding of labour into an account of social structures. There is a clear reason why this is so, and this is because of his understanding of moral language. The authorization to speak relativizes all human authorities. No human authority can claim to be absolute. God's mandate is for church, family, labour or government, and does not spring from human well-being, such as the claim of the instinct of self-preservation. All that labour (or any of the other mandates, which are family, church and government) can do is to give effect to God's command. It can give effect in conjunction with the other mandates: as Bonhoeffer writes, God's commandment 'juxtaposes and coordinates these authorities in a relation of mutual opposition and complementarity and thus it is only in this multiplicity of concrete correlations and limitations that the commandment of God takes effect as the commandment which is manifest in Jesus Christ'.[57]

Bonhoeffer transformed the theological understanding of 'commandment' into a positive content, wherein humanity is given permission to live life to the full. It is, however, concerned with the individual as she seeks to live out that fullness. Bonhoeffer could write that 'action which is in accordance with Christ is in accordance with reality because it allows the world to be the world; it reckons with the world as the world, that is a limited statement'.[58] For this world cannot be seen apart from the reconciliation given it in Christ. The 'world' is thus the sphere of concrete reality given in Christ. In Bonhoeffer's words, it is a 'concrete and therefore limited responsibility . . . which acts within the world in accordance with this knowledge'.[59] The problem with this is not in its understanding of vocation, responsibility and conscience. The influence of Bonhoeffer on what he called 'man come of age' is enormous. Rather, the problem lies in the focusing of the world into the concept of responsibility. 'The "world" is thus the sphere of concrete responsibility which is given to us in and through Jesus Christ.'[60] Responsibility and action eclipse any further understanding of the world. Social structures become the stage on which responsibility is exercised.

Bonhoeffer's *Ethics*, from which this account has been taken, was one of the few theological studies at that time which took political and economic life seriously. Since Luther and Calvin's understanding of vocation had been formed in the sixteenth century, Protestant theology had written little on the public realm. This theology is analysed in chapter 3, on work, but Bonhoeffer came to feel that there was too great a distinction between law and gospel in Luther's theology. Bonhoeffer's Christocentric theology did not allow him to confine the presence of Christ to his saving work in word and sacraments, but drove him to see Christ at the centre of a redeemed humanity. Fritz De Lange writes:

In the Ethics, the incarnation is the theological paradigm through which Bonhoeffer analysed European culture, and with which he justified his Christian apologetics. The incarnation of God made Europe what it was – a historical, political and cultural unity . . . The incarnation of God is not only the starting point of European history, it is its purpose, its substance, its aim. And now Jesus Christ has made of the West an historical unity. . . The unity of the West is not an idea but an historical reality, of which the sole foundation is Christ.[61]

The advantage of this Christocentric theology is that personality and sociality are developed together. The person who is open to the call to take up responsibility for others which comes in following Christ finds that their personality is now shaped by the command of Christ. Life becomes living in communion with 'the man for others', and fulfilment is found in carrying out that command, which Bonhoeffer calls deputyship. The sphere of the world in which it is exercised is the mandates, as described above, and the constitution of these mandates is what is meant by sociality. Hardy gives a fuller description of them later in this chapter. However, there is no predetermined ordering of these mandates.

The whole realm of ordered wholeness in the various areas of human life on earth (even, it should be noted, the order of the Church which is one of the mandates) becomes not an ordained structure, but a divine calling and a human secular responsibility. Only the 'domains' are presupposed, not how they shall be ordered. The ground under our feet is not orders of economic life, marriage and family, state, church or culture, but human relations justified and illuminated by Christ, in all of these spheres and beyond them.

There is then no sociality which can be described and then related to Christ. There is only the human task given by Christ.[62]

Three comments can be made about this understanding of social structures given by Bonhoeffer. The first is simple. Bonhoeffer is at his most socially conservative in the *Ethics*. Larry Rasmussen has described how Bonhoeffer responded in his visit to New York City in 1931 to many aspects of American culture which challenged the highly sophisticated cultural formation he had been shaped in as a child. Alongside classical music there was the discovery of jazz, and as well as the theatre there was now the cinema. But, by 1943, Bonhoeffer had returned to an aversion for mass, consumer culture and in his letters to the conspirators against Hitler and in the *Ethics* he pleads for an elite to take on this responsibility of resistance. René von

Eyden, who is related to Bethge, the biographer of Bonhoeffer, has also written of this conservatism. Why, she asks, is there so much emphasis on the above/below relationship of rulers/ ruled, husband/wife, the elite and society? In his rebuttal of Nazism, which Bonhoeffer saw as paradoxically a movement which was highly authoritarian yet supported, at least before the war, by mass, popular opinion, Bonhoeffer became suspicious of anything which challenged the highly cultured, socially responsible world of the elite which he had known as a child. This was an unusual elite. For centuries from the Reformation it had developed economic power, but had been denied political power by the aristocracy which held to their dominance in the many small states which made up Germany. Even after German unification, the Prussian aristocracy and military leaders formed an alliance with the new leaders of German business. This led to the First World War, with little power shared with the German national parliament or local state parliaments. For a brief while, after 1918, there was a flourishing of middle-class political hegemony in the Weimar Republic. The collapse of this, first economically in the 1929 Wall Street crash, and then in 1933 in the Nazi seizure of power, returned the German cultural elite (*Bildungsbürgerstum*) to a deep antipathy with politics. What is so striking is how the German political resistance drew from this class, but its political instincts for Germany purged of Nazism by a political *coup d'état* were deeply conservative. Mass political culture, mass consumer culture and the exploration of different gender roles, which all flourished briefly under Weimar in the 1920s, were alien to it. This explains both Habermas' intense concern with the legitimation of political rule, which is so predominant in *Legitimation Crisis*, and the distance of any political thought from 'below' found in Bonhoeffer's *Ethics*.[63]

A second comment is about how Christocentric Bonhoeffer's theology had become by the time of the *Ethics*. Charles Marsh, in his recent theological study, is concerned at this aspect, even if it also yields enormous insights. Marsh writes: 'Yet Bonhoeffer seems to push too far his emphasis on Christ as the centre of the real . . . Does he not push the theme of recapitulation in Christ to such a point that the difference between Christ and world is jeopardized (despite his criticisms of Hegel on precisely this point)?' The danger is that of a monistic language, where Christ self–empties his being into the world which He redeems in what Marsh calls 'an extreme Kenoticism'. Certainly there are times when the *Ethics* can sound like this. 'The whole reality of the world is already drawn into Christ and bound together in Him, and the movement of history consists solely in divergence and convergence in relation to this centre.' That is certainly very monistic, but, in the same section of the *Ethics* there is a passage which, as it were, draws back from Bonhoeffer's identification of world and Christ as one reality:

The unity of the reality of God and of the world, which has been accomplished in Christ, is repeated, or more exactly, is realized ever afresh in human life. And yet what is Christian is not identical with what is of the world. The natural is not identical with the super-natural, or the revelational with the rational. But between the two there is in each case a unity which derives solely from faith in this ultimate reality.

However Bonhoeffer never elaborated how this faith-given unity might have been expressed, and realized afresh. The *Letters and Papers from Prison* offer hints, but it remains an unrealized programme.[64]

The third comment is on the theme of this programme. Bonhoeffer seems to lay so much stress on the responsibility which a person must exercise that it is difficult to see what else there is to say about the world. Peter Selby, in *Grace and Mortgage*, rightly draws attention to the earlier theological writings in the same way as Charles Marsh does in his study as being of decisive importance for our understanding of Bonhoeffer. In his *Christology*, which is the lectures which he gave in Berlin in the early 1930s on the theme 'Who is Jesus Christ for us today?', Bonhoeffer sharpens his criticism of liberal theology. We cannot know who 'we' are and then accommodate 'us' to Christ. Instead, Christ judges us in our self-definition. This implies that developing a theology which addresses social structures may lead to criticizing structures which define our identity. It is in this sense that Selby attacks the existence of the market, since 'the attraction of the market is that it appears to offer a method for deciding who "us" is apart from Christ'.[65] Bonhoeffer can certainly be read in this way. Selby's description of the criteria which Bonhoeffer provides for speaking about Christ is of central importance:

They must speak in language that has not been co-opted into the exclusive realm of religion, speaking to humanity, that is to say, in individualistic and inward ways; contact must be re-established between the language about Christ and the language of the world about us and its realities. Secondly, it must address humanity in its strength, not relying on a sense of alienation or weakness to gain a spurious purchase on human life but both appreciating and confronting a humanity come to maturity, answerable for itself and not dependent on religion for either survival or explanation. That exploration, those questions and those criteria have brought us to the place where Christ is quite literally in the marketplace.[66]

Nevertheless, this challenge to the reality of the powers which determine our existence does not remove the necessity of evaluating and describing what our society might become, in a theological manner. Too much Christian social ethics juxtaposes a theology of Christ with a sociology, or politics, which is deeply secular.

Is there another way by which social structures can be evaluated, without collapsing theology into sociology? Hardy's analysis of social structures provides an alternative. Hardy provides an effective critique of Bonhoeffer. Bonhoeffer derives social structures (the term used is sociality) directly from relationship with human sociality is inseparable from community with God; human and human–divine community are mutually necessary'.[67] It is important that Bonhoeffer points to ethical holiness for society as much as for individuals. However, there is no explication of the necessity of social community with divine community. It is simply stated to be the case, for 'social community is the response to the gift of God, fulfiled in his achievement in Christ'.[68] Hardy also notes that the Church is the place where this response is made. The Church is seen 'as apostle to society as a whole'.

In one way this is a great step forward. Seeing the Church as inextricably connected with the well-being of society allows the Church to become involved in social action and social concern. It legitimates prophesy, and Bonhoeffer has been much used to justify such theological and ecclesiastical developments. In another way, the effects of these views is damaging. It is worth spelling out Hardy's critique of Bonhoeffer in detail.

First, social relations (or sociality) present in the human condition are eliminated, since their place is always taken by the gift of God in Christ. The way in which created nature, and human society as part of that creation, has an underlying truth of social relations (technically, a 'social transcendental') is ignored for an emphasis on Christ's revelation of God. Secondly, it should be possible to analyse how this sociality can be seen as true, but again the emphasis shifts to the apostleship of the Church and the Christ event. The effect of this is twofold. First, Christians, by moving specifically to God's work in Christ, 'lose their commonality as created social beings with the society to which they speak. They put themselves outside the society to which they speak.'[69]

Secondly, they narrow God's work to that of redemption, without relating it to that of creation. Christian faith may stress its commitment to social well-being with great sincerity, but individual Christians 'privatize the Christian contribution to sociality'. It also allows those who see religious faith as absolute to deny that it has any contribution to the contingencies of modern life: 'not only those which have to do with the disappearance of external natural resources but also those related to crises in institution and personal freedom and meaning'.[70]

Hardy points out that social theorists claim that religions are obsolete because they have ceased to be able to deal with these contingencies of human society. At the most, as one of the historians of the Frankfurt School from which Habermas came has claimed, religion offers a 'contingency management praxis' through the 'bourgeois stabilization of capitalistic action systems' which does not lead to successful identity formation.[71]

How then must we find an effective relation of sociality to the truth of God present in creation? Hardy points to the logos of God operative in creation. Sociality, or the social transcendental, is formed from geographical conditions, such as 'location on a delimited land area and the natural resources which are available there'. There are however also conditions in human society, such as:

1. those of social institutions, the presence of laws, customs and political organizations, with the constitution of leaders such as rulers, governors or a 'superior' class;
2. those of economic arrangements, including those of production and distribution;
3. those of personal relationship, including natural bonds (whether of blood affinity or loyalty) and those constructed bonds of a more 'spiritual' kind such as friendship or compassion; and
4. those of communication, such as language, symbols and culture.[72]

Such conditions are both the product and the producers of a world history where their effects have become more distributed and complex. Human society thus reforms itself in ever changing ways. The social cosmology of laws, customs and political organizations has been transformed again and again in recent centuries. Hardy echoes some of Habermas' critique of modern capitalism, while not explicitly naming him.

Hence the institutionality of society has its own historical dynamic. Indeed, it must have if it is to escape the premature stability of which modern social theorists complain, or the injustice of repressive societies to which those concerned with social liberation are opposed. For these are complaints about the fixation of society in inadequate forms which can be answered only by recovering the dynamics of institutionality.[73]

What has happened to modern social structures is analysed in a further article by D. W. Hardy, which was written five years after the one above. Here Hardy traces the relativizing of social structures and the marginalizing of God as closely related features of contemporary society. Again the article illuminates Habermas' work, in ways in which Bonhoeffer's writings have not always succeeded in doing. Hardy begins with an account of social change in recent years. Modern states have become concerned with human beings as a collective whole, and use social administration and the management of wealth, to increase social well-being. At the same time, human beings resist

the excesses of states, and appeal to the concept of individualism. States come into existence as a result of individuals freely
contracting with each other to ensure individual well-being.
Therefore states need to be restrained by constitutions and laws
which limit the exercise of arbitrary power. What has declined
in social significance is the informal and local range of units,
such as voluntary societies.[74]

The managerial notion of the state leads to a belief that
human beings can be treated as externally related by reference
to a common process. This process is characteristically that of
wealth creation and social control. The two are related and
human beings are explained, manipulated and changed
through this process. The same is true of education. 'Right'
education 'socializes' human beings, ameliorating social relations, such as those from class structures: 'Throughout, people
are seen as related to each other through the characteristic or
process by which they are "managed".'[75]

In a similar way, human beings can see themselves as
individuals, where each individual is ontologically prior to
society, and may be defined without reference to other human
beings. Each individual is related to others by their own choice,
or by historical accident. They are endowed with certain rights
such as liberty. Society arises out of the contingent relations of
such individuals. 'The civil state is constituted by individuals
when they freely hand over certain natural rights, renouncing
their right to punish intrusions upon their life, freedom and
property; but it exists for the sake of individuals.'[76]

Both notions of individuality and states lead to an external,
extrinsic notion of human relationships, and to a downplaying
of informal, voluntary groups. At the same time, the goal of
human life shifts, and certain forms of social structures are
idealized in their own right. States appeal to human beings in
general, and win their approval by promoting particular ideological processes. Thatcherism, for instance, constantly justified
itself by a self-referring ideology, since the market was the best
way of organizing states, 'the implicit suggestion is that this is
the most equitable way of securing the interests of most of their
citizens and is therefore most likely to succeed in securing their

approval'.[77] At the same time individualism argues that: 'true society is seen best to be achieved through securing a greater sense of responsibility on the part of individuals. Adherents of each often fault those who follow the other for their inadequate view of society.'[78]

Hardy argues that such social movements of extrinsic relationships and self-justifying ideologies are not simply the historical accompaniment of the marginalization of Christian understanding of God. Conceptually also such views outlined above deny the 'presence in human social structures of the social coherence which is embedded in God's very being and work, together with the deeper and more varied form of human rationality which that presence implies'.[79] The marginalization of God from social structures began with the eighteenth-century deism which disengaged God from nature. At the same time, evangelicalism domesticated religion by confining God to a personal relationship between him and particular individuals, based on a theology of choice and human election. We have seen Bonhoeffer's attempt to bring back the importance of social relations in Christianity, and the advantages and limits of his theology.

An alternative position would be one in which God and humanity participate in the historical process, and seek for a justice which relativizes all inadequate forms of political and social organization. We will return to this later in this theological discussion on the possibility of the continuing validity of political theology. However, it is worth noticing that the relativism and increased simplicity of social structures in advanced industrial society reflects an impoverished conceptualization of the nature and activity of God. Hardy points out, following the political theorist and historian David Nicholls, that the *monarche* of God is transferred to states and individuals. The monarchical view of God in western thinking, not simply in Christian theology, portrays God as absolute and simple, related in the same manner as the ultimate explanation of all creation. 'Because such a view disallows all diversity or particularity as fundamentally unreal, the complexity of nature and humanity is unintelligible. When this view is extended to social structures, what results is that simpler ones are considered preferable, and this authorizes the preference for either monolithic states or those based on solitary individuals.'[80]

At the same time, the differences in personal and social relationships, with the complexity and unity which occur in this differentiation, become problematic. Extrinsic relationships deny the complex differentiation in intrinsic relationships which anthropology and political theory clearly reveals. The theological response turns back to the divine simplicity, where the divine will fashions everyone alike, 'repetitions of God (or his will) in finitude whose destiny is to be reincorporated in an absolute unity with each other and with him'.[81] Likeness disavows complexity. This transfer of a monarchical view of God to states and individuals means also that social structures determine their own social coherence. Any other set of values becomes marginalized, as does pluralism, variety, complexity and changeability in society. 'Justice is seen as conformity, as requiring a return to the norms of the society, its identity and its enduring character.'[82] Society comes to prefer its self-sustaining unity, whether through particular ideologies or processes. A totalitarianism pervades the understanding of the relationship of social institutions.

Hardy therefore suggests that what is needed is a properly developed theology of social structures. Just as Habermas sets the tone of this book by his analysis of 'lifeworld' and 'system', even if not all his conclusions are acceptable, so Hardy moves theology into a dialogue with social structures. The rest of this book will follow this agenda. It is, however, important to follow up the implications of Hardy's analysis for theological method.

Let him put it in his own words. 'The development of more adequate social structures is correlative with uncovering the presence and activity of God in them.'[83] God's presence and activity is found in diversity and change, and not primarily in the simple social structures which domesticate the conception of God. Hardy follows the social anthropologist R. N. Adams, who sees society as fields of relationships, throwing up social units and evolving into new forms.[84] Such recreation of social order requires an energy which works in unstable, unpredictable and non-linear ways. As we will see later, this echoes the well-known management theorist Charles Handy who entitled one of his books *The Age of Unreason*.[85] There is no reason why social change should be linear, and, in fact, it is more likely to be randomly variable. The technical term is stochastic, and it fits very well the random set of variations characteristic of British urban and economic life after the late 1970s: the rapid emergence of small firms, leisure and entertainment, mass poverty, alienation and information technology.

Our primary concern at this point in the argument is with theological method, and not with social analysis. If social life is made up of interacting units, they are both internally and externally related. Unlike much of the above description, human beings and social units are bound up intrinsically with one another. They are structured by formal, informal and individual structures, with a self-constituting existence through processes of rapid (even bewildering) change. Social structures, as Habermas has consistently maintained, are either benevolent or harmful. The way in which these social changes take place is the energy of a society, which again can be positive or destructive of social and human relationships. There are also external relationships, where self-maintaining structures can continue its distinctive unity, while engaging with other structures.

God is equally self-structured, self-determined and self-identified. His energy structures and maintains his cohesion. This is not a concept of God as simple, but as highly complex. This God maintains also 'an energetic faithfulness in his dynamic relation to the world'.[86] Hardy postulates the nature of God in Trinitarian terms. The energetic unity of God is the Holy Spirit, arising in its initial genesis in the Father and ordering its energy through the Son. However it would be wrong to see this as a description of the being of God. Rather it describes God's interrelatedness with the society He loves.

God and society are both complex, dynamic and changing sets of relationships. In God's dynamic relationality 'there is an infinite possibility of life'. Yet there is more than this. God self-structures his being in the midst of a continuing relationship with the world. All human activity, either as individuals or in social structures, is caught up in this dynamic. Hardy summarizes the complexity of his theory in words that are best quoted in full:

It is in the energizing of his relationality that God reaches his fullness, and in this ordered relationality interacts energetically with human beings to enable them to structure their life together. In their turn they exist in a relationality whose form is derived from God: their self-relationality is also their sociality, both together being structured by the presence and activity of God ('love the Lord thy God . . . love thy neighbour as thyself'). But their relationality (self-relationality and sociality) is also given its dynamic energy from God; their moving toward themselves and towards others are energized by God. They need not attempt to 'process' their relationships, by relativizing particular forms of social structure and by domesticating the notion of God and transferring it to themselves. They need instead to rediscover their own relativity to God in their relativity to each other, and thereby find new social life from God.[87]

Hardy provides us with the beginning of a theological understanding of economic and bureaucratic systems. The remainder of this book will explore the nature of that relationship to God and each other in the worlds of the global market (chapters 4 and 5), the nature and experience of work (chapter 3), and the pervasive effects of consumerism on human identity (chapter 2). At each point there will be an exploration of the conditions in human society, or sociality, which shape human relationships with particular reference to economics and the market world. What will also be attempted is the analysis of how social structures and ideologies justify themselves. We turn next to the question of language in Habermas, and his hostility to theological discourse.

Habermas' use of public language has been discussed by theologians, especially by David Tracy.[88] He acknowledges that his own public theology has the danger of becoming trapped in the problem of correlating theology and society. Theology can be correlated with social experience using the symbols of the religious tradition and contemporary culture. The danger is that this cultural insight ignores the conditions of that culture, such as the market and bureaucracy. Habermas demands that there are certain conditions of possibility for all communicative action. All such action must be comprehensible, true, sincere and right. Tracy is aware that a transcendental philosophy of consciousness will only lead to greater privatization of communication in the public realm. For Habermas reason functions as reason only through the persuasive force of the argument. Critical theory has always been concerned with coercive power, whether socially in totalitarian ways, or individually through the internal imposition of neuroses. Public language must be committed to the unveiling of coercion, and to showing by persuasive argument how different understandings of relationships and rationality are formed by different social practices and institutions. This language is implicitly democratic, since out of the conditions of communicative action there come the concepts of equality, reciprocity and individual dignity.

Nevertheless, Tracy raises severe questions about Habermas' argument. The lack of attention in Habermas to ideas of myth, symbol and interreligious dialogue means that his theory of social evolution is overprescriptive. Habermas' belief that social evolution is concerned with the cognitive and sociological autonomy of the three spheres of science, morality and art is, as Tracy says, 'too neat a response to the disturbing contrary hypotheses of modern anthropology, history of religions, and philosophical hermeneutics.'[89] However it is not with his theory of social evolution that we are concerned now, but with his use of public language.

Tracy presses Habermas with the claim that symbols can have a public character which is open for dialogue. Furthermore, truth can be seen as a notion which manifests possibility. It is not the case that the classic works of religion and art are available simply for private edification. In particular, Tracy looks at 'the utopian impulse found in [the] eschatological symbols',[90] and sees in them a disclosure of possibilities which are not simply expressive. Tracy returns to the early thinkers associated with the Frankfurt School, such as Ernst Bloch and Walter Benjamin. Their use of symbols works in two ways. They describe the past suffering of those who have been destroyed by the encounter with war, poverty and social oppression in which capitalism has been deeply implicated. Secondly, they offer utopian possibilities for a better life in society. Tracy instances the concrete examples of Reinhold Niebuhr using the symbols of grace and sin to illuminate social, political and economic life in the United States in the 1930s, and provoke a public debate around the validity of the 'New Deal', which, of course, directly confronted the failure of capitalism. Another example instanced by Tracy is that of Martin Luther King in the 1960s, who again redefined the discussion of justice and social relationships by invoking the language of biblical imagery and American classic political symbols.

However, Habermas' challenge to public language is not only about the place of myth and symbol in public discourse. It is also about the relationship of concepts of what is right to what is good. Since liberal theories of justice stress the priority of the former over the latter, it 'concedes that diverse conceptions of the good life exist.'[91] Given Hardy's defence of the complexity and variety of human society, this need not be a problem. What is distinctly more problematic is the idea, shared by John Rawls and by Habermas, that theories of justice can develop conceptions of justice independent of theories of the good. Indeed, Habermas goes further than Rawls. Rawls stops at the idea of an overlapping public consensus, but Habermas argues that conceptions of justice should challenge what can be legitimately claimed to be part of the good life.[92] Justice is always more fundamental as a concept for Habermas than ideas of human flourishing.

As Duncan Forrester points out, in his book *Christian Justice and Public Policy*, there are certainly similarities between Habermas and Rawls, although both thinkers have evolved their ideas over time. Habermas' ideal speech situation has no intimidation, or pressure. This position is superficially like Rawls' Original Position, but the differences are striking. The appeal to complete ignorance in Rawls is not matched by Habermas. Habermas requires a great knowledge of possibilities for a discussion to be fruitful. Forrester believes that there is a quite substantive content in Habermas, but it has to be teased out of him. A just society will have the minimum of coercion, and 'where manipulation and ideological control are systematically discountenanced, where people are able to relate freely and openly to one another, where people learn to "speak the truth in love" '.[93]

Forrester is concerned about his confidence that it is possible to overcome the distortion of ideology and interest: 'A theologian might echo Anselm in suggesting that he has not yet considered the gravity of sin and its pervasive distortion of human judgements.'[94] However, Habermas is a universalist, and believes that a society can be structured according to ideas of justice. What is more uncertain is whether one can speak, as Forrester does, of Habermas' commitment to the 'good society'. As pointed out in the previous paragraph, justice challenges our ideas of what the good life is. Perhaps the most which can be said is what Forrester claims. This is that unlike Rawls justice is not 'a principle or principles, . . . or a simple set of procedures governing a part of social life'.[95] That would be true of Rawls, referring to principles, or Hayek, referring to procedures, but not of Habermas. Instead, justice is a form of social order. Here the impersonality of life is overcome, and individuals exercise their choice from their deepest convictions. These choices are not determined by tradition, or relationship. He is suspicious of social structures, and wishes for participation as deeply as possible. Nevertheless, one cannot say what choices will be made, or whether goodness is a term that can be given specific content.

Fiorenza instead believes that there is a mutual relationship between goodness and justice in Christian faith. This is a claim, central to Christianity, that a vision of the good for humanity can combine with ideas of justice. He argues that the theological understanding of justice is embedded in a theological cosmology, so that, for instance, eschatology now contains an ideal vision of justice and peace. 'The religious belief itself is not simply an image of the ideal good life; it is an image radically constituted by principles of justice and equality.'[96] Fiorenza sees churches as communities of interpretation within their religious tradition. Political theology must use public language which is nevertheless related to the conceptions of the good held within that religious tradition. Such a conception cannot simply be a historicist one, relating particular notions of justice to particular cultures. It will need to engage in an internal dialogue between what is publicly normative through principles of justice and what is normative in a tradition about the good life. Habermas, of course, remains unconvinced. Conventional ethical life (*Sittlichkeit*) is motivated by dogmatic evaluations of the good life, with an irrational acceptance of prior traditional authority in an uncritical way. The 'sacral realm' for him is no longer a distinct form of discourse.[97] All that Habermas will accept is a formulation of justice in terms of communicative dialogue, and without any reference to concepts of what is good. If religions hold substantive views of what is good, this is a sign of their acceptance of traditional authority.

The argument between Habermas, Tracy and Fiorenza remains undecided. There is the danger that a phenomenology of culture may become preoccupied with its own life. However, Habermas would appear to be a candidate for what Rowan Williams has called 'a naive evolutionism which sees the development of religious language as a progressive emancipation from myth and metaphor'. Tracy draws attention to eschatological symbols, and the reality of imaging utopia. Symbols only function within communities which can interpret them. This is what enables Fiorenza to hold together themes of justice and of the good life. Human flourishing is capable of being given substantive content, in a theory of justice. Such content is only possible because it is placed in the context of a community. A community that understands itself in the light of belief in God, within the Christian tradition, will show how certain lives are shaped by the symbols of the Christian faith. Habermas resists this.

Habermas, as has been discussed above, believes that the ideal of action is that which is carried out in accordance with norms established by free and public discussion. The rationality of speech is released to fulfil its potential. There is still a defence of the ideal speech situation in *The Theory of Communicative Action*, although it is now set in a theory of universal pragmatics. McFadyen points out that Habermas fails to establish why the ideal conditions of communication should be accepted, since all there is remains 'a closed reference to actual practice'.[98] What could take place is the grounding of the ideal conditions of communication in properly transcendental realities, such as God's creation, and the nature of eschatology. This would enable the dialogue between Habermas, Tracy and Fiorenza to be resolved. Symbolic language, such as eschatology, is nevertheless more than symbolic. It is transcendental, and yet open to Habermas' communicative ethic.

In the preceding pages, Fiorenza's appeal to the symbols of American life and biblical tradition has been mentioned. One continuing symbol has been that of the covenant. The western theological tradition has grounded the possibility of communicative action in the dialogue which is made possible because of the divine covenant with humanity. Political theology continues to have a place in the public realm through the language of covenant, kingdom and hope. Such language need not be apocalyptic, neither need it represent a permanent form of counter-culture to a dominant technical rationality. In particular, the language of the covenant offers rich possibilities for political theology.

The covenant at Sinai must be understood to legitimate the new Christian covenant, the Reformation debates on political liberty and the American constitution. In each new development, there are different actors with significant power (those who rule, or who rebel), and new technological and social circumstances. Yet each event was seen as the reinterpretation of the basic covenant. The 'true' meaning of each event is determined by its relation to the basic symbol of covenant. Each new event resymbolises the old one, and the historical agents reinterpret its meaning. The exodus and the covenant set up a unity of significance which maintains the continuity of western Christian social identity. There is liberation and salvation, where freedom could be reconciled with justice. The Israelites seem unique in the ancient near east in seeing their social identity in terms of a transcendent mission, and not through a cosmology of religious and cultural practices, such as the Babylonian Empire. Equally, imperial societies saw kingship as a divine office which mediated the cosmos, and thus justified hierarchial societies. Israel instead existed in a tension of prophetic–cultic dialogue, where prophet and priest served the Lord who promised in the covenant a liberation that would give Israel its future. There is, in short, a messianic dimension in the political thought that runs through the Reformation to the American Republic: one that can be called eschatological, where there is a reinterpretation of the symbol of liberation.[99]

Habermas offers the theologian a way of discussing the complexity of global capitalism in a way that is at least implicitly also eschatological. His ideal speech situation is a concept which he modified the 1980s. The concept however is eschatological. The power of ideal speech is the power of communicative action. It is more than a regulative ideal. But how can this be so? Adams sees Habermas' theory as similar to that of many of the German political theologians of the 1960s, such as Jürgen Moltmann, Karl Rahner, and Johann Baptist Metz. Rahner saw the future as 'addressing' the individual or community, through the promise made to us by God. When addressed, we are both addressed by a person and by the words uttered. The effect is that we focus on what our response should be. So Habermas' 'ideal speech situation' describes that communication where there is no compulsion save that of the compulsion of argumentation itself. No domination exists in the dialogue, and there is genuine symmetry among the participants themselves. Internally, such dialogue should be sincere, truthful, intelligible and morally right. Much of the discussion of strategic rationality in the first part of this chapter is about domination and distorted communication. Hence, when we respond to the ideal speech situation as a dimension of the symbol of liberation described above by Ricoeur and others, or as part of the narrative of eschatology, we are 'addressed' by it and respond in one movement.

This leaves both the western political tradition of liberation, seen in its broadest terms as including the English Civil War and the American Revolution, and Habermas' ideal speech situation as ways of communicating which challenge their audience. They do not simply speak of an ideal, but of a power, which can motivate the power of true communication or of protest against oppression and poverty. It is a future hope, stemming from the juxtaposition of exodus and covenant.

The covenant as a theological concept refers back to the presence of the logos of God in creation. As I have outlined above, Hardy traces the promise of God's presence to the presence of a Trinitarian indwelling of creation, including social structures. This presence is a covenant of promise, to use Hardy's words. Political theology is about the continuing possibility of change and transformation, in political institutions.

Such political change must take place within institutions, as well as outside them. Adams writes of 'areas where money and power have done their colonizing worst. It is under these circumstances that, perhaps, we can and should narrate and debate the ideal speech situation as a parable of God's future for humankind. And submit humbly and hopefully, to its judgement.'[100] This is a justification of political theology in terms of its continued validity as a vehicle of protest against the impoverishment of society. The problem is that this can become a permanent marginalization from society. Part of the challenge of Habermas' account of the self-stabilizing nature of modern economic systems is that it forces one to ask what alternatives might be possible to contemporary economic paradigms.

Here the understanding of political discourse as reinterpreting the basic Sinai covenant is relevant. For what is needed is a form of economic liberty which is theologically grounded in the Sinai covenant, with freedom and justice as its norms. McFadyen has offered one definition of sin as 'the absence of genuine communication'.[101] How can institutions open themselves up to change? What can enable dialogue within institutions, and between institutions and individuals? Most pressingly of all, can the theological language of covenant and kingdom facilitate this challenge? This is a question which must be returned to in later chapters.

What of the question of justice in Habermas' thought? One problem which Forrester identifies is the increasing remoteness of his theory from any identifiable practice, in spite of much talk by him about the unity of theory and practice.[102] The 'new social movements' have not been able to achieve much purchase on social change, although it is possible to use his ethics as a model of dialogue between administrators and those affected by their decisions.

However, there are two fundamental criticisms which must be made of Habermas' theory of justice. One concerns the relation to substantive accounts of the good, and the other relates to worship. Articulating the faith requires a means of handing it on, and seeking the future of the faith. This dimension of the faith, which is seen in public worship, nevertheless recognizes the dialogical nature of all communication, even in religious faith. It is not possible to exclude those with whom one disagrees ethically from worship, nor to control the situation. The contemporary German Lutheran theologian Trutz Rendtorff puts it well: 'The knowledge that faith lives through a reality that it does not control must be clearly portrayed by the church.'[103] This excludes both legal force as punishment, and a demand for ethical conformity which is absolute. 'Freedom of belief is always basic to the church's ethic.'[104] Here freedom is taken into the heart of worship in a way which respects the openness for which Habermas has always striven. Nevertheless, the transcendent element remains central in a way which Habermas denies.

Secondly, justice has a substantive meaning, and is related to community. Forrester cites the anticipation of the Kingdom in the Eucharist as the sign of the church's commitment to a just community. This avoids identifying the community which instantiates justice too obviously with any one empirical manifestation, such as a particular church, while not denying that in its deepest reality the church is a social space where divine justice is manifested.[105]

CONCLUSION

In conclusion, Habermas offers the possibility of understanding our society as shaped by the power of the state and the market. What is distinctive about this understanding is that it embraces modernity, rationality and epistemology. In terms of the market, this leads to an increasingly complex search for self-identity in what is paradoxically an ever more stable global market place. Habermas' fear is that self (or ego) identity can become problematic in a culturally impoverished society.

I have emphasized the growth of political apathy in my account of Habermas, since I find the interpretation of Habermas as providing a radical blueprint deeply suspect. The nature of consumption, and life style, gives this study one of its enduring themes, and this will be taken up in a later chapter. A theological study of consumerism is long overdue. Another theme is that of the role of the state. In spite of political apathy and the role of spin doctors, there may nevertheless be more chance than before to regulate the market. Again this will be taken up in a later chapter. A third theme is what has now replaced the Protestant work ethic. As shown above, Habermas has greatly modified the centrality of this concept from Weber's understanding of it. He does not discard it, but it is placed in a much wider context.

The importance of Habermas is that he holds together in a unified whole a vision of modern economic life, rationality and human consciousness. Out of this there came the questions of consumerism, the state, and the meaning of work. His theological significance is equally profound. I have not engaged directly with his epistemology, as McFadyen and others have done. Instead, I have attempted to discuss the nature of social structures. What does it mean to speak of 'social sin'? Bonhoeffer and Hardy have been the theologians I have found most useful in understanding the complexity of society. In particular the concept of 'socializing' human beings by managerial techniques is one that marginalizes God as a remote, benign figure. Hardy proposes instead a Trinitarian, dynamic concept of God who interacts with society.

Next there is the question of theological language. Here I have followed Tracy and Fiorenza in arguing that there are still possibilities for theological symbols and metaphors in public life. Symbols only have value if they are sustained by living communities. There is a place for Christian groups to keep alive the debate on social reform, and later in this book I will look at examples of church reports. My concern is with the language which is used, and the place of theology in such reports. How far theological language can impinge on the secular sphere remains a pressing problem.

Finally there is the question of social justice. The elaboration of a substantive theory of justice will be elaborated in the next chapters, with specific reference to the components of the market world. A theological account of justice will be in tension with Habermas, who offers a secular, procedural account of justice by referring to just communication or dialogue. Nevertheless, the importance of not excluding those with whom one disagrees needs to be constantly remembered by the Church.

CHAPTER 2

Consumerism and personal identity

Consumerism is a central phenomenon of modern society. It can be explained by a hedonistic theory of social action, which is fundamentally different from utilitarian-based perspectives found in contemporary economic theory. Consumerism was a feature of late eighteenth-century English society, and has persisted until the present day. As the central study on this subject, by McKendrick, Brewer and Plumb, has argued: 'It will be one of the major burdens of this book to show that consumer behaviour was so rampant and the acceptance of commercial attitudes so pervasive that no one in the future should doubt that the first of the world's consumer societies had unmistakably emerged by 1800.'[1] Consumerism is a product of a romantic ethic, and thus can be traced back through the intellectual history of the seventeenth and eighteenth centuries. Colin Campbell has provided a fascinating study of this period which traces the emergence of consumerism from the reaction to Calvinist orthodoxy in the late sixteenth century.[2] The intellectual movements of the Cambridge Platonists, Latitudinarian theology, sentimentalism, Romanticism and the final emergence of aestheticism in the late nineteenth century all show that the relation between moral idealism and hedonism is not straightforward. Yet out of this tension there emerges the moral and social justification for consumerism. It is true that consumerism can simply be equated with a 'soulless' utilitarianism, but this ignores the subtle interplay of intellectual thought and popular taste in the preceding two centuries. Furthermore, utilitarianism was often anything but soulless, especially when it was concerned with the cultivation of moral feeling in the hands of J. S. Mill or Henry Sidgwick.[3]

The crucial distinction in a hedonistic theory of social action is that between pleasure and satisfaction. Once individuals live beyond the level of subsistence, which was increasingly the case by the eighteenth century for a growing percentage of the population, they can distinguish between traditional and modern hedonism. Traditional hedonism saw 'pleasures' as discrete events, found in sensory experience. The hedonist, often a well-to-do aristocrat, would become preoccupied with sensory experience. Modern hedonism, which spread throughout the middle classes by the end of the eighteenth century, was marked by a preoccupation with 'pleasure'. This was a potential quality in all experience. The individual constructed her own environment of pleasure by the creation of illusions. To speak of 'illusions' is a severe way of describing the emotional dimensions of consciousness, with illusory as well as real stimuli. The attention was focused on the meaning and images given to a product. Novelty became a central feature, as did the search for pleasure. Consumption became a creative process, self-directed and voluntaristic. Consumerism came into being. The consumer created wants, and then abandoned them. It became a never-ending process of autonomous energy. The whole phenomenon was a dynamic one, disacquiring as much as possessing. This is because the purchase of goods could swiftly lead to disillusionment, and because longing could give us as much pleasure as gratification. From this perspective, the fashion industry and the Romantic cult of personal self-expression became aspects of this intense focus on personal subjectivity. So, too, did the stress on romantic love, where again the joy of longing could exceed that of possession of another.

CAMBRIDGE PLATONISM AND SENTIMENTALISM

The Arminian reaction to Calvinism, together with the theology of Leibniz and the theology of the Cambridge Platonists, allowed an emphasis on benevolence and an ethic of feeling. There were three key strands in Cambridge Platonism. First, the image of God in humanity was held to be the goodness and love of God found in humanity. It was this, argued Isaac

Barrow, which was most divine in human life. Secondly, Barrow was of great importance in popularizing Platonism. This goodness was held to spring from feelings, and was not simply made up of philanthropic actions. It anticipated the later 'moral sense' school of Shaftesbury. Natural benign feelings should be expressed in actions, but the existence of feelings was again taken as a divine quality. In particular, an ability to feel sympathy and empathy was a quality implanted by God, an argument found in many of the influential clergy who were affected by the Cambridge Platonists, among them Samuel Parker, William Clagett and Isaac Barrow. Thirdly, and of decisive importance for this argument, it was held that an inherent pleasure accompanied both benevolent emotions and charitable action. As John Tillotson, who edited Barrow's works and became Archbishop of Canterbury, wrote: 'There is no sensual pleasure in the world comparable to the delight and satisfaction that a good man takes in doing good.'[4] Barrow expressed a similar view, writing in 1671 that: 'As nature, to the acts requisite toward preservation of our life, hath annexed a sensible pleasure, forcibly enticing us to the performance of them: so hath she made the communication of benefits to others to be accompanied with a very delicious relish upon the mind of him that practices it'.[5]

Cambridge Platonism acted as an opposition to the materialism of Descartes with regard to the inanimate world, and to the doctrine of election found in Calvinism. Their mystical view of reason reinterpreted it into an abiding direction of will and affection. Since they gave such emphasis to affection, they introduced into theology and Christian ethics the centrality of feelings and emotion. It was because of this change that Weber's account of the Protestant ethic is insufficient to account for the growth of industrialization in England. The problem with Weber's theory is that industrialization was accompanied by consumerism. Weber identified the 'Protestant ethic' as rationality, industry and achievement. When this development of English Puritanism met Enlightenment scepticism, Weber argued that the result was an empiricism which finally became one of the sources of utilitarianism. Weber demonstrated the asceticism of Calvinism, which disciplined 'the spontaneous enjoyment of life and all it had to offer'.[6] Puritanism was hostile to opulence, seeing it as 'vain ostentation', for it feared the enjoyment of possessions. The accumulation of wealth was justified, but the pursuit of riches for their own sake was condemned. The ordered and disciplined life promoted by Puritanism led to the repudiation of indulgences, 'wasteful expenditure and worldly pleasure'. Only 'rational recreation' was accepted which served a useful purpose. Pleasure, as such, was tolerated if it accompanied acts willed by God or shown to be rationally necessary.

Yet this evaluation which Max Weber made of Puritanism cannot account for the development of consumerism. Consumerism justified everything which Puritanism condemned. It is deeply ironic that it was an alternative Protestant ethic which justified consumerism. It begins with Arminianism, and then incorporates the benevolence of the Cambridge Platonists into an approval of emotional behaviour. This, in itself, would not explain how consumerism became the central feature of the late eighteenth century. The answer lies in the growth of the cult of sensibility and the ethic of feeling, as sentimentalism replaced Calvinism, and the 'religion of benevolence' gradually took the place of the intellectual rigour of the Cambridge Platonists.

Eighteenth-century aesthetics rested upon a concern with the pleasures of feeling, and the innate goodness of humanity. Sensibility was seen as a susceptibility to tender feelings, which some novelists like Lawrence Sterne (himself a clergyman) saw as a divine gift. The Calvinist doctrine of signs becomes transformed into an emphasis on virtuous feelings, such as pity, sympathy and benevolence. At the same time the metaphor of inscription in the religious arguments of the latitudinarians, which claimed that the moral law was written upon the heart, could become simply a doctrine of the heart itself. Once this belief could be extended into aesthetics, the way was open for a unification of pleasure, morality and goodness. Weber simply failed to take account of this in his account of the development of the Protestant Work Ethic.

Shaftesbury's *Characteristics of Man, Manners, Opinion, Times,* published in 1711, marked a decisive shift in the attitude to pleasure. The moral sense is the basis for ethical decision making.[7] The 'virtuous soul' would depend on the intuitive moral sense in morality, and in aesthetics. Again it was by feelings that the insights into beauty would be gained. Furthermore, pleasure could accompany these feelings, both in regard to goodness and beauty. Ethics and aesthetics became almost interchangeable since sensibility was able to cover them both. Responsiveness to beauty became a crucial moral quality, while virtuous behaviour was seen as an expression of 'taste'. A moral lapse became a sign of 'bad taste'. Jane Austen's *Sense and Sensibility* (a century after Shaftesbury) uses 'taste', 'sensibility' and 'virtue' almost interchangeably. Self-conscious responsiveness and excessive emotionalism become the hallmarks of the main character. Imagination becomes paramount, and the justification of emotional behaviour is taken from a reliance on one's inner self.

Out of the moral importance of expressing the correct aesthetic judgements as proof of virtue, there came the importance of expressing sensibility. Ascetism ceased to have the importance which it had in the early to mid seventeenth century. Instead, the link between moral stature, taste and aesthetics was forged. The expression of good taste was a manifestation of one's sensibility, which, in turn, required the consumption of goods. Taste was both an ethical and aesthetic concept, and it became indispensable to consumer behaviour. It was responsible for the development of fashion, which enabled the creation of new wants and guided the choices of consumers. Fashion became the *de facto* answer to the search for a commonly agreed, aesthetic standard. It also served as the basis for an ideal of character, which could advance the appreciation of beauty. Aesthetics, with its emphasis in the eighteenth century on the appreciation of beauty, became interwoven with criteria of true, emotional genuiness. Genuine emotional sensitivity and responsiveness were the key to the appreciation of beauty.

Sentimentalism eventually transformed itself into Romanticism, although the history of aesthetics and culture lies beyond the scope of the argument. What is crucial is that the emphasis on emotion, and on pleasure as an emotion which accompanies virtue, is continued through Wordsworth and the Romantic poets in England into the nineteenth century. Consumerism was well established in England before then. However, the eighteenth-century critique of the nobility by sentimentalism became irrelevant. Sentimentalism had criticized the aristocracy for their 'emotional stoicism', and their lack of concern with spiritual values, as well as for their arrogance. The new enemy in the early nineteenth century lay in the utilitarianism of social reforms, philosophers, bankers and business men. Consumerism became financed by the latter, but drew its moral justification from Romanticism. Romanticism emphasized a theology of creativity rather than of benevolence.

VEBLEN'S THEORY OF CONSUMPTION

Consumerism is fuelled by a desire to experience in reality those pleasures created in imagination. The theological emphasis on emotion in the Cambridge Platonists led into sentimentalism, with its full-blooded ethic of feeling. It enabled consumerism to justify itself, because of the need to experience in new ways the beautiful and the sublime. Traditional hedonism is not the same state of being as the hedonism which underlies modern consumerism. The argument up to this point has distinguished between traditional and modern hedonism, and shown how modern hedonism is both related to sensibility and to its theological predecessor, the liberal, Anglican reaction to Calvinism in the late seventeenth century. What we must now do is clarify the relationship between imagination and modern hedonism, which underlies consumerism. In brief, the argument will be that consumerism, as one of the central phenomena of modern societies, is a manifestation of imagination and the imagining self. It is as part of the preoccupation with consciousness, and the definition of who one is, that consumerism takes its place in modern society.

There are, however, dangers in making this statement. 'I shop, therefore I am' is the stock-in-trade of moralistic accounts of the 'self-indulgent' society of western Europe or America.

Such arguments draw on the sociologist Thorstein Veblen. However, Veblen's theory has been too easily adopted by theologians anxious to strip away what is perceived to be the facade in front of the hollow core of contemporary society. What is needed is, first of all, a rigorous assessment of Veblen's perspective. Secondly, the nature of imagination must be considered in consumer behaviour. Thirdly, theologians who rest their case without question on Veblen's theory will be criticized. In particular, the widely influential book *God the Economist*, by M. Douglas Meek, seems to me to make just this mistake. Finally, there will be an attempt to criticize consumerism from the perspective of debt (Peter Selby), over-consumption and greed. Even if consumption is part of a search for identity, there are moral limits to this behaviour.

As this chapter turns from the intellectual history of the late seventeenth to the mid nineteenth century and considers instead the nature of modern consumption, it is important to emphasize that the consideration of the history of English moral philosophy and aesthetics is not an interesting diversion as the argument engages with contemporary life. It is central to the argument, as it is in John Milbank's *Theology and Social Theory*, that the justification of argument and behaviour in modern society is rooted in the development of the previous three centuries. The great centre of imagination, feeling and consciousness today is not primarily found in art (music, painting, sculpture or even cinema, theatre and media) but in consumerism, fashion, design and hedonistic behaviour. Art is a manifestation of this in culture. The source and origin of consumerism lies, as I have tried to argue, in the cult of sensibility and feeling which superseded high Calvinism in the mid seventeenth century. It is therefore because of developments in theology and intellectual history, dating back three centuries, that the fascination with the self, imagination and a series of forms of self-expression has come to dominate fashion, design and (it need hardly be said) cinema and music. Theologians who seek to understand this culture of the late twentieth century (and very few have in any depth) must pause before condemning it as a degenerate preoccupation with unbridled capitalism and personal expenditure. Consumerism is the expression of a particular search for the self, but as Habermas has argued, the search for 'ego-identity' is very problematic in the fast-changing world of fashion and culture typical of late capitalism. It needs to be met by an alternative Christian anthropology which does not condemn the search for identity out of hand.

This caveat needs to be made before we turn to the work of Veblen. Veblen accepted a neo-Darwinian account of natural selection, which implanted in human beings basic predatory instincts. Industrial society made possible the expression of these instincts on the most unprecedented scale. His anthropology held that there were two forces rooted in human beings. One was 'the instinct of workmanship', which drove technology forward. The other was the 'instinct of emulation'. Commodities had importance as signs or symbols in socio-cultural terms. The central problem for Veblen is how certain objects in contemporary society take on meaning, and how behaviour in relation to these goods also becomes significant. Central to Veblen's argument is the importance of consuming goods, neither in terms of satisfying physical needs nor in terms of the construction of personal identity as has been argued above, but in terms of social status. Veblen offers an alternative account to the Marxist struggle for power between social classes. In Veblen's classic work *The Theory of the Leisure Class*, he argued that consumption indicated how much wealth a person possessed. Wealth for Veblen was 'pecuniary strength', and this was a key indicator of social status. Consumption, in Veblen's neo-Darwinian account, was therefore a sign of social status, and of success in the struggle for social selection. Veblen wrote:

No class of society, not even the most abjectly poor, forgoes all customary conspicuous consumption. The last items of this category of consumption are not given up except under stress of the direct necessity. Very much of squalor and discomfort will be endured before the last trinket or the last pretence of pecuniary decency is put away.[8]

Veblen was seen by his admirers in America in the nineteenth century, and indeed up to his death in 1929 in California, as pioneering American sociology and political economy. Some aspects of Veblen's work now compare badly with Max Weber, his German contemporary. Diggins refers to the way in which Veblen was 'imbued with the idea of science as the harbinger of progress', and describes how Veblen 'saw technology as liberating man from the domination of leisure-class values'. This led to Veblen's unusual combination of highly polemical literature and empirical research – what Diggins calls his blend of 'determinism and scientific objectivity . . . [he] chastised the capitalist in the most severe moral terms'.[9] It is clear that Weber's fear of rationalization was incomprehensible to Veblen.

This led to an attack on Veblen years later by another German philosopher and social critic, Theodor Adorno. While in exile from the Frankfurt School of Social Research during the Nazi era, Adorno worked in America. Veblen, who was by then dead, was born in America, but was the son of Norwegian Lutheran immigrants, and was brought up in the Norwegian-speaking Lutheran community in Minnesota. Both were intellectuals with a common heritage in Northern European Lutheranism, and both had become deeply secular, while retaining an interest in religion and aesthetics. Both were highly critical of capitalism, although Veblen was equally scornful of Marxism. Adorno felt, however, deeply unhappy at Veblen's acceptance of mass, consumer culture. Veblen saw conspicuous consumption as mere ostentation. Adorno saw a need 'to transcend the drudgery of industrial life. Veblen's attack on status emulation and conspicuous consumption aroused the antipathy of Adorno'.[10] Adorno valued aesthetics very highly.

Veblen's attitude to Christianity was predominantly hostile, although throughout his life he read Lutheran theology and hymnody. He distinguished between traditional Christianity and 'natural Christianity'. Traditional Christianity was doomed; it was institutionally archaic, had a pre-modern view of science and providence, and its clergy were like leisured, upper-class women: 'Conspicuously exempted from any useful industrial pursuits'. Over against this was the 'Christian impulse of brotherly love'. This 'natural Christianity' was potentially revolutionary, and emerged at times in the early church, the pre-Reformation and Reformations sects concerned with social equality, and with the eighteenth- and nineteenth-century experiments in communal living. Some of these had, of course, established themselves in the United States. He felt that 'future social developments may well be substantially influenced' by these forces, and such a society would 'be characterized by an absence of the ethics of pecuniary competition'. Veblen had a positivist view of human nature, seeing it as 'composed of irreducible traits, instincts or native propensities'. These included self-regard, parental care, intellectual curiosity, aggression or pugnacity, and a sense of workmanship.[11] It was this view of human nature that made him critical both of artistic culture, to Adorno's disappointment, and of institutional Christianity, which he saw as largely irrelevant. His preference was for a social democracy shaped by secular ideals of community, craftsmanship and scientific inquiry. He accepted the mass culture of America (although he was himself at times a strange recluse, scornful of attempts to make his own personal life style conform to the expectations of his academic peers), but hoped to humanize it in ways that would destroy the dominant culture of the social elite which had come to power in America. Veblen was contemptuous of the ostentatious wealth of the new capitalist elite which, ironically, endowed many of the universities in America where he taught in the early twentieth century, until his behaviour ended his career.

Veblen was sceptical of the fact that the rapidly industrializing economy of the United States was efficient. Both in his book on the leisure class, written in 1899, and in *Imperial Germany and the Industrial Revolution* (1915) he examined the growth of a leisure class which he called parasitic. Its interests dominated cultural life, determined the division of labour and condemned the poorest members of society, especially women, to a hard and unrewarding life of toil. Each class becomes dominant, displays its wealth in conspicuous consumption, and is swept away by a new industrial elite. So the cycle turns continually, driven by a theory of technological determinism. Beads and war paint in early hunting societies are the counterparts of large estates and houses today. In particular, women were employed as trophies in tribal warfare in pre-industrial societies. The early twentieth-century wealth of the modern bourgeois expressed its ostentation through the leisure and clothes of their women, which Veblen regarded as no different from barbarian tribal polygamy. Conspicuous waste and idleness was encouraged by American and western European social elites.

Veblen felt that he had solved the problem of social meaning, and given an explanation of the restlessness of contemporary society. Economists have adopted Veblen's theory to explain phenomena which lie outside the nature of marginal utility theory. They have adopted his theory in two ways, thus modifying the individualist, rational and utilitarian model. 'Veblen effects' refer to cultural significance and social emulation. The price of a commodity is set by its cultural significance and not simply by its economic worth or utility. Increasing the price of an object may make it more desirable, and the demand for it may increase, when consumption exists to show 'pecuniary strength'. Some car advertisements have long traded on the price of a vehicle as signalling objects of desire. Secondly, economists also recognize that individual's consumption behaviour is deeply affected by the behaviour of other consumers. This can work either way, since it may be governed by wishing to be part of a social movement (the 'bandwagon' effect) or to be different from everyone else. If it is the latter, once a design has become popular, a cultural elite may move on to a new fashion or service (the 'snob' effect).

It is now time to examine why this apparently plausible model will not do. There are serious problems with Veblen's theory. Campbell speaks of the 'extreme simplicity' of these modifications to utility theory. Consumer products have complex symbolic meanings, which are communal and not simply individual. Fashion, taste and style reflect self-understanding, and communal imagination, which need not be seen in the rather condemnatory way in which Veblen described them. Imitative and emulatory group behaviour is complex, and is not to be described so simply. There are certainly ambiguities in Veblen's own account.

The first problem is whether he used the term 'emulation' to refer to a competitive striving for status or to a desire to achieve the ideal way of live embodied in those of higher social status. Is it the influence of the leisured classes which allow their moral and aesthetic standards, embodied in a way of life, to become an ideal for all of society? Veblen could write in this vein:

The leisure class stands at the head of the social structure in point of reputability, and its manner of life and its standards of wealth therefore affords the norm of reputability in the community . . . the norm of reputability extends its coercive influence with but slight hindrance down through the social structure to the lowest strata. The result is that the members of each strata accept as their ideal of decency the scheme of life in vogue in the next higher stratum, and bend their energies to live up to their ideal.[12]

It is not clear in this passage whether 'Ideal' refers to what people seek to aspire to, in terms of the superior status of a particular way of life, or whether it refers to aesthetic or moral standards which are embodied in a way of life. Veblen felt that the cultured leisured elite, because they valued aesthetic excellence so greatly, did seek to live up to their aesthetic (and sometimes moral) ideals, but also were in a competitive struggle to prove their aesthetic superiority, embodied in their privileged life style. The ambiguity of cultural significance is clear, as it embraces both meanings, sometimes at the same time.

Indeed, Veblen could also see 'emulation' as referring to the attempt to reach an 'ideal' which was for the moment out of reach. At the same time, this striving is competitive and aggressive, resulting in conspicuous consumption between individuals. He used the term 'outdo' to speak of competition. There is always in Veblen a sense of inferiority, envy and dissatisfaction. He wrote of 'emulation – the stimulus of an invidious comparison which prompts us to outdo those with whom we are in the habit of classing ourselves'. Veblen held this competitive sense of 'emulation' alongside the 'imitative', because he felt that there was a leisured elite which set the standards of a cultural ideal. Each class then attempted to reach these ideals, and felt that the class above it embodied these values more fully. Therefore the Marxist concept of the class struggle is replaced by Veblen's account of a struggle by social groups to be socially and culturally superior.

There is clearly a historical and sociological debate to be had at this point. A. H. Halsey in *Change in British Society* writes of the way in which working-class boys in Salford in 1900 read comics extolling the virtues of the public school.[13] Halsey notes that the Catechism of the Anglican Prayer Book was not wholly forgotten in the urban working class, at this time: 'To submit myself to all my governors, teachers, spiritual pastors and master. To order myself lowly and reverently to all my betters.'

Halsey shows that there was deference in Victorian England, and this was reflected in patterns of consumption. This appears to prove Veblen's point. But was this competitive or imitative? The criticism of Veblen is complex. First, deference to imitative social ideals and ideologies need not be competitive. There certainly could be acceptance of the ideals in their own right. Secondly, groups may choose to ignore the behaviour of a wealthier class. In others, there will be social mobility without necessarily being competitive. Nor need a lower social class be always combined with imitative behaviour of a higher social class. There may well be a fierce local pride, as Halsey reveals. It is also the case that where competition does exist then innovation through socially entrepreneurial behaviour may bring greater success. Imitation may not be a good strategy to adopt. In other words, one social class may simply adopt new patterns of behaviour which are more satisfying than the attempt to imitate a wealthier class. This was certainly the case with fashion and the British working class in the 1950s.

A second problem with Veblen's thesis is that society may contain groups which disagree over how status is to be defined. Perhaps there is no agreement over how social values are formed. Wealth might indeed be a highly suspect social value for some groups, especially those with a commitment to ideals of equality, social reform or justice. If consumption is not indicative of status but of cultural values which express the search for personal identity and self-definition, the picture changes. Where fashion, cultural leadership and style emerge from in today's western society is not easy to determine. Some groups sociologically are noticeable for a propensity to conspicuous consumption, but in contemporary British society such groups may be influential but are certainly not typical of all of society. Nor are such groups themselves culturally self-contained. Groups which do display great wealth are themselves influenced by a small collection of designers, fashion consultants and decorators. Status and taste exist in uneasy tension. Finally, it is very doubtful whether in contemporary Britain there are dominant social groups that set the pattern of consumption for lower groups.

Veblen also fails to account for two very significant features of consumption. Consumption may not be socially visible, but instead be rather private, inconspicuous, inner-directed. Such consumption (one obvious example is the purchase of books, or expenditure on extensive, private travel) may be highly meaningful in the search for self-expression. Since Veblen confined consumption to competition between peers for status, he was primarily interested in other-directed behaviour, and defined consumption in this way. Secondly, Veblen does not distinguish contemporary consumption from traditional hedonism. Veblen, as already mentioned, could equate barbarian, tribal groups with the early twentieth-century elites who fill the pages of Henry James' novels. Each society for him was preoccupied with status, which is expressed through the emulation of ideals embodied in behaviour. Veblen claimed that technology and social competition explained the basic dynamic of society. However, it is the characteristic of modern society that it is concerned with a search for novelty and insatiability. This is a feature of private consumption as much as of public consumption. Fashion is not simply to be explained as the means by which a social elite maintains its dominance. That argument is quite circular. An elite is said to set a fashion as a response to emulative behaviour by others, while emulative behaviour is explained as the response to a new fashion. What is missing in this argument is an explanation of behaviour which is independent of emulation, either as imitative or competitive in its emulative form. Fashion-oriented behaviour instead derives from the cultural logic of modernity, which encompasses both scientific experiment and instrumental thinking on the one hand, and creative passion on the other. The romantic embodiment of imagination and dreams exists through fashion and consumer behaviour in contemporary experiences of pleasurable activity.

Veblen is useful in explaining some aspects of consumption. There can be no doubt that some consumption is competitive, and that some consumption exhibits conspicuously the status of the purchaser. All this is undoubtedly a gain, and Habermas' explanation of the worker becoming a consumer in the late twentieth century takes on added depth in the account given by Veblen. Nevertheless, it is fundamentally a deeply flawed theory. It ignores the way in which emulative behaviour need not be competitive, and is not clear whether it is ideal standards or ways of life which embody these standards which are being emulated. Veblen certainly wanted to emphasize the competitive aspect of emulation, but this is problematic. Secondly, there may have been social coherence up to a point in the late nineteenth century (Halsey would seem to confirm this), but there certainly is no agreement on social values in contemporary western society. It makes no sense now to try, as Veblen did, to believe in a social elite in a nation state which sets the trend of conspicuous consumption as a means of proving its competitive status symbolically. In other words, in a book concerned with the dual issues of identity and justice in consumption, Veblen is unsatisfactory because he overplays the concern with social competition and undervalues the search for private identity, expressed both in fashion and consumption. Thirdly, and most importantly, Veblen ignores the sometimes private, always novel, drive to try out new identities and find who one is and what might be your identity in the world of fashion and design that marks western society at the end of the twentieth century. It is a long journey from Cambridge Platonism to the apparently secular world of the shopping mall, but the concern for self-identity remains.

IMAGINATION AND CONSUMPTION

Wordsworth and Shelley were deeply critical of those who searched for new pleasures for 'idle' reasons, where 'excitement is carried beyond its proper bounds'. The purpose of the artist who gave pleasure was to convey truth as well, or to create a moral sensibility. Indeed, the early Romantics who stood in the intellectual tradition of sentimentalism and aesthetics were often concerned about modern culture. Pleasure-seeking, fashion, tawdry Gothic novels which flooded the market were condemned as the fruit of unhindered, commercial forces. Behind this was a utilitarian, *laissez-faire* philosophy.

Nevertheless, Romanticism recognized that it could also be in tune with popular sentiment. When Wordsworth argued for the language 'really used by men', or Coleridge wrote of far-off places, they opened up a market for mystery and romance. Popular, vernacular culture began to be the subject of increasing artistic attention. It was only a small step to the commercial artist, who, allied to the vast power of the Industrial Revolution, could be reproduced in a thousand living rooms. Romanticism became the ideology of Victorian art, and while Victorian artists ceaselessly inveighed against soulless materialism, they were also repeatedly exploited by the market. Campbell writes: 'Compared with neo-classicism, however, Romanticism involved concessions to popular taste, concessions which served to ensure the continued economic survival of the artist under the new "free market" conditions.'[14]

Out of Romanticism there came a series of factors which determined the nineteenth- and twentieth-century's concern for consumption. First, there is the political context. As sentimentalism gave way to Romanticism, the Industrial and French Revolutions swept across Europe. The end of the eighteenth century saw an enormous social upheaval, in which the aristocracy were eventually displaced as the paramount social and economic group in society. Sentimentalism had criticized the aristocracy for its lack of spiritual depth, stoicism, arrogance and extravagance. Increasingly, the new enemy was seen to be economic materialism, or the assigning of primacy to wealth, economic success and the creation of greater industrial or commercial strength. Wordsworth and Shelley were alarmed by a society which gave the paramount place either to wealth creation or to the consumption of goods. They stressed instead a doctrine of moral renewal through art. The political critique of society came through the belief in the solitary individual, who was made better by poetry. Shelley argued for the necessity of imagination to transform society. Society was not changed because of a lack of imagination. 'The cultivation of the mechanical arts' was promoted in society, while imagination was not.[15] 'There is no want of knowledge respecting what is wisest and best in morals, government and political economy . . . We want the creative faculty to imagine that which we know; we want the generous impulse to act that which we imagine; we want the poetry of life.'[16] Poetry, for Shelley, was cast in the role of God, while the principle of self was seen as Mammon. The poet and the reader are cast together in a philosophy of creativity and recreativity, which lays great stress on the moral force of creativity.

Nevertheless, the failure to carry through its social vision led to an ironic consequence for Romanticism. Romanticism throughout the nineteenth and twentieth centuries could result in moral idealism and a search for personal identity. The example of California, with its ambiguous character in the 1960s of student revolt, personal self-expression and rampant consumerism, is the most obvious example. Where the romantic world view fails, however, then as Campbell says romantic literature, music and art 'will be employed as little more than the raw material for a leisure and recreation industry; with dreams used less to raise the vision of an imaginatively apprehended ideal world with which to counter this one, than to overcome boredom and alienation'.[17]

The irony of social action is that altruistic idealism becomes instead hedonistic self-interest. The fundamental condition of consumerism is its apolitical nature, but this is not because politics is ignored in order that attention can be focused on consumption. Instead, it is intrinsic to consumption that imagination is at work, but this imagination is cut off from a political and moral vision of a better society. The failure of the imagination to envisage personal or social change becomes the prerequisite for recreation, and the imagination of a new self-image through consumption. This is not, however, a one-way process, for moral idealism can arise out of hedonism. Hedonism, self-idealism and Romanticism exist in a symbiotic relationship of a search for pleasure, a concern for ideals and the cult of imagination. What this implies is that consumption may be channelled into political behaviour, either through 'ethical consumerism' or through the promotion of ideals connected with mass leisure activities. The example of pop stars, and especially Linda McCartney, who have promoted environmental concerns, or the close link between HIV-awareness and the music business makes this point clearly. 'Green consumerism' is a continuous dimension of modern retail activity. Consumption may also become completely apolitical.

Secondly, consumption, and the justification of it in consumerism, is highly individualist in its behaviour. Romanticism stressed the uniqueness of personality, with a concept of the self which saw it as a potentially creative artist. Self-expression and self-discovery were at the centre of their creed, although the individualism was a dynamic one. There was a belief in the importance of learning to feel, or to see, what was true from the visionary power of the Romantic prophets themselves. 'The vivid scenes which their imaginations revealed were taken to be both things of exquisite beauty in themselves and glimpses of an ideal reality.'[18]

In particular, the importance of dreams was stressed in Romanticism as being revelatory of truth. The failure of individuals to act politically was, as noted above, seen as due to a lack of imagination. Translated into consumerism, the individual focuses her interest on to the creation of images, meanings and novelty within a product. The problem becomes that of failing to live up to an ideal self-image, especially as compared to others. Introspection can stand alongside the pursuit of external display, both displaying a search for the embodiment of ideals and dreams whether in one's feelings or one's behaviour, dress and life style. It goes without saying that the great consumer temples of the twentieth century, such as cinemas or shopping centres, appeal both to the imagination and to the individual as participants in the world of images and dreams.

Thirdly, there is the ambiguity of creation and recreation inside consumerism. Romanticism created a theodicy of creativity which took the place of benevolence. The justification of pain, suffering and moral evil was that they were the birth pangs of a new creativity, and a world struggling in labour to be born. Wordsworth and Byron placed the creation of a new social order as the justification of personal suffering. Sentimentalism in the eighteenth century could still embody the benevolence of the Cambridge Platonists, but by the nineteenth century utilitarianism took over benevolence as an ideal and transformed it into social utility: the usefulness of a belief or institution for society. Instead, God became for Romanticism the creative, supernatural force which was present throughout the natural world. Such creativity within the individual could be represented as genius. It could be described as a new triad of nature, self-consciousness, imagination. Creation becomes the ability of the self to create beauty, linking the aesthetic and the spiritual, through the imagination. Weber contrasted prophetic religion and art in *The Sociology of Religion*, seeing them as deeply opposed, but Romanticism united the two.[19] Once again, the limitations of Weber's typology of religion is revealed.

Romantic thought was sceptical of religious orthodoxy within Christianity, but emphasized the congruence of the creative spirit with nature. Religious experience was equated with participation in nature, in a mystical or pantheist sense, although this was not true of Coleridge, nor of the later Wordsworth. The centrality of creativity, both in productivity and in originality, became the fundamental understanding of divinity. Creativity was located in the inner self, whereby each person could foster their own divinity.[20]

Increasingly this emphasis on creativity became changed into a philosophy of 'recreation' where self-expression and self-realization are legitimated within a search for pleasure as good in itself. At the same time the enduring emphasis on 'creation' ensured the continuation of new cultural products to stimulate the individual in her search for recreation. Imagination and the experiencing of pleasure became commensurate, with individuals seeking enjoyment in the display of the imagination. This could, of course, oppose itself to the utilitarian ethic of work, utility and materialism, for a world of play, leisure and the pursuit of imagination. As Campbell argues, consumption is a self-directed, creative process in which ideals are sought but never fully realized. The cult of romantic self-expression, romantic love and the modern phenomenon of dynamic fashion became linked with autonomous hedonism.

We have now reached an understanding of consumption, and the process of consumerism, which places it in relation to political and social involvement, the individual self and creativity. Campbell puts it well: 'The cultural logic of modernity is not merely that of rationality as expressed in the activities of calculation and experiment; it is also that of passion, and the creative dreaming born of longing.'[21] There is a tension between them which drives the dynamic of western society.

Consumerism is a search for novelty and pleasure. The creation and recreation of illusory stimuli brings pleasure out of everyday experience, which it transforms into an environment of continuous pleasure. The emotive dimension of consciousness is central, and consumerism is always in danger of becoming fantasy, that is, illusory experiences completely separate from everyday life. Originality, pleasure and self-expression break through the traditional restrictions on the expression of desire in both Christianity and utilitarian philosophy. Consumption can be defined as 'the use of goods in the satisfaction of human wants'. The issue for consumerism after the Romantic movement was how human wants were seen as tied up with a whole worldview of self-identity and of meaning. Identity becomes central to the process of consumption: justice was concerned with the distribution of the satisfaction of wants, but identity defined the nature of what was wanted.

If consumerism is seen in the way the previous few pages have suggested, it becomes a cultural product which has arisen out of the creation of feeling and aesthetics on the one hand,

and creativity and personal imagination on the other. There is within consumerism a failure all too often to engage with political and social change, as well as a pervasive individualism and concern with recreation. What the argument above has sought to bring out is that these are not accidental, or contingent, characteristics which could have been otherwise, but are intrinsic to its nature. Consumerism is therefore an ambiguous phenomenon, capable of expressing the identity of the self, and indeed capable of being taken up into social renewal, but also capable of a purely individualist pursuit of pleasure. Such an analysis as I have offered (deeply indebted to Colin Campbell) brings out the implicitly theological dimension, and origin, of consumerism. It would be too simple to see it as an alternative to religion, for it stands in the broad stream of western cultural development.

There is, finally, an alternative explanation which is offered of consumerism. It has been left to these concluding paragraphs of this section, so that the strength of the counter-argument may be brought out. This is the argument given by J. K. Galbraith in *The Affluent Society*.[22] Galbraith, writing from the 1970s, was attacking the desire for growth in economic production in the western economies of Europe and North America. Galbraith was deeply influenced by Veblen, and in some ways their careers were similar. Both were highly critical of the excesses of capitalism, and both left academic life to write as social critics and journalists. Galbraith, however, was also an ambassador. Galbraith argues that classical economic theory was wrong not to investigate where the origin of consumer demands arose from. It is not the case for Galbraith that all production increases are desirable. This is not simply because some products are intrinsically or potentially socially harmful, such as pornographic videos (intrinsically) or weapons (potentially). It is also because production satisfies wants which it may be would be best not satisfied. At the least, Galbraith feels that there is a contradiction that modern economic theory accepts that the urgency of consumer wants remains as intense even as they are satisfied. Galbraith disagrees with what he perceives as the social origination of wants:

If the individual's wants are to be urgent, they must be original with himself. They cannot be urgent if they must be contrived for him. And above all, they must not be contrived by the process of production by which they are satisfied. For this means that the whole case for urgency of production, based upon the urgency of wants, falls to the ground. One cannot defend production as satisfying wants if that production creates the wants.[23]

Galbraith gives three arguments to support his position. All rest on positions developed in the social sciences. The final one is that associated with Veblen, which has already been discussed at length above. The other two are 'instinctivism' and 'manipulation theory'. Instinctivism is deeply held within economic theory, which speaks of 'latent wants' and 'latent demands'. Wants are placed in the human, biological inheritance. There they manifest themselves as needs. Human behaviour does biologically have a need for food and shelter. However, the behaviour which these drives create is quite unspecific. It may range from aggression to cultivation of the environment. Modern consumption is very specific, on the other hand, and exhibits particular conduct in pursuit of determined wants. The problem is to find a way of moving from the biological basis of needs to the motivated action of consuming specific goods. It is also the case that consumerism involves disposing of goods. Galbraith argues that biological need is independent of culture and the activities of others. Such a need, if left unsatisfied for too long, becomes urgent. Urgency is a criterion of independence. Wants do not have to be created in consumers, for they exist anyway and will manifest themselves when the relevant goods are supplied. Galbraith further follows Abraham Maslow in listing the needs which are turned into wants. The most basic needs are biological, whereas the higher ones are psychological. These are safety (security, protection and routine), love (affection and affiliation), esteem (self-respect and prestige) and self-actualization (self-fulfilment).

However satisfactory this psychological theory is in explaining human motivation, it runs into the problem that consumer wants are not universal. They also are subject to great change and variation. Change can take place in wants during an individual's lifetime. One society may put far more emphasis upon one set of wants than another. There is a circular argument at work here. The behaviour explained by the concept of latent want is also evidence for the existence of the concept of latent want. Finally, there is the issue of the cessation of wants. Consumers can cease to be interested in a product. This can happen either after consumption of a product, or after a cultural change when the product becomes unfashionable. However, biologically based needs/wants should continually reassert themselves. It is not just Galbraith who follows this argument. McKendrick, in *The Birth of a Consumer Society*, explains the growth of sales of printed calicoes in the late seventeenth century as the 'unleashing of home demand', or 'the unleashing of acquisitive instincts'. Nevertheless, the arguments fail to be convincing. While there are biological bases for human action, consumption is to be explained by changing values and attitudes, which are justified by new intellectual movements.[24]

Galbraith's other argument is 'manipulation theory'. In some ways this argument contradicts the one above, although this does not prevent the two arguments being used together. Individuals are seen as lacking motivational desires until they are manipulated by advertising agencies. Individuals are filled with a desire, or a want, not only through advertising but through the mass media of cinema, television, newspaper and magazines. The consumer is seen as passive, until new desires are created. Once again, however, this argument has been strongly criticized. First, market research and advertisements only represent a small part of the culture in which an individual lives. Secondly, the audience for any medium is very diverse, and therefore it will be received differently by different groups. Thirdly, there is much evidence that individuals are not passive recipients of any medium. They respond in a highly pro-active fashion. Individuals have their own beliefs, attitudes and values. No doubt these are continually being reformed by the surrounding culture, but the underlying motivational structure does not change so easily. That is the product of years of experience and relationships. If manipulation occurs at all, it can only happen by taking into account the desires of the consumer. It is also the case that advertising does not manipulate consumers directly, nor their desires. What occurs in advertising directly, or in exposure to the media indirectly, is that a symbolic message is attached to a product. Desirable images are associated with consumption, or ownership, of a product. Symbolic meanings are connected with gratification far more than the intrinsic utility of a product. This is closely associated with imagination and emotion, and not with rational utility. Yet it is not the case at all that a person seeking gratification of emotions or of imaginative self-expression is being 'manipulated' when advertising appeals to the consumer in an emotional, and symbolic, way. If one argues that manipulation ceases to be present only on the strict condition that all the arguments in advertising on behalf of a product are rational arguments put forward about a product's intrinsic utility, that is a stipulative definition of 'manipulation'. Consumption is about emotion as much as rational thought. The crucial question is left unanswered. That is how the desires of groups and of individuals identify with the symbolic meaning of products promoted in the media or advertising. How is this done successfully, and how far do individual consumers play an active role in that process?

Insatiability and satiety are fundamental features of contemporary society. At the same time there is a 'revolution in rising expectations' as a social class or group begins to envision new wants for itself. This has been especially true of the British working class since 1945.[25] Here, in this social group, the challenge to Veblen's theory of competitive consumption is seen. From the 1950s Mods and Rockers onwards, it set its own fashion, culture and life style, which innovated far beyond an imitation of the tired way of life of a British social elite. Indeed, the term 'working class' is now a considerable anachronism in large sections of society. Consumption can be defined as the use of goods in the satisfaction of human wants, which usually is the result of consciously motivated behaviour. What I have sought to argue here is that consumerism is explained neither by Veblen, nor by Galbraith's appeal to instinctual drives and the manipulation of the media. Consumerism, and the activity of consumption, is neither governed by custom nor tradition. That was the case in the largely non-literate, pre-industrial societies which existed in western Europe and North America until the end of the eighteenth century. The central difference between these societies and our own in terms of consumption is that the older society would find it impossible to imagine, let alone tolerate, an endlessly changeable and novel pattern of consumption. Yet this is exactly what the classless, style-conscious person in western Europe espouses at the end of this century. She is fundamentally concerned with the question of social and personal identity.

Pre-industrial societies had a notion of the 'limited good' which is directly opposed to the existence of modern consumerism. It is here, and not in Galbraith or Veblen, that the mystery of modern consumerism exists. In the previous society, the traditional way of life has divine approval, and there is an expectation that change is to be resisted. While this began to break down from the Renaissance onwards, if not from the acceptance of Aristotle into western theology, change was accepted far more in the world of ideas than of social behaviour. Social behaviour in pre-industrial society is largely continuous with previous generations, with change being slow, and evolutionary. Most crucial of all, if there is a 'limited good', with the belief that all the desired objects are always in short supply and are of finite quantity, unlimited consumption by one person or group threatens the entire community.

Consumption in pre-industrial society is related closely to production, except for a few elite groups. There is a biological basis for consumption in the pattern of life of pre-industrial societies. If the way of life is understood as a whole, consumption falls into place. Wants are fixed, limited and understood. All this changes in an industrial society, but it is not because of the expansion of production that this happens. It is the connection between literacy and industrialization, which is a contingent fact but a continuous one in western history, that allows the imagination free reign. Consumption is a feature of the imagination at play, and in contemporary western society fashion and consumerism are its manifestations.

CONSUMPTION IN WESTERN CULTURE IN THE TWENTIETH CENTURY

The development of consumption parallels that of consumption theory in the twentieth century. From 1880 until the First World War, and, to some extent, until 1939, there is the first stage of mass industrial society. The first city-centre department stores are laid out, and people in the suburbs flock into the new stores by the equally new public transport: trains, motorized buses and underground trains. It is the era of the vivid underground posters in London in the 1920s, beautifully designed in a modern style, exhorting the delights of the city centre: theatres, shops, music-hall and later cinema. This is also the era of T. Veblen and G. Simmel. Simmel analysed the inhabitants of the ever-growing city of Berlin, as migrants poured in from the East before 1914. Simmel felt that the 'deepest problems of modern life derive from the claim of the individual to preserve the autonomy of his existence in the face of overwhelming social forces'.[26] The individual is levelled down by the city, and its indifference and impersonality. Consumption expressed both the belonging to a particular group and yet also individual preferences. 'Making a striking impression in the briefest possible time',[27] such as a visit to the theatre in the centre for a few hours before returning to the suburbs, becomes the aim. Veblen's views on the consumption patterns of the leisured class have already been mentioned, with expensive home furnishings, clothes, jewellery and food, typically described by Henry James. The opulence of this era is recaptured in Martin Scorsese's film of James' *The Age of Innocence*, where the camera lingers on the artistic display of each plate of food at a banquet. Neither Veblen nor Simmel described capitalism as a system, holding together economic, political, cultural and social forces. Instead, it was a cultural analysis.

Alongside the themes of Simmel and Veblen, and the consumption patterns of the modern city, there was articulated a very distinctive form of modern art and architecture such as, quintessentially, the work of Charles Rennie Macintosh in Glasgow with his 'art nouveau' tea rooms where the middle class Scottish ladies could meet after shopping. Equally the 'skyscraper' develops in Chicago at this time: architecture, capitalism, culture and consumption form a whole. Behind this glittering façade lay poverty, and the much more stereotyped world of the factory-worker and the agricultural labourer. This was not centred on home or family, but on the pub, football matches and community which was a male world. Typically this world was one of steel, coal and ship-building.

It was the decline of this world which issued in the second stage of consumption, partially in the 1930s (in affluent parts of England or the United States), and much more so after 1950. The economic affluence of the working class became dominant, with popular music, travel and shopping. The home became central, as did youth culture. Gender issues became important. There was a strong debate in the 1950s and 1960s on the affluent worker, and the socio-political implications of this. Goldthorpe, Galbraith, Gamble and the Marxist cultural historian Raymond Williams described a 'way of life'. This was more than a common-sense analysis[28] of different styles of consumption. It linked together the routine of work, leisure, moral values, and ways of articulating emotion. The most sophisticated analysis of this was in the post-structuralist writer Pierre Bourdieu, who wrote in France in the 1960s to the 1980s. In *Distinction: A Social Critique of the Judgement of Taste*,[29] Bourdieu analysed how different social groups emphasized their distinctiveness by patterns of consumption. He distinguished between economic capital (the new rich, with conspicuous consumption) and intellectual capital (the old elite). Consumption does not merely express differences, as Veblen had argued. It also establishes it, and consumption played a central role in this. Education was vital, for it allowed access to this world.

The third stage in consumption takes us into the present day, and the post-modern. People are distinctive individuals, not primarily members of a group, or if they are members of a group it is the flourishing of a 'gay culture', or the 'pink pound', which allowed the establishment of a gay identity through gay consumption. Indeed, what is developing now is the emergence of an Asian or non-western gay culture, following a decade or so behind the western one. (The invisibility of gay people in Africa says much about the hostility of some African church leaders to the gay issue.) At this point consumption becomes directly about the creation of a particular identity. The writing of Jean Baudrillard sees all consumption as the consumption of symbolic signs:

Symbols, or signs, do not express an already pre-existing set of meanings. The meanings are generated within the system of signs/symbols which engages the attention of a consumer. So instead of seeing the process of consumption as one based on the satisfaction of an already existing set of needs, as in classical liberal economic theory, and in some other authors as a set of needs noted in human biology, Boudrillard proposed a different approach. Consumption is to be conceptualized as a process in which a purchaser of an item is actively engaged in trying to create and maintain a sense of identity through the display of purchased goods.[30]

Identity in today's society (or, as it is called, the post-modern world) is no longer given by ethnicity, class, gender or social status. People find out who they are or who they want to be, by consumption. Baudrillard echoes Philip Oppenheimer, who will be described later, in the sense of emptiness that often follows consumption. Consuming is something that creates enjoyment in anticipation (the search for a new pair of shoes) as much as in the consumption (wearing the shoes for the tenth time). In economic terms, marketing no longer appeals to socio-economic status, or the virtues of patriotism, but to life style and identity.

This means that people must learn to become consumers. Formal education may give people intellectual capital, as well as scientific, vocational and technical skills, but there is equally a social education at adolescence into the values of consumption. Such education continues during one's life. People move away from social status groups, explored by Bourdieu, and even from their ethnic groups into their own self-definition. Confusingly, consumption patterns that began by defining one group (e.g. black music, Asian food) may develop across the whole society, although some cultures, such as those of France or Italy, are more resistant and have maintained more of an indigenous style. Family structure is more stable there as well, and there is more national patriotism.

Lastly the work of Jacques Lacan, the French psychoanalyst who died in 1981, should be mentioned. Lacan believed that we do not inhabit simply a biological body, but that we develop conceptions or images of the body by social interaction. Rituals, costumes, and ways of living our bodies all structure how we see our body. The body has basic drives, or instincts, but they become desires by being attached to symbols and cultural concepts. The body's capacity for sexuality and aggression is transformed by symbolic images: as the new-born child enters into culture, and the symbolic, the unconscious is formed. This is not the private possession of the individual, but is interwoven with cultural symbols, 'structured like a language'. Consumption patterns affect these symbols deeply. Symbols are often pre-linguistic, depending on images, which are highly visual. For Lacan, the failure to deal with the non-rational elements of social life is shown in the disasters of Fascism and Nazism.[31] Symbols do not, however, represent what is present but what is absent for Lacan. Human language, and the imagery (to be distinguished from the imaginary, where the new-born child has no sense yet of her personal body) of visual symbols, show us what is not there at the moment. So the 'Real', the full world of people and things in all its depth, is known only through the glimpses afforded by language and symbols. Therefore we construct our identity, and view our bodily drives, through the world of language and symbols.

Lacan adopted a synchronic approach, examining the unconscious outside historical time. What is needed is a diachronic structure, which can express historical change. Since Lacan did not do this, he never analysed consumption as such. Yet it is clear that the logical expression of his work is that our lives are lived out by expressing our desires in consumption, and that the unconscious libido is shaped by consumption. John Fiske has said that: 'Commodities are not just objects of economic change; they are goods to think with, goods to speak with.'[32] Male behaviour has increasingly shifted from production at the beginning of this century, when women shopped as consumers, through the period of men as fighters and warriors, to the late twentieth-century stress in western capitalism where masculinity and consumption are now intertwined. In other nations, where war is still present, there is a tension between masculinity as willingness to fight (e.g. in Iraq, or Bosnia) and the psychological expression of masculinity as consumption in the West. Soccer has become a vast, public expression of highly ritualized masculine experiences, now increasingly involving the observation of women as well. Symbolism and consumption run very deep here, affecting entire national identities, binding together ethnic groups in one nation, and providing role-models for constructing individual identities. Male imagery becomes narcissistic, objects of consumer desire, and visual: 'There is an increasing number of men who now define themselves through their patterns of consumption rather than through a work – role identity. Work provides money for purchasing the consumer goods required to construct and maintain identity.' Frank Mort contrasts working-class Tottenham in North London in the 1950s and the 1980s. Football is still watched, shopping goes on, but the clothes and hair reflect consumer display in a manner unimaginable thirty or forty years ago: 'hair: wedges, spiked with gel, or pretty hard boys who wear it long, set off with a large ear-ring'.[33] The cathedral of consumerism is the shopping mall, and it is increasingly policed to exclude deviants, who include the poor and the unemployed.

Social psychologists have studied the fascination with identity, presentation and appearance in this world. Anthony Giddens, as a sociologist, refers to this as life-politics, which goes beyond the protest movements of the 1960s–1980s described in chapter 1 by Habermas.[34] Life politics involves the person who challenges the perceived exploitation of life by negotiating personal identities.[35] People feel ambivalent about their involvement in consumer culture. There is an awareness that the poor and unemployed are excluded, that consumerism is not environmental, and yet there is the task of constructing one's own identity and maintaining it across time and place. 'People's involvement with material culture is such that mass consumption infiltrates everyday life not only at the levels of economic processes, social activities and household structures, but also at the level of meaningful psychological experience – affecting the construction of identities, the formation of relationships, the framing of events.'[36]

Finally, it is worth mentioning how the entire culture of a community or society can be transformed by tourism. Tourism is deeply embedded in the consumer industry, and it is doubtless with irony that John Urry entitles his story of tourism *Consuming Places*. The very identity of a community can be consumed by tourism. This, in turn, affects the person: 'Rather the very nature of the personal is transformed in modernity. . . Mobility is therefore responsible for altering how people appear to experience the modern world, changing both their forms of subjectivity and sociability and their aesthetic appreciation of nature, landscapes, townscapes and other societies.'[37] It is not simply the local community which is environmentally and socially overwhelmed by hotels and the tourist industry. The tourist also is changed: 'Many of the objects of the tourist gaze are functionally equivalent to the objects of religious pilgrimage in traditional society. When people travel (make a pilgrimage) to the great tourist sites of the modern world . . . They are in effect worshipping their own society.'[38]

What happens to religion in such a world? How do religious bodies, such as churches, see the transformation of identity brought about by consumerism? Although there has been little study of this subject by theologians, there have been some works which have been very influential. One example, which will be analysed in detail, and which stands for a whole genre, is that of M. Douglas Meeks. But it is worth emphasizing, before we move on to Meeks, that consumerism can replace religion altogether. Urry hints at this, and the highly sophisticated analysis by the Norwegian Bishops Conference makes the point explicitly. This looks at the ritual involved in giving consumer gifts, such as at Christmas and birthday, which express the motives of the giver. This is ritual action, which can displace the very event (Christmas; birthday) being commemorated itself. But there is more than this:

Ritual symbolic actions are, however, also exercised after the gift is received or the item is purchased, when it is shown off, evaluated, compared to other items etc. When a man fondles his new car or a woman takes good care of her jewellery, they invest meaning in the items, an investment that is strongly influenced by the power of advertising. The items give the owner resources, qualities and qualifications, they live within him, bless him with vitalizing effects, give him identity, self security and social identity. Because of these aspects consumption gets a lot of the functions that religious used to have in earlier times.[39]

THEOLOGY AND CONSUMERISM

The most sustained theological critique of modern consumerism, and indeed of the whole notion of an economy which has consumption at its very heart, comes from M. Douglas Meeks in his book *God the Economist*.[40] It has attracted widespread attention, and has been praised by such theologians as Jürgen Moltmann and Rebecca Chopp. It is written from an American Protestant perspective, and was published in 1989 towards the end of the Thatcher/Reagan decade of unparalleled consumption and affluence for those who were the economic elite. Meeks uses a Trinitarian critique, and moves away from the traditional concerns of social ethicists on the economy, which are commutative and distributive justice. Commutative justice is the evaluation of how relations are formed, such as fair bargaining, while distributive justice examines the eventual outcome in terms of distribution. Meeks has a different perspective. He believes that the concepts of scarcity and satiety in contemporary economic life need a fundamental re-examination from a theological perspective.

Meeks argues from a Christian socialist perspective, deeply influenced by two presuppositions. First he believes that the '*oikos*' of the divine economy, or the household of the Church, can and should give Christians the key to understanding the nature of a properly ordered economy. Indeed, at a number of points in his book, he alleges that the predicates of the Christian God have been smuggled into contemporary thought about both economics and economic life. It is necessary to reclaim such language, and subject economic activity in western society to a stringent critique. Secondly, he accepts the neo-Marxist account offered by MacPherson that the seventeenth century was a time when possessive individualism excluded the poor from any intrinsic, inclusive use of property. The seeds of modern capitalism lie in the revolution in political thought, which destroyed the pre-industrial organic political community.[41] Slowly this transformation added to itself the attributes of divine action, in a secularized sense. The argument has been criticized by such writers as Atherton and Preston, in the liberal, English, Anglican tradition, but it is clear that such criticisms cut no ice with this attempt to reconceptualize a Christian political economy.

Atherton and Preston are concerned with a Christian social ethics based on the middle axiom tradition stemming from J. H. Oldham and William Temple. They take the existence of the market seriously, which is a point made by Atherton repeatedly in his book *Christianity and the Market*.[42] Meeks is concerned with a theological sociology, which conceptualizes the whole of modern society from a theological viewpoint. Like this book, Meeks is concerned to present both an ethic of social justice and an understanding of Christian identity. Unlike my own study, Meeks ultimately depends on a biblical presentation of the nature of God to mount a sustained criticism of contemporary society from the standpoint of a Trinitarian theology. There is a coherence about Meeks' work which is impressive, but it eventually fails to account for the way in which a Christian understanding of human identity and of social justice must arise from an interplay of secular thought and action, on the one hand, and the Christian tradition, on the other.

Meeks has a carefully worked out methodology which is significant. The first three chapters lead into a biblical chapter which determines the content of the book. This is then followed by three chapters on the relationship of this God to property, work and needs (which is a reference to consumption). So the whole book has a coherent shape, whereby the case for a biblically grounded understanding of economics is made; this is then expounded as a biblical account; and then the implications for contemporary economic life are set out. The case for a biblical understanding is because of the 'ambiguity of the liberal tradition'.[43] It has provided us with the conditions for democratic society, the discourse of rights and a liberation from despotism and poverty, at least in theory, and sometimes in practice 'for a portion of the populations of the democratic, industrialized nations'. However, there is a hidden domination caused by its own assumptions, and this domination is mediated by traditional God concepts. Rights defined by the privileged in the economic sphere of life define rights in other areas, especially in legal affairs and health. (This is an American book.) Liberalism, like Marxism, has a unitary view of power, juxtaposing the power of the state and the market over against each other. Neither sees that their preferred option can itself produce domination.

Meeks claims that divine language legitimates this improper domination. Hence the recall of divine language to its true perspective is an act of liberation for society. Meeks' argument depends on the secular use of divine language to legitimate the economy. The state of American society is not a good one, he claims, writing in 1989. There is a sense of the finitude of all resources, and a feeling of inability to solve economic and technological problems. This leads to an awareness of the need for survival, competitiveness and less compassion. There is also a pervasive sense of satiation. People consume too much, and become exclusive. Finally there is a feeling of the need to gain security: 'Societies ridden of scarcity and satiation will devote an inordinate amount of energy to defending gains and possessions . . . Compulsion to security leaves no energy for imagining a different, more just world. The conspiracy of scarcity, satiation and security issues in a society without memory and hope.'[44]

The problems of political economy are threefold, which need to be demythologized by the doctrine of the Trinity. First, there is the view of economy as fate determined by unchanging laws. Such a view of the immutability of economic doctrines is supported by a conception of God as an unchanging, eternal substance or absolute self. Secondly, the domination of capital within the economy, and of the economy within society, is 'supported unconsciously by deformed God concepts'.[45] Thirdly, there is the pervasive individualism of economic life which is grounded in the theological attempt to describe God in terms of pure subjectivity. Finally, there is the assumption of scarcity. Here economics does not take off an unconscious use of divine language, but of the failure to criticize a central economic assumption. Scarcity is seen in modern economic thought as fundamental to economic relations, because there is no limit to human wanting and production is always insufficient. Scarcity is the universal presupposition of exchange relationships, but the righteousness of God means that such assumptions are fundamentally wrong.[46]

The doctrine of the church is the doctrine of the economy of God's household (Col. 1:25; 1 Cor. 9:17; Eph. 3:2). Because the church exists for the sake of God's love of the world (John 3:16) there can be no sound teaching about the church that does not include the relationship of the church to our society's economy and the world's economy. The church is meant to be that place in history where God's interests for the world meet the interests of the world in the presence and power of the Holy Spirit.[47]

A transformative praxis from theology aims to transform human action 'in critical solidarity with victims of the way property, work and consumption are practiced'.[48] It is not only the poor who are the victims, but all those whose lives are distorted by the present market system – which includes almost everyone.

In his third chapter, 'God and the Market Logic', Meeks sets out his closely argued intellectual case against the market. After analysing this, we will then move directly to his argument on consumption, ignoring his writing on property and work. He begins with a historical account of Smith and the nineteenth century, relying on Polany's account of this transformation. Market relations are entered voluntarily, and without coercion, on this theory and the ancient understanding of economy as concerned with livelihood is replaced by the modern notion of exchange.[49] Transformation of goods and services from one form to another involves a gain in value, which includes an economic price for something that is valued more. All economics involves this costly choice, and it excludes the concept of livelihood from the argument: 'This is the most fateful development in modern economy. It accompanies the eclipse of God from the market.'[50] Land and labour became commodities, and social institutions are determined by its economic systems: 'The economic laws of the supply–demand–price mechanism and the human incentives of hunger and gain would decide who could have access to the oikos/market.'[51]

This leads, in Meeks' view, to poverty and social exclusion. Capital is a social process which uses wealth as an 'expansive value' instead of the traditional 'use value'. Here Meeks turns to Heilbroner's *The Nature and Logic of Capitalism* to defend his argument that capitalism is both dominating[52] and continually transformative. Wealth is always involved in the accumulation of more wealth. This means that wealth is a social category in a capitalist society inseparable from power, through its control of access to the goods that enable livelihood. This is done by control of property rights. There is a social relationship between the owners of capital, and the users of these embodiments, which allows a right of exclusion. Domination, despite liberal theory, is based on the fundamental inequality of social relationships. This is true in property rights and wage labour, 'poor labour markets throughout the world are therefore a negation of freedom'.[53] Coercion is present in exchange relationships 'by means of the determination of the actual relationships of property and work. Economic dependency is no less an antithesis of a community of free people and thus of democracy than personal political bondage.'[54]

The apologia for this is based on human nature. Meeks therefore confronts this understanding of identity, and of the economy, with the conceptions derived from the understanding of God. 'The working of the market depends on coercive conceptions once applied to God but now given as presuppositions of the market human being'.[55] The attributes of market domination are the remains of western ideas about divinity which still are uncontested in our society. Once they justified unlimited political power, but they controlled the economy. Now they are reversed, and justify unlimited economic power.

There is nothing particularly theological about much of this account, and there are a series of assumptions about economics which will be challenged later. What is distinctively theological are the arguments about God language. Three God–economy correlations are cited. First, the concept of God as plenipotentiary meant that there was a monistic conception of God as one simple being, behind the Trinitarian language. Many of the classical views of the Christian deity, in fact, reflect a pre-Christian understanding of God through his transcendence being defined over against the human experience of immanence.

According to this method God is said to be infinite, immutable, indivisible, immortal, independent and self-sufficient (having aseity or having no needs), and impassible (incapable of suffering). The God defined in this way does not go outside of himself and does not have relations with other human beings for he is self-sufficient. He has no needs outside of himself. These attributes . . . are the political attributes of domination. They are the set of attributes that constitutes dominium and imperium, which are at the heart of many historical and contemporary notions of economics, especially property.[56]

One instance is the way in which the divine freedom is related to the absolute power of the disposal of property. However, the modern situation is worse than the ancient one. In ancient times the absolute authority of God was transferred to the emperor. There was therefore both absolute power in imperial role, but also a sense of limit over against the working of the economy, which was not in imperial hands. Today, argues Meeks, the absolute power of the economy inherits this sense of absolutism, but there is no corresponding sense of limit in modern economic anthropology 'because of the eclipse of ancient metaphysical notions of God'.[57]

It is this argument which is at the heart of Meeks' conception of human identity and social justice. The concept of God underpinned the political authority which placed limits on the economy. 'Eliminating such a God concept seemed to be required to make way for an anthropology adequate to a market economy.' The market psychology of the participant in the market economy means that the human being has a new image of personality. It is this person which takes over the qualities of formerly attributed to God. 'The human being is now viewed as an infinite acquisitor, an infinite appropriator, an infinite antagonist against scarcity, and an infinite consumer . . . In market anthropology it is assumed that the unlimited human capacity for production/creativity grounded in progress overcomes absolute scarcity.'[58]

So Meeks claims that the market human being reflects the emperor deity, producing growth, efficiency and wealth, calculating costs rationally, and having unlimited power to dispose of property. God concepts become functionalist, where pure choice is seen as sheer potentiality. This leads into an account of how this anthropology determines behaviour in the three areas of property, work and consumption. I will look at the third area here. Human nature, argues Meeks, was portrayed as naturally insatiable, by conflating needs with bodily appetites. Natural bodily life aims at the satisfaction of pleasure, and the attempted resolution of this aim creates tension until the process is successful. This crucial point of the argument is based on a nineteenth-century economist, Alfred Marshall, who taught economics in England at Cambridge. In his seminal work, which laid the foundation for much neo-classical economics, entitled *Principles of Economics*,[59] he used the analogy of physiological needs and their satisfaction: needs create an appetite, caused by a deficiency in the body. This appetite produces a tension and a drive which seeks satisfaction. A temporary equilibrium results. However Meeks sees this analogy as being transformed by the concept of insatiability. There are three concepts about divinity which transform Marshall's argument. They are divine aseity and the liberty of the independent human being; divine sovereignty and needs as necessity; and divine infinity and human insatiability. There is a compulsion to meet every need, but only the private individual knows her own needs. This is a belief that private wants are always superior to public needs, and leads to a lack of belief in the public realm. It trades on the original understanding of God as a being without relationships, meditating upon his inner perfections in his radical, individual essence. Such a conception of God was taken from Aristotelian philosophy, surviving the transition to Christianity because of the failure to begin with the social experience of the Spirit: 'Thinking of God without the experience of Jesus and the Spirit leads to thinking of God as the unrelated self.'[60] So Meeks claims, following Christopher Lasch's cultural study of America, *The Culture of Narcissism: American Life in an Age of Diminishing Expectations*, that 'intimate experience of the self's wants is the only measure of reality'.

His second argument examines divine necessity. Divine sovereignty was regarded in terms of divine freedom. However this divinity, expressed in terms of the ability to make unfettered and free choices, also expresses itself in terms of a necessity. God can only be who God is. Thus there is a necessity about how God acts, and the acceptance of God's will is accepting the necessary logic of the world. So today society sees the necessity of satisfying needs. The self and the objective world are united, and the need becomes absolute. A society which does not consider goals makes needs an absolute. Needs replace moral discourse, and yet these needs are manipulated by corporations and social ideology. Meeks considers the option offered by neo-Marxism which conflates capitalism, psychic repression with manipulation, and false consciousness. The problem with this theory is that it is not ethical. By arguing that the unconscious is penetrated by the socio-economic structure, in such a way that desire becomes at the service of that structure, all instincts such as love, security, sexual desire etc. become marketable. The artificial needs of capitalism are identified with the psychic needs of the self, and marketed. Alienation remains as a general malaise because in spite of greater and greater material satisfaction a 'deep discontent' persists. Unlike Freud's belief that civilization was based on the repression of needs, neo-Marxism argues that capitalism continues because society's members repress their awareness of the inhumanity of capitalism so that they can continue to enjoy gratification. Meeks argues that this theory, in some ways close to his own on the evil of uncontrolled desire and competition, fails ultimately because it places the false needs in the unconscious or even the instinctual structure itself, and 'therefore beyond scrutiny, control and responsibility of the individual and society. The theory leaves unclear how people could resist ideology at all. It depends on the notion that there must be a social system in which all false needs must be eliminated.'[61]

Meeks resists the theories of Marcuse, Reich and Fromm, preferring to look at a theological response for reformulating our slavery to needs, which I will examine later. Nevertheless it is striking that Meeks almost concedes the neo-Marxist argument: to the claim that humanity has lost its freedom he responds with the claim that responsibility cannot be given up, so freedom must be present and the theory false. It is a dangerously assertive argument. He argues that there is a social necessity about the satisfaction of needs – and then pulls back from the full implications of necessity, which is the loss of freedom.

The third, and final, argument used by Meeks is that the concept of divine infinity has been transferred to the concept of human insatiability. Just as divine aseity is a corruption of the Trinity, so a description of God as pure Spirit is equally a distortion. The Spirit on its own is described by its effects and power not by the person of the Spirit. The dynamism of this concept, found either in individual experience or in social relations, becomes the capacity for pure decision making, or unhindered choice. 'The God who is sheer spirit and the corresponding human being who is sheer spirit support a society that focuses all of its economic problems on the spiralling increase in insatiable wants and the doctrine of growth which has become the secular religion of our society.'[62] Again Meeks returns to Marxism, this time to Marx himself, on the *'boundless'* nature of the hoarding drive. All of society is reduced to ways of making a profit, and all life is potentially commodified. All needs are interpreted because of the intensity of the market as the need for commodities.[63]

The Trinitarian answer to this is to re-emphasize the cross as the central concept for understanding the Trinity. Given a Trinity in which the son dies and is raised from the cross, every concept of the divine can be criticized which is not fully Trinitarian. Divine aseity and pure Spirit are equally invalid.

However, a fully Trinitarian account is about access to life through the Spirit given in the divine righteousness shown in the Father's raising of the Son from death (Rom. 1:4). The central point in Meeks' argument is that this includes a critique of the death implicit in capitalism. At the heart of this death are two realities. One is the empirical reality of poverty, starvation and lack of resources for the poor. The other is the economic definition of scarcity. The market requires scarcity in the sense of withheld access to the means of livelihood and work. Scarcity is the condition of private property, but it is justified by the understanding of the human being as infinite desirer and acquisitor. Human fulfilment is only found through work and acquisition on this account, so we cannot work and consume enough. This belief allows the creation of a system of debt. A deep sense of scarcity is born: 'consumption is the messianic message of salvation'.[64] Through sexuality and conspicuous consumption a connection is made between capitalism and scarcity. This is because society can no longer create notions of scarcity by spiritualizing work and money. Meeks advices two reasons for this. First, he conflates sexuality with 'intimacy . . . friendship, love, self-esteem and happiness'.[65] Here competitive work and consumptive pleasure fill the void created by the constant presentation of spiritualized images of sex. Equally, 'names and images . . . are identified with the intimacy and happiness which we lack'.[66]

Secondly, he turns to the school of thought begun by Veblen. The emphasis is on satiation, an intensifying sense of scarcity, and relative deprivation even amongst those who are affluent. 'They stress the joylessness of a consuming public, the harried-ness of today's leisure class, and the inevitability of frustration in positional goods.'[67] Meeks answer to this is to recount the biblical message with Christian tradition and to juxtapose this with contemporary problems. In terms of the analysis of theo-logical method presented in the Introduction this is an iso-morphic strategy, with a correlation between the biblical narrative and present-day experience of the Spirit. Further-more, this experience of the Spirit is then taken as the valid norm for an ordering of economic life. Hence Meeks examines the fullness of life in the Spirit (1 Cor. 2:12 and 4:8); the self-giving of God and the emphasis on relationships rather than needs; the condemnation of the rich landowner who builds barns in the parable found in Luke 12, where hoarding leads to self-deceit; and the need to have no anxiety faced with the challenge of the Kingdom (Luke 21:34). Following Michael Walzer's argument, he argues that needs and rights should be complemented by an emphasis on the meaning of social goods. Social goods refers to a definition given by Walzer, which I refer to in the later chapter on globalization. 'Goods with their meanings – because of their meanings – are the crucial medium of social relations; they come into people's minds before they come into their hands; distributions are patterned in accordance with the shared conceptions of what the goods are and what they are for.'[68]

Meeks argues that justice, in terms of production, distribution and consumption, depends on understanding the true shared meaning of social goods. So all distribution must be preceded and controlled by both the conception and creation of goods. Justice for a community is when 'its life and arrangements are faithful to the shared understanding of its members. We cannot expect a radical redesign of the economy without radically changed shared meanings of its members.'[69]

The social meaning of goods is given in scripture, for the biblical narrative renders God at the same time as providing 'the communal shared meaning of social goods'. All questions of justice and identity are not settled by reference to abstract right or subjective need, but by the narration of historical relationships. The Eucharist uncovers the fundamental shared meaning of all social goods, and the logic of their proper distribution. This logic criticizes the market economy. Meeks ends his study of the divine economy with an appeal for change:

Economic action is not an end in itself; it is a means towards communal human praxis determined democratically. Economy should serve democratic community, which in turn serves the creation of conditions of human beings finding their calling. The great success of the market economy and its tendency to draw everything into commodity exchange relationships has conditioned us to treat ever more dimensions of life as private, that is, unaccountable. The future of our society and its possible constructive contribution to the global household depend on our learning to restore many aspects of economy to community accountability. If we rightfully appreciate the market's logic of the exchange of commodities as a tremendous instrument of economy, we nevertheless have to be aware that there are many social goods whose shared communal understanding should require different logics of property, work and distribution. This means that the market should be blocked in some spheres of society. This, of course, cannot happen without democratic politics, which, in turn, are impossible without communities of shared values.[70]

It is difficult to be sure what the relationship of Meeks' argument to political economy in fact is. He argues that he is using the term 'God the Economist' as a metaphor, although at other times he refers to God concepts. Certainly there is an interest in the correlation of 'God' and the economy, which takes place (is 'lodged') within the church. This church is the divine attempt to build a household ('oikos') that will co-operate with God 'in making the world a home'.[71] Within this church there should be self-giving to one another, or, in theological terms, *diakonia* as praxis.

Economists have certainly discussed the nature of metaphor in the increasing awareness of language and rhetoric. Economic metaphors, such as 'the market', are figures of speech, and they are not 'true' in any simple way. They are useful for a purpose, and rhetoric can provide standards of likeness. The social construction of economics goes on, and economists decide how useful a scientific metaphor is. McCloskey criticizes the trend to modernism in economics after the 1950s, catching up belatedly with the cultural modernism of the 1920s. Modernism confined the discipline of economics to fact and logic, ignoring the values of stories and metaphors although these continued to be used. McCloskey pleads for a sensitivity to the use of such intellectual tools.[72] Meeks is concerned, however, to change the whole framework of the discussion. In the words of Richard Roberts, writing on theological social ethics, it is 'not so much formal analyses of contemporary capitalism in various stages of its recent evolution as partial insights and attempted corrections, which 'seeks to persuade, to posit and to sustain "rhetorics" of the ethical and the human in the face of the dehumanising power of the capitalist project and its consequences'.[73]

There are three levels of rhetorical discourse in Roberts' analysis of theological texts in capitalism. On a first-order level, Meeks engages at several points with contemporary American capitalism, and hardly uses a rhetoric which involves literary devices. His 'rhetoric' involves an engagement with the literary scope of theological language inside economics, such as when he considers the semantic fields of theology and economics (faith, debt, redemption etc.). This gives Meeks the justification to introduce an analysis of biblical narrative in a salvation-history (*heilsgeschichte*) form alongside a presentation of the experience of salvation in sacramental, liturgical and non-liturgical ways. This juxtaposition of experientialism and biblical narrative encompasses and out-narrates the story of capitalism, which again is recounted in largely historical terms. There is a direct clash of rival strategies, with much use of powerful, emotional language.

The second order of rhetoric is the organizational paradigm and implicit presuppositions of the work, or what Roberts calls the 'systematically exploited commonplaces . . . of a given discipline or sphere of discourse'.[74] Here biblical theology provides an overarching framework, while there is a denial that capitalism has to function in the way that it does. I have already noted how close Meeks comes to accepting in neo-Marxism a blend of Freud and Marx as an implicit presupposition, and the rebuttal of this seems close to revealing a hidden, less Christian understanding of social forces. Meeks is weakest on the third level, where culture as a totality is considered. Rhetoric is not an individual matter, for there are rhetorics of organizations, social movements, professions, scientific disciplines, the mass media and even of cultural epochs. All these are examples of collective rhetoric. Unlike V. A. Demant, who in *Religion and the Decline of Capitalism* provided an entire cultural analysis which was 'the base and the dialectical ground of the whole argument', Meeks says nothing of global culture.[75] There is no analysis whatsoever of how this church, which is the *locus* of his argument, is located in time and space; how it might relate to any culture. Demant based his opposition to capitalism on the bases of a shared culture which capitalism relied on for its initial success. Like Meeks, Demant argued that capitalism destroyed social relationships (although Demant would never have used Meeks' neo-Marxism in its Frankfurt School guise, which he could have done: the contradiction with Christian theology was too great), but he believed that this culture could regain ascendancy over capitalism. As Roberts points out, the parallels with the establishment of the British Welfare State in 1949 are very great. Demant provided a detailed account of 'the formidable task of re-creating a more natural community so well grounded in its biological, community and spiritual foundations, that it can use technique and exchange as enrichments without drying up the sources of social living'.[76]

Meeks has no discussion of what an alternative, or renewed, culture might mean, which is deeply ironic. For Demant avoided discussion of the epoch making era in which he wrote, yet he provided a clear and defensible (even if deeply archaic and economically flawed) account of both culture, state socialism and social values. He was well aware of the tension between four factors: bourgeoisie society, traditional social values, the market and state socialism. None of this appears in Meeks, and it becomes an exercise in first- and second-order rhetoric.

However, even at this level, there are questions which could be raised. First, there is the lack of awareness of the different shifts in government towards consumption and the economy and the fact that the role of advertising in relation to the market has led some sociologists to a more intense role for government. There is a good discussion of the New Deal's intervention in the 1930s by Irving Michelman in *The Moral Limitations of Capitalism*, and the relationship of government to capitalism.[77] Meeks relates heavily on Heilbroner's strongest criticism of capitalism, but ignores totally his argument that political intervention (such as Roosevelt's) will shape the future of capitalism, especially in his recent *21st Century Capitalism*, where he expects the *laissez-faire* attitude of Reaganomics to recede in the face of the threat posed by the damage to the environment and society by global capitalism. A more interventionist government is likely. From a similar perspective, Walter Owensby (a former civil servant, and now staff officer in the American Presbyterian Church for their public-policy office) charts how much the American government affected the economy towards unbridled capitalism in the 1980s.[78] Finally the non-Marxist school of left-wing Keynesians, such as J. K. Galbraith in *The New Industrial State*, Joan V. Robinson at Cambridge, England, R. H. Chamberlain and A. Hansen argued that competitive markets did not exist.[79] Unlike Meeks' view that each individual decided for herself what her needs were, this neo-Keynesian school argued that advertising (and monopoly power in alliance with government) rendered competitive markets a fiction. If the market could not be relied upon to set prices fairly and efficiently, government intervention is called for, which would lead to a just, democratic socialism. This argument, typical of the 1950s to the 1970s, has passed Meeks by. His reliance on the rhetoric of the exclusivity of private property and the neo-Marxist–Freudian embodiment of consumption in human and social identity leads him instead to prophesy doom. Political reform might be more appropriate.

Secondly, there is the question of the role of the market, and the reality of scarcity. It is here that Atherton and Preston concentrate their criticism. Relative scarcity is a concept in economics that ensures that resources can be used more efficiently in filling our wants, while the function of profits is both as incentive and as provider of information. As Atherton says, they 'generate a criterion to test the extent of that achievement'.[80] Equally conflict between groups in the market is deeply affected by price changes, for the price mechanism provides an objectivity against which people have to adopt. Atherton denies that Meeks' promotion of the superiority of 'household' economy over contemporary market systems is a valid economic viewpoint. It is an 'inability to come to terms with the reality (of) . . . the market'.[81] Preston makes similar criticisms as well.[82]

Thirdly, there are theological questions about the Trinitarian theology, adopted by Meeks. Marshall helpfully asks why the social model of the Trinity should be applied in the way Meeks does, when other theologians work in a different way with a Trinitarian social ethics.[83] Meeks, for instance, appeals to the pleroma of fullness of life in the Spirit. Christoph Schwöbel articulates a Trinitarian economy where human nature, even after redemption, remains fundamentally finite. The goodness of God is shown in the reconstitution of finite and created freedom. The imprisonment metaphorically of human beings by their attachment to finite goods is removed, and this deceptive freedom to choose is shown in its true colours, but it does not deny the reality of finitude. It is exactly the opposite, since the network of human and created relationships exists before we act. We act into that network, and, indeed, the purpose of redemption is so that we can participate more fully in it. This means that the finitude of human relationships is accentuated, not removed, even with the participation of the Spirit. Talk of the divine pleroma removing scarcity is simply assertion. This would mean that the self-limiting, or *kenosis*, of God in the Incarnation is taken seriously, in a way Meeks seems to ignore. Divine omnipotence and infinitude is self-restricted 'to allow the other the free response of love'.[84] Our own redemption by the Spirit is the same. 'The liberation from the abortive attempt of the self-constitution of human freedom discloses the reality of the other person and of the non-human creation as the one to whom good action is directed.'[85] So all human agency is restricted, conditioned by 'a limited space for action, a limited time to act, and the restrictions of fallible, finite knowledge'.[86] Even divine action, as personal and intentional action, within creation is conditioned by these factors, although of course Schwöbel says that the personal attributes of God are then qualified by the metaphysical, divine attributes. For this reason, divine agency is perfect, and self-regulated, unlike human agency. God is omnipotent, omniscient and eternal. The creation and redemption of human sociality is part of this work.

It is striking that Meeks stands in the Reformed tradition. There is no reference in his writing to the Lutheran depiction of work as one of the orders of creation, where its finitude is affirmed by the gift of the law, and Christians individually are redeemed by grace through the gospel. That tension of law and grace is absent in Meeks, and the description of work becomes impoverished for it. As Preston says:

This double aspect of work as toil and a joy is brought out in the biblical 'parables' of creation and fall in Genesis. The Bible has a realistic attitude to work and is not at all fastidious, unlike the Greeks . . . The Bible may not do enough justice to creative art, but it certainly sees the vast bulk of the world's work positively under God.[87]

Meeks only values work, or consumption, if it is Spirit-led. This seems to overemphasize the role of the Kingdom.

The fourth, and final, criticism of Meeks is in the symbolic understanding of consumption and especially in his use of Veblen. Meeks is convinced by the school of thought begun by Thorstein Veblen that the meaning of an object is given by its consumption. As already analysed in this chapter, Veblenian social theory analyses the crisis of meaning for the over-affluent: the joylessness of overconsumption and the decrease in leisure time leads to the portrayal of a disintegrating culture among the social elite. Satiety, the self-defeating struggle for possession of the best position in society (positional goods, such as the desire to own the house with the best view can end up spoiling it for all) and a frenetic life style lead to the judgement that consumption economics is a destructive force. It is an endless search for meaning in a meaningless world. Veblen and his followers (Scitovosky; Linder) see consumption as fundamentally non-economic behaviour expressing the search for meaning, status and worth; but this also degenerates into the isolation and mutually competitive behaviour ('one-up-manship') of suburbia which destroys true social relationships.

Socially, Veblenian analysis fails to realize that post-materialism is a growing feature of society. The intrinsic problems with Veblen have already been noted: there are also problems of contemporary application. There is much evidence that society is not homogeneous, uniform and satiated by consumerism. Sociological studies of working-class youth find, alongside the anger and despair of unemployment, an increasing concern for personal relationships among peer groups which

reject material consumption as the goal of human development. This can go so far as a reflection of the need to work at
all, although this can often be held alongside a hedonistic life
style which requires a considerable income to support it. At
the opposite end of the social scale, the inner-directed individual driven by particular values may well enjoy an affluent
existence, but there is no necessary correlation (indeed,
perhaps a dichotomy) between the search for individual values
and the affluent life style. Consumerism is no help here, and it
is certainly false to posit consumerism as the end-goal of that
search. It is interesting that the books cited by Meeks from the
Veblen school all date from 1970–1976. Meeks does not discuss
feminism at all, nor Niklas Luhmann's or Peter Berger's
disassociation of the search for meaning and the existence of
the market. As James Beckford puts it, discussing Berger's
work, capitalism is incapable of legitimating itself in mythic
terms.

Indeed, even in modern advertising there is an awareness
that social groups have more complex values than Meeks
admits of. Such advertising divides groups into those maintained by a vision of the past, who are often insecure financially
and committed to a survival ethic, with fairly clearly defined
and strongly maintained values and beliefs (the old working
class, gradually declining in numbers, but preponderant among
the elderly); the consumers, who fit Meeks' description of
conspicuous affluence where consumption does express a particular life style, and search for meaning; and those inner-
directed, who find their satisfaction in post-materialism and
their self-identity, although insofar as they also seek goods
which are valued for their position they still depend on their
affluence: but this group need not be affluent, as the increasing
number of those interested in personal spirituality outside the
churches, the environment, feminism and other causes demon-
strates. Religion can appeal to any of these groups, and their
relationship to organized Christianity will be very different.
Equally, the market will also interact with these three groups
differently: for only one of them is Veblen's theory of consumption appropriate.

HUMANISM AND CONSUMERISM

The other great criticism of consumerism comes, not from a theologian, but rather from an intellectual in the tradition of western civilization, Paul Oppenheimer. Oppenheimer's book *An Intelligent Person's Guide to Modern Guilt* examines the phenomenon of guilt from Augustine and the Reformation through to the guilt-obsessed creations of Dostoevsky.[88] Oppenheimer argues that at the root of modern guilt lies the reality of infinite desire and a society preoccupied with legalization. There is much in Oppenheimer that is reminiscent of Habermas' concern with 'juridification', which is the ever-increasing control of daily life by the creation of more and more laws, and with Habermas' awareness that the fragility of personal identity is taken over by the phenomenon of consumption. What is distinctive in Oppenheimer is his sensitivity to the religious dimension of western culture.

It is clear that Oppenheimer regards the fascination with guilt in Augustine as a serious mistake. There are many possibilities of creating a religious world view without this fascination, although Oppenheimer concedes that western guilt stems from belief in a personal God with its awareness of disobedience and estrangement. Oppenheimer believes that the decline in belief in a personal God should lead to less concern about guilt, yet this is not the case. Guilt persists in fiendishly intense form in modern, western, secular societies. It is a creative stimulant on film, music and art, yet it also weighs society down. It stems from 'the infinite desire', which is neither genetically nor socially determined. Although we are limited beings with limited needs and potentials, infinite desire always is present. Oppenheimer again points, like Campbell, to the Romantic movement as the origin of this infinitude. He describes Shelley in Rome in 1821 who 'evoked a similar capacity of human desires to expand infinitely'.[89] Oppenheimer compares these desires, and the adult desire of Baudelaire in his poetry of the mid nineteenth century, with the infinite reaches of the solar system mapped by Galileo two centuries earlier. The universe, says Oppenheimer, is 'too large, bare and trivial to be

emotionally satisfying'. What is more absorbing are the desires
of the self so that 'the human imagination . . . may actually seek
to overwhelm space-time and physical reality altogether, by
ignoring and exceeding them, belittling them with grander
infinitude of desire itself, and with a form of desire that may
prove self-centring and abasing'. For Shelley, infinite desire was
a novel revelation, utterly unknown in medieval Europe. Eter-
nity was the rival concept to personal and physical infinity,
standing outside time and referring to the indescribable mind of
God. Shelley's universe is one which is infinite, filled only with
the desires of the awakened self.

As Oppenheimer argues: 'In the modern western world,
infinite personal desire has replaced God.' What distinguishes it
from the old Judaeo–Christian faith is 'a vastly and paradoxically greater capacity to inspire guilt. It is infinitely subtle . . .
its adaptability, its complete elasticity, is one of its most com-
mendable and bewildering qualities.' Oppenheimer sees this
power as assuming a Christian, Jewish or Islamic disguise for
those who for social and psychological reasons wish to call
themselves Christians, Jews or Moslems.[90] The divine incarnation of solipsism both gives its followers a sense of release from
superstition, and a greater sense of freedom than religious
adherents felt in previous centuries. Nevertheless, there is
always the 'paroxysm of unavoidable guilt' because it is 'impossible to appease the new stupendous desire – God'.[91] Oppenheimer puts his finger on the Achilles' heel of the new
consumerism. Since it is always chasing some new novelty, and
some fresh expression of personal identity, there is no way in
which one can be finally satisfied. Oppenheimer dwells too
heavily on the frustration and impotence which those involved
in consumerism must feel. For many, especially in younger
generations, there is a sense of personal identity which is both
given and challenged in the world of music, fashion and
contemporary relationships. This is the defence of consumerism, and explains why it has become so dominant and all-
embracing. Nevertheless Oppenheimer's insight stands as a
valid condemnation of consumer behaviour. If one cannot be
satisfied, then one will feel guilty.

In any materialistic society, materialistic desires rapidly come to assume an exaggerated importance. This is probably self-evident. What is perhaps not so obvious is that in any such society desire itself must soon assume this type of strange importance, that spiritual desires too may now become exaggerations, paralysing in their sheer hugeness . . . It is precisely this new western (and spreading) exhibitionism of desire, in which it comes to lack anchors in values, in which it becomes a force too great for the human heart to bear, and for the human mind to grasp, that is the new human condition. It is also the root of the new, tormenting features of modern guilt.[92]

Oppenheimer feels that this guilt is pervasive in western industrial society. This desire is never seen as obsession, but rather as a form of health. What is most difficult with this secular manifestation of desire is, as Oppenheimer shows, a theological issue. Prior to the twentieth century in the West it was assumed that a broken pact with God must be the source of feelings of guilt and worthlessness. This implied atonement, and the possibility of acceptable forgiveness. The presence of the new God of infinite desire means the loss of finitude, the meaning of atonement and the possibility of forgiveness. There is as a result a 'rampage of modern guilt through modern societies'.[93] Oppenheimer is clear that psychiatry is not the answer to the issue of unsatisfied ambition, desire and the search for self-satisfaction: 'Society, culture and the state may seem alien. Their disconnectedness, or one's own, will have nothing to do with wealth, with money. No amount of money or economic security, or bankruptcy, will affect one's irremediable, unending guilt.'[94] Oppenheimer opens up the central paradox of consumerism. It arose out of the Romantic discovery of the possibility of infinite desire, and the solipsistic fascination with one's soul. By art, and by hedonistic consumption, it seemed possible to achieve a resolution of personal identity in a civilization that had largely abandoned faith in the Judaeo-Christian God. The irony is that this search for identity destroys itself, for the infinity of desire cannot be satisfied. Hence, the irony is that the psychologist accepts that a sense of guilt is part of the modern condition. 'A well-honed guilt sense, or at least a sense of guilt empathy, is considered normal and a promoter of social peace.'[95]

Oppenheimer believes that traditional religion will seem too unsophisticated to deal with 'the modern dilemma of facing and submitting to the demands of the desire-God'.[96] His solution is to accept that humanity will eventually attain a new ethic to adapt to release themselves 'from the shadowy threats of modern guilt'.[97] For the moment he believes that the human spirit is 'experiencing . . . a period of dramatic adjustment to its new knowledge about its environment'. There is a time-lag between scientific knowledge about infinity and the fundamental psychological and spiritual reaction to it. Arguing for the validity of spiritual beliefs, both from their antiquity and their survival in the face of persecution this century, Oppenheimer foresees new developments in spirituality and organized religion to cope with the changed state of human consciousness. At the moment there are, as always, early and extreme reactions to this new consciousness: 'Even extreme reactions have their values. Thus the violence with which the Church greeted the new astronomy, and the new fashion of infinite desire, has acted as a spur to art, science and the spread of democracy.'[98]

What exacerbates this situation is the bureaucratic spread of laws which are ironically created by those self-same democracies. In an attempt to right perceived social and economic inequalities, greater legislation has been passed by modern legislatures than in any period in history. The fundamental shift in jurisprudence is from the view that judges with strictly limited powers could discover the law to one where law is enacted by the courts. The influence of the Justinian Corpus Juris in Europe, and the closely defined activities of Anglo-American law led to the concept of legal 'discovery', or Justinrecht. Today, the complexity of modern technological society, as Habermas has already noted in the discussion in chapter 1, means that modern legislation is absolutist: what Oppenheimer calls 'the seizure of increasingly sprawling guilt-inducing powers by legislatures and parliaments'.[99] The result is a blizzard of litigation on the one hand, and a profound alienation from legislation on the part of most citizens on the other. Social change (produced for well-meaning reasons to improve social welfare) which proceeds by means of legislation leads to 'a continuously heightened sense of social construction, then of alienation and then of potential guilt'. This explains the much documented popular reaction to the 'social engineering' of the 1960s, still prevalent in some societies, and to the widespread populist reaction of less taxes and less social control: a feature found in Scandinavia, and in contemporary Britain, despite the election of the present government. There is a continuous disrespect for the laws and nature of government itself. As Oppenheimer points out, this virus of cynicism can affect a prosperous society as much as an impoverished one, perhaps more so in some instances, such as in California. At the same time, the problem of overlegislation, and the celebration of criminality in modern cinema (such as *Bonnie and Clyde* in 1967), reinforces the sense of guilt and inadequacy in personal well-being and spirituality produced by the spirit of infinite desire.

It is now surely clear, from this example, why the two issues of human identity and social justice must be held together. Just as Habermas identified the problem of modern western societies as both that of social fragmentation and social inequality, with the alienated individual content not to intervene politically but to accept her powerlessness by enjoying a life of personal hedonism and consumption, so Oppenheimer shows how guilt both accompanies the personality of the modern individual and is orchestrated by the ever-growing activity of the modern legal–political establishment. Personal identity and social justice go hand in hand, but the answer is not necessarily more legislation. For Oppenheimer, the immediate solution is to enjoy a quiet Epicureanism, valuing the pleasures of daily life and of personal freedom, ignoring the pressure of the desire to express oneself in new and unexplored ways.

Oppenheimer's reaction is in many ways reminiscent of that of the English political philosopher John Gray, in his book *Enlightenment's Wake*.[100] Gray's horrified reaction to the impact of the global economy, and his defence of the local and the traditional in western social democracy is analysed in chapter 4 on globalization. The challenge to the theologian writing from an English, Anglican perspective is to ask whether the description given by Oppenheimer can produce an answer to the problem of infinite desire.

CONCLUSIONS

It is time to review the argument of this chapter. The history of the rise of consumerism has been charted, and the basic thesis advanced that consumerism is a displaced search for identity, from the religious vocation found in work in previous centuries to a combination of hedonism and self-expression in consumption. Put bluntly, the search for fashion does not just make people feel good, it defines who they are. Alongside this argument I have been critical of Veblen, although there is some truth in his arguments. It is, however, a confused thesis, and one that is overplayed by social moralists. Amongst them are a fair number of church people. The critical factor is that of imagination, and I will argue in the chapter on the market that recent developments in market theory again do not see it as merely teleological, seeking a state of economic equilibrium, but as concerned with imagining new possibilities, including new forms of identity and self-expression.

I have next described the current state of consumerism, and of consumption theory. There is much evidence of greed, waste and over-consumption, driven in part by the increasing inequality of the most economically skilled in our society. It is also the case that across the developed world two massive shifts are happening. One is from an industrialized to a service economy, and secondly there is a transition from an economy based on production (what we can produce) to a consumption (what people require) economy. Even in the field of medicine, in the 50th anniversary year of the National Health Service, in Great Britain, there has been much reflection on the shift from production (more operations, technology, pharmacology) to consumption (more primary care in the community, health life styles and support groups for the chronically ill). Consumption is a fact of life, in both the industrialized and service sectors. It is also a major factor in cultural development. This requires a much more intensive study than can be attempted in this chapter, but it is worth saying that so far Christian social ethics has remained largely in the realm of production and industrialization, rather than in the fast-developing world of consumption and the service sector.

Finally, I move to two major critics of consumerism, Meeks and Oppenheimer. I have dealt at length with Meeks, for although there are some important insights and it is a skilful presentation, I would agree with Preston that:

Meeks is playing with the concept of God as an economist rather than providing illumination . . . he does not understand what economics is about . . . The doctrine of the consumer as king in the market reflects the idea of the authoritarian monotheistic God. This is a highly implausible theological basis on which to criticize the idea of the market, which in so far as it derives by several removes from Christian theology is much more related to the concept of personal responsibility.[101]

Meeks has been a highly influential theologian in some Christian circles, but there is a failure to engage seriously with contemporary economic life. Oppenheimer is another intellectual who sees the damage done by the current state of western culture. His book is a *tour de force* of cultural history, moving between historical periods and societies with great ease: Oppenheimer is concerned to present a problem, which he puts very well. This is that the search for identity found in the interplay between hedonism and aesthetics which is called consumerism is self-defeating. One of the intrinsic features of consumerism is the search for novelty. However, this is self-defeating, because the response to this search must be the cultivation of the phenomenon of infinite desire, which, in turn, leads to satiety, guilt and a sense of failure. Indeed, it is compounded by the spread of legislation and litigation in western society, which heightens the sense of guilt. I find the arguments of Oppenheimer very persuasive, not least because in a different way he echoes much of the concerns of Jürgen Habermas on identity, consumerism and overlegislation of daily life (juridification in his words).

What then should be the response to this shift to consumption and the service economy? This is both a theological issue about identity, and an ethical one about debt and patterns of consumption. There are three ethical concerns. One is about ethical consumerism, and the impact that a well-directed consumer campaign can make to global living standards. Secondly, it is about self-restraint and the value of a simpler life style. This is also a taxation issue, where the shift from income tax to taxation on the consumption of goods and services (e.g. VAT) is well advanced. Hypothecation (allocation of specific taxes on certain activities of goods for particular spending outcomes by government) is also frequently discussed. Thirdly, it is an ethical issue of debt, credit-scoring and advice on spending. The theological issue can be stated simply. The historical part of this chapter shows that consumerism came out of a move from a theological, moralist association of work, religion and identity to a synthesis of aesthetics, emotion, subjectivity and identity. What is constant is the concern with identity, and the issue of relationships. It is unlikely that much progress will be made by appealing back to the Victorian values of work, religion and personal freedom, although Mrs Thatcher certainly tried to do just that. Instead, we need to find a new context for consumerism, which preserves the concern for identity and relationships, but puts them in a transformed reality of transcendence, wider social relationships and service of others as well as self. Part of this would include leisure.

The ethical questions are ones which Christians have on the whole been more actively involved in. There are several studies of debt, including a recent one by the Anglican Church in Wales, and a publication from the Centre for Theology and Public Issues at Edinburgh University, significantly entitled *Domestic Debt: Disease of Consumer Society?*[102]

Ethical consumerism has been promoted by many charities and lobbying groups. Oxfam, for instance, ran the Clothes Code Campaign, highlighting the poor conditions and low pay of women textile workers in developing countries. They used a television celebrity, Caryn Franklin, who presented a fashion show called *The Clothes Show* to give added impetus to the campaign.[103] It became a particular gender issue, with women buying many of the fashion goods, a woman celebrity fronting it, and women benefiting in developing nations. Christian organizations in Britain, such as Traidcraft, Tearfund, CAFOD and Christian Aid have all linked awareness of global poverty with lobbying campaigns. These have been reinforced by movements to spread wealth on fairly grown and fairly traded commodities (such as tea and coffee) and craft products. Ethical consumerism has also been active in the environmental movement, with a concern to label goods for their energy and environmental impact. This strategy agrees with one aspect of the regulation of the market, which is for government to make available much more information on products in the hope that consumers will respond.[104] Governments have also used fiscal policy to shape consumption patterns, as for instance in the British government's policy of putting higher taxes on leaded petrol, which led to a steep decline in sales of such fuel. How far government policy should try to influence consumption is a heavily debated issue, not least in such areas as smoking and alcohol. Finally, there is the strategy of the boycott. In Christian terms this goes back to the end of the last century, when the Christian Social Union compiled blacklists of products produced for low pay or in poor conditions. In recent years there have been extensive boycotts of companies investing in South Africa (Barclays Bank in Britain, Polaroid in America), or harming the environment (Shell earned much bad publicity over the Brent Spar disposal row) or involved with oppressive governments (Shell, again in Nigeria). The combination of trade-union pressure, lobby groups and consumer power can be devastating if properly co-ordinated. It can also be allied with stock-market investment policies, and the increase in ethical investment portfolios in this decade has been enormous. The media have an enormous role to play in uncovering abuses of working and pay conditions. It is important that Christian support of ethical consumerism in all its forms continues to develop. The Nestlé baby-food controversy is the most contentious in Britain in this decade.[105] The consumer movement has changed dramatically since the American lobbyist Ralph Nader published a series of reports on unsafe products, including the famous attack in the 1960s on unsafe cars called *Unsafe At Any Speed*. The National Consumer Council in Britain also widens concern with consumption by representing user groups of privatized utilities.

The second area is that of restraint in consumption. One of

the best-selling books in the early 1990s in America was Duane Elgins' *Voluntary Simplicity: Towards a Way of Life that is Outwardly Simple; Inwardly Rich*, which promoted a simpler way of life. The memorable aphorism 'Even if you win the rat race, you're still a rat' sums up this insight. Some adopt restraint out of concern with the environment. Others realize that the pressure of economic life puts intolerable strains on social relationships. It is no surprise that two of the cities in England with the highest divorce rates, Guildford and Cambridge, also have some of the fastest economic growth rates, most mobile populations, highest earners and those working longest hours. The family bears the brunt, as the recent Church of England report on the family *Something to Celebrate* points out.[106] (This is not to deny, of course, that poverty, bad social conditions and enforced stress from economic insecurity in the most declining economic areas, such as parts of north-east England, also lead to marriage break-up.) The third reason for 'downshifting' was a response to a spiritual need. Elgin emphasizes the link between voluntary simplicity and the Aristotlean gold mean, the Platonic emphasis on the transcendence of sensory desires and the Buddhist 'middle way'. He claims that 90 per cent of those involved in a less intensive consumer life style are involved with 'spiritual growth activity' from New Age to the world faiths.

Juliet Schor, a Harvard economics professor and author of *The Overworked American*, points out the many ethical difficulties with this approach. The labour market is still organized around full-time work, especially at the higher earning level. It is very difficult for individual consumers by their actions to influence society's perception of what material goods are required for a fulfilled life style: we return to the neo-Keynesian point made by J. K. Galbraith about the power of advertising and the influence of corporations on the market. Adopting a simpler life style can also lead to personal economic instability. What might change attitudes is the perception that slower rates of growth might lead to greater social cohesion, which again might improve health and reduce criminality. It is, almost certainly correctly, a tentative argument with a series of conditional hypotheses.

Another difficult ethical question is that the emerging middle classes in the developing world have only recently acquired the consumer goods now being rejected by some in the industrialized world. Finally, the logic of economic restructuring is leading to greater social and economic inequality, not less. Daniel Cohen's recent book, *The Wealth of the World and the Poverty of Nations*,[107] argues that team work in the western world requires the highest level of competence. The best lab technicians are required in space exploration, and the best secretaries are needed by top law firms. Advanced economics increasingly are driven by technology into adding more and more value, since low-value production shifts increasingly into emerging economies. Therefore, the work of adding the highest value requires the highest level of team competence. The infamous example usually cited is the explosion of the space shuttle Challenger in 1986, which was caused by the failure of a simple rubber seal known as an O-Ring. The investigating commission reported that the workforce had come under too much strain, the seal had been wrongly designed and fitted, and one small fault had destroyed the quality of the entire finished product of the error of a few team members. Advanced economies pursue higher and higher quality every year. This requires better and better team members: 'It means that very slight differences in skill and performance are magnified into big disparities of income. There is no longer a single market for any particular type of skill.'[108] What is occurring is not simply disparities of income between high-skill and low-skill employees, but also that in different professions with similar skill levels individual competence (or sheer luck) is rewarded far more in some companies than others. Earnings within the legal profession, and within secretaries, are widening. In 1967, the richest fifth in the United States earned 43.8 per cent of all income. By 1993, it had risen to 48.9 per cent.

Higher salaries lead to greater displays of conspicuous consumption, a pattern described in *Economics for Prophets* and in a recent collection of American essays on consumerism entitled *The Consuming Passion: Christianity and the Consumer Culture*.[109] The ethical questions raised by a simpler life style are about the shift to a culture less obsessed with material goods. A social ethicist will, however, want to ask if consumption of non-material activities (visits to theatres, travel and recreation) is only a substitute for material acquisition. Questions like this are raised by Ronald Inglehart's book, *Culture Shift in Advanced Industrial Society.*[110] Nevertheless, the correlation of happiness, social well-being and economic growth by the New Economics Foundation shows that economic growth does not produce greater social well-being in advanced economies, nor does it allow for a growth in criminality and other social ills. The NEF is now beginning a series of social audits which purport to give the 'true' reading of a society's welfare. It is in this direction, allied with an increasing interest by individuals in a personally simpler life style, that the ethical challenge to the phenomenon identified by Cohen is put at its sharpest. On the one hand, as the journalist Diane Coyle puts it commenting on Cohen's book: 'Once an economy has started down the path of inequality, when the organizational, legal and cultural barriers to some categories of people receiving higher and higher incomes have vanished, it is impossible to turn back'.[111] Punitive taxation on high incomes is very unlikely, and company codes of conduct rarely set an upper limit on salaries. Performance-related pay is not always transparent either. On the other hand, the impact of voluntary self-restraining, 'post-materialism' (the phrase refers to the shift in consumption from material goods to non-material ones), the necessity of social cohesion and new forms of social auditing may lead in the contrary direction. The example set by Christians, both as individuals and as a communal body in churches, is clearly of the greatest significance.

Finally there is the question of domestic debt. In the seven years 1989–1996, the total amount of credit outstanding in Britain more than doubled; the number of mortgage repossessions rose almost eightfold in the same period; and more than half of unemployed families with children are in debt. In the late 1980s and early 1990s, personal bankruptcies also increased dramatically. Graham Blount is a Church of Scotland parish minister who has researched and written extensively on debt. Another person who has worked extensively in this area, using

Blount's research as well as his own, is Peter Selby, Bishop of Worcester and previously Professorial-Fellow at Durham University. He published his findings in *Grace and Mortgage* (1997).[112]

Blount is clear that a cautious, even suspicious, attitude in the British commercial attitude to credit used to restrict the offering of credit very severely. Now the role of the law is to ensure the functioning of the credit market. Controls on credit were scrapped as an instrument of economic policy. Blount makes an ethical distinction between credit and debt. Credit becomes debt when repayments are not met. There are two explanations for unpaid debt. One is the moral argument, stressing the failure of the debtor. The other is an economic explanation, stressing the economic circumstances in which the debt took place. Blount argues that different kinds of debt also reflect different causes:

Fuel debt and rent arrears, for example, may well be closely linked with poverty; credit card debt may offer more scope for explanations in terms of financial management; and analysis of mortgage arrears and repossessions may show a clearer link with events such as redundancy or relationship breakdown. Thus Rowntree usefully distinguishes primary, or long-term debt (linked to chronic low income), from secondary, or short-term debt, which is likely to be more closely related to disruption in income.[113]

Credit is clearly popular, in that it allows access to consumption, spreads the cost of large items, and ends the queues that were common only twenty years ago in Britain for a loan from a building society to buy a house. It is worth remembering how difficult it was for working-class families two decades ago to obtain a loan to buy their own home. Mortgages were often issued to those who had been saving with a building society for some time, those whose job seemed secure or fell in accepted categories, often professional and those whose parents owned their own home and could provide surety. All this reflected a cautious, and class-based approach to credit which is good to have disappeared. In 1975, J. K. Galbraith, who was no friend of organized capitalism and felt that it rigged the market, could still argue for wider access to credit. Credit had, he said, 'a remarkably egalitarian' function for it is credit which 'allows the man with energy and no money to participate in the economy more or less on a par with the man who has capital of his own'.[114] Blount helpfully notes different attitudes to credit, which are often age-related. Pensioners are far more critical of debt than young people, and Berthoud writes of it being regarded as on the same level as 'soft porn'.

Peter Selby has given a good analysis of the relationship of credit to poverty and debt. He points out that one of the least noticed, but most crucial, developments in Britain in the 1980s was that participating in the culture of debt and credit is 'now for practical purposes an index of participation in society at all; even the social fund, which replaced emergency grants to those in receipt of family credit, can be seen as a way of integrating claimants, the poorest members of our society, into the credit economy'.[115] This meant that the lowest income group saw an increase in credit from 22 per cent of that group to 69 per cent in the decade 1980–1990. Indebtedness, and house repossession, grew dramatically in this period. Even despite the fact that inflation fell and personal disposable income for those in work rose, savings fell throughout the decade. Consumption grew 25 per cent faster than the gross domestic product.

There are a number of ethical issues which are raised by this. One, most obviously, is the difficulty for people on low incomes to obtain credit at all. A second question is why poverty has grown so much in a wealthy country like Britain? A third is that of the appropriate response to such a burden of debt in Britain. The first is the question of access to banks and credit. The closure of banks in poorer areas, and even the difficulty of opening a bank account because of low or irregular income, means that there is still a two-level system of credit in Britain. It is no longer class-based, as in the 1950s, but one which turns on poverty, regular income and geographical location. What this means is that even if a person gets a part-time job, or occasional casual work, the level and irregularity of income places them outside the sphere of normal credit. For a low-income family, especially in an inner city or outer estate, this means social exclusion: 'Debt functions as an effective termination of social as well as economic participation for many.'

There are many stories of the social isolation which this can cause, which are often exacerbated if the person is a member of a minority ethnic group. Peter Selby describes the profitability of companies which will lend to low income groups avoided by banks and building societies. Such companies can charge interest rates of more than 100 per cent, but demand for their services is growing.[116]

A second ethical issue is the way in which poverty has grown in Britain, and people have been forced to borrow at these rates merely to survive. The annual rate of change in inequality in income inequality in Britain from 1977 to 1990 was 0.75 per cent per annum, which was a faster rate than any other country except for New Zealand from 1985 to 1989 (a much shorter period). Countries like Italy, Ireland and Denmark experienced reduced inequality, and even France and Germany only increased inequality by 0.1 to 0.2 per cent per annum. Indeed, after housing costs are taken into account, the poorest tenth of income groups saw their income fall by 17 per cent from 1979 to 1991/2. This decrease in income leads to greater poverty, greater indebtedness and a growing sense of social exclusion.[117]

How then should society, and Christians, seek to respond to this 'disease of consumer society' to quote the title of the report on debt from the Centre for Theology and Public Issues? Part of the answer must be to argue strongly for a decrease in poverty, more social inclusion and better paid work for those on the margins. This was the response of the Methodist Report, *The Cities* (1977), and the ecumenical British report from the churches, *Unemployment and the Future of Work* (1997). Partly the suggestion by the National Consumer Council should be taken up: 'that, above a certain level, credit agreements entered into with no reasonable enquiry as to ability to meet them should be unenforceable at law'.[118] There are also Credit Unions, which are co-operative societies with a common purpose uniting the members such as living on the same estate, members of the same church or workers in the same company. They offer members loans out of the pool of savings built up by the members themselves. Here the criteria of the market, such as credit scoring, are replaced by the common bond and personal trust. There is a necessity to be a saver before one can borrow, which will discourage some. It is very striking that, at the end of the 1980s, 30 per cent of the Irish Republic, and 30 per cent of Catholics in Northern Ireland, belonged to Credit Unions. The maximum rate of interest cannot exceed 1 per cent on the reducing balance. However, only a tiny proportion of the population of Britain belongs to a Credit Union. In 1987, 108 existed with no region involving more than 1 per cent of the population.

Why do few so belong to this answer to poverty?[119] It requires a high degree of idealism, with a debate inside the movement between those who are idealistic and those who see the objective in strictly practical terms. Is it there to create a community or to enable money to be borrowed at the lowest cost? These aims are not exclusive, and members of such unions value the sense of community. However, they tend to be used by those who are not the poorest members of society, and they will not bring about the radical change of society wished by some. Nevertheless, they play a vital role, and above all they represent a challenge to society. There is a deep Christian involvement in many such Credit Unions. This leads into the question of theological responses to the consumer society in which we live. How does a person as consumer respond to the divine calling which is presented in Christ? Of course there will be other roles which the person will perform (parent or child, worker, citizen, neighbour), but the importance of consumption cannot be denied. Consumption is centrally about feelings, affectivity, style and desire. It is primarily (not entirely) an urban, cosmopolitan phenomenon, focused on novelty and the conferring of identity. Again, it is natural that a different set of emphases can be placed against it which relativize it: tradition, locality and rootedness, the will. Nevertheless, once again, the reality of consumerism (shopping malls, cinema, clubs and recreation) remains, even after all the qualifications have been made. For some people, especially young people, it is overwhelmingly central to their lives.

It is, then, with desire that a theology of consumerism must begin: 'If you do not want to cease praying, do not cease

longing'. wrote Augustine in his discourse on Psalm 38. Desire
certainly matters, and the adoption of an affective norm in
sexual matters (that is, the centrality of consent between adults,
and the importance of personal relationships) has been justified
by appeal to the centrality of love and personal relations in the
Gospel accounts of Jesus. However, this chapter has shown how
intransigent is the problem of 'unlimited desire' especially as
described by Oppenheimer. What is needed is a recognition of
the unity and materiality of the human person, where 'the soul'
refers to the essence of the person, including her bodyliness.
Perfection is found in and through participation in the world.
Such an approach was, of course, part of the old work ethic
which consumerism has now supplanted. How then does a
theory of personal identity speak to this quest for identity in
consumption?

First, personhood can be seen as self-transcendent. The
'infinite desire' in consumption can be transformed into the
unbounded openness and quest for the infinite, but with this
infinity placed in God. Jesus as a person becomes the symbolic
point of encounter between divine self-giving and human self-
transcendence. The artistic metaphor, issuing in a sacramental
vision of imagination, creativity and incompleteness, can take
seriously the central concerns of consumerism while placing
them in a larger whole. That whole would be a community of
persons which make up a local society,[120] and the local church.

Secondly, Rahner's emphasis on how historically conditioned
we are must not be forgotten. Language about sexuality, authority and money is always inevitably embodied in concepts that
are culturally conditioned. The implication for the church is
that the meaning of poverty must be rethought. Rahner's essay
on 'The Theology of Poverty' explored this tension:

When Jesus called his disciples to poverty, it was not in order to
inaugurate a social programme. His was not a radical rejection of
possessions or an idea of a universal economic or social transformation. His call was to an act of faith in the definite fulfilment of
human existence that comes from outside our human situation as a
grace. Amid the abundance of our consumer-oriented society, religious poverty means that most being satisfied with a relatively modest

way of live. Similarly, Christian discipleship today means that the church is now called to provide an example of consumer ascesis in non-conformity with modern mass consumption.[121]

An aesthetic Christianity, which appeals to the heart by symbols and transforms the imagination would be one answer to the identity question posed by consumerism. The work of Christian groups that work with secular and Christian artists, such as the Arts and Recreation Chaplaincy with Canon Bill Hall in north-east England, is the way forward. Here is the answer to the answer of infinite desire: to place the search for novelty in the community of those who find their identity in the longing for God, which is answered by divine grace. Such a longing would be marked by simplicity, community and imagination, not denying the reality of consumerism but transforming it through symbols of love and hope.

Thirdly, there is the need to strengthen personal identity to resist temptation (it is not too strong a word) posed by the consumer society. A Christian philosophy of education would see that the task is no longer the cultivation of a social elite, and the culture which mattered so much to Newman and T. S. Eliot. Nor is it simply the inculcation of scientific and technical expertise, important though these are in the era of the global economy. Instead, a philosophy of education will not deny the validity of these first two points, but concentrate also on what it means to live well in a consumer society. How can the character of individual persons be shaped so that the intrinsic values of community, relationships and personal vision be embodied in those who will experience the unceasing challenge of a con-sumer society in which identity will equal consumption? This is a distinctive task for Christian schools, so that the moral values can be preserved in which a religious vision might take shape, not in a sectarian manner, but in one that is hospitable to religious dialogue: 'Forming people in the intelligent search for the coherence of conceptions and use of money with theological conceptions and norms is an exceedingly important task.'[122] 1 Corinthians 12:12-26 describes a human being as part of a body: 'If one part of the body suffers, all the other parts suffer with it; if one part is praised, all the other parts share its happiness.' This can be applied not only to the church, but also to the organic relationship between a person and reality. The reality of humanity is three levels that interconnect and interact. These are the natural or biological, the social and the cultural. Through all three God encounters the human being, as it is self-transcendent and historical. What has happened in consumerism is that the quest for self-identity has been focused overwhelmingly on the social and the cultural realms through the unlimited desire for what is novel, exciting and stimulating. What has also taken place is that the fragility of the human person has been revealed in this desiring. The danger is that we (for it includes us all) have become dependent on the stimuli which the consumer society gives to us. As we become more addicted to such stimulation, our inner identity is threatened and weakened. It is not that we are dominated by goods which we 'worship' (I disagree with Meeks here profoundly), but that our inner identity is in constant need of reinforcement by the stimulation of consumption. As the Norwegian Bishops put it, perhaps too trenchantly, but certainly in a way which needs hearing:

The individual that lacks security in himself has to obtain it from his surroundings, by trendy fashions and the magic of the consumer goods, which give him security . . . The important thing is our own need for investment, that the culture of consumption is dominated by fantasy, and that it is characterized by the narcissist removal of the borders between the ego and our surroundings.[123]

The individual identity which participates in the body which is the natural, the cultural and the social becomes swamped (overwhelmed, in the words of one recent theology[124]) by culture. As Job 15:33 puts it, human identity becomes 'like a vine that loses its unripe grapes'. By overstimulation, the identity withers away.

This is the reason for not only considering the ethical challenge of consumerism. Alongside that challenge, so powerfully stated by Peter Selby, there is one of human identity. I do not believe that the consumer society can be wished away, or condemned outright. If anything is pure fantasy, that is it. What is needed is attention to the theological issues of identity, desire, self-transcendence, creativity and education. This task of posing a creative alternative to consumerism, through the creation of a different community which expresses its longing through the symbols of freedom and love, will enable human identity to find a new vocation different both from the vocation of consumption and the old work ethic. It is to a consideration of what remains of that work ethic that we turn in the next chapter.

CHAPTER 3

The work ethic

> Baptised in the icy waters of Calvinist theology, the
> business of life, once regarded as perilous to the soul,
> acquired a new sanctity. Labour is not merely an
> economic means; it is a spiritual end. R. H. Tawney.

Max Weber published *The Protestant Ethic and the Spirit of Capitalism* as a two-part article in the 1904/5 issue of *Archiv für
Sozialawissenschaft und Sozialpolitik*. It was published as a single
volume some fifteen years later, with rebuttals to earlier criticisms. This revised edition was translated into English by
Talcott Parsons in 1930. Habermas' critique of it has already
been mentioned in chapter 2, where he refers to its excessive
concentration on economic issues.

   In this chapter, the impact of Weber's study will be taken up
again. Weber's influence is usually taken as referring to The
Protestant Work Ethic (PWE). There are two debates which
Weber started, and it is primarily the second of these which will
be of interest. The first is the accuracy of Weber's hypothesis. In
addition to the philosophical criticisms made by Habermas,
amongst others, there have also been historical criticisms of his
work. This chapter will survey the debate briefly, but the real
focus of the chapter is on the second debate begun by Weber.
This debate is about the understanding of work in an industrialized society. Does work equate with paid employment? Why do
people feel the need to work, and what are the beliefs and values
which sustain this need? Are these beliefs any longer shaped by
religion, or has the PWE (as it will now be referred to) become
part of the lumber-room of history? There are four sections to

this chapter. First, Weber's original theory will be discussed. Secondly, psychological and sociological studies of the work ethic are analysed. Thirdly, the future of the work ethic is examined. Finally, and only then, is a theology of work described.

Ever since the 1950s, with the work of Alan Richardson[1] through to Pope John Paul II,[2] there have been theologies of work produced either by individual theologians or by the denominations themselves. Very few of these, if any, pay much attention to the empirical reality of working life. Some have done so, especially those associated with the Industrial Mission Association in Britain, but they are all too few. A notable exception was the 1997 report, *Unemployment and the Future of Work*, written by a working party from the Council of churches for Britain and Ireland through the working-party secretary, Andrew Britton. He is a distinguished economist who has combined a career as an applied economist with his role both as a lay reader in the Church of England and a member of several church committees on social responsibility.

A theology of work must wrestle with the issues which have been mentioned above, such as the present state and the future of the work ethic. If the meaning of work, whether as paid employment or as activity focused on a goal, does not take account of its subjective meaning for individuals and groups, then the theology is inevitably distorted. There is also, of course, the economic and sociological reality of what is happening in the world of work, and the theological exploration of that reality. Alan Richardson, for instance, draws heavily on the 'biblical theology' school with its emphasis on the 'works of God' in salvation history, but ignores totally the psychological and sociological reality of work. The meaning of work must also be considered for its participants, and the lack of this lends to much theological discussion about work an abstract feel, which is to its detriment.

WEBER'S PROTESTANT ETHIC THESIS

Max Weber began *The Protestant Ethic and the Spirit of Capitalism*[3] by defining in a provisional way the phenomenon which he sought to explain. This was the spirit of modern capitalism. He challenged another German socilogist, Werner Sombart, whose study *Modern Capitalism* (*Der Moderne Kapitalismus*) appeared in 1902.[4] Sombart investigated the self-sufficient, handicraft economic systems and then moved onto early and 'high' capitalism. Each of these was made up of values for economic behaviour, a way of organizing economic activity, and a technique of how to work. Pre-capitalist systems are traditional, and satisfy fixed needs. They are closely tied to the exploitation of natural resources. Sombart saw in capitalism not only new techniques and the use of new technology, but also a new value system. On the one hand, there is the spirit of dynamic enterprise, and, on the other, the rational spirit of the new merchants. Unlimited expansion and economic rationality were signalled out by Sombart as the ethos of modern capitalism. This first appeared in thirteenth-century Italy (before the Black Death of 1348), then paused for a long while, finally began to grow in the sixteenth century and was fully triumphant by the start of the nineteenth century in Europe. Sombart traces the emergence of this spirit to the influence of Judaism in western medieval Europe. The Deuteronomic commands permitted different commercial dealings between Jew and Gentile, such as the use of usury. This was forbidden between Jews, but allowed between Jews and Gentiles. Medieval and Renaissance Judaism was deeply indebted to a legal and national way of ordering its life. Its style of life was sober, and it was excluded from church and state, still more from the military aristocracy of western Europe. So it turned in upon itself, developing both study and the organization of its own life. There is a splendid description of medieval Jewish welfare in Michael Walzer's *Spheres of Justice*. It also began to create great wealth, in finance and in trade. Sombart maintained that Jewish merchants carried this economic ethic across Europe. Sometimes they propagated it, and sometimes it was imitated by the indigenous business communities where they settled. From 1903 to 1914, Sombart published a series of further texts, including *The Jews and Modern Capitalism* (1911) *Luxury and Capitalism* (1912) (the relationship of this to Veblen's work discussed in chapter 2 is clear), *War and Capitalism* (1912) and *The Quintessence of Capitalism* (1913). Later he republished *Modern Capitalism* in two volumes, with the final volume appearing in 1927. At the same time Georg Simmel published his *Philosophy of Money* in 1900, where again the attitude to wealth in different cultures was explored. Simmel's study in consumerism has already been mentioned in chapter 2.

When Weber published his famous essay in 1905, he was therefore writing within a highly developed sociological and historical tradition. Weber's intention was to challenge Sombart directly. He not only wanted to relocate the origins of the capitalist mentality from Judaism to the Protestant Reformation, especially in Calvinism in Northern Europe, he also wanted to redescribe the nature of the spirit of capitalism itself. First, he denied that Sombart's description of the spirit of capitalism as ruthless, restless acquisition was modern at all. This could be found throughout economic history. Weber also wanted to redefine the spirit of capitalism itself.

First of all, modern capitalism is not based on the oppportunist, nor the bold adventurer, which have always existed in history. It is found instead in risk-minimizing and profit-maximizing strategy, although the empirical evidence for Weber's argument was not substantial. Secondly, modern capitalists were pecularily ascetic, restricting his consumption of capital once it had been earned. The great shift, for Weber, occurred in the fifteenth century. Up till then the merchant could live his life without sin, but could not intrinsically please God, since money making was fraught with danger. The honest earning of modest profits was tolerated in medieval Europe, as it had been in patristic Christanity at the end of the Roman Empire.[5] Now the emphasis changed. Weber posed the challenge to Sombart, 'How could activity, which was at best ethically tolerated, turn into a calling in the sense of Benjamin Franklin?'. Fourteenth-century Florence was the greatest western capitalist centre, and money capital of all the great powers. There was much criticism of this wealth, even if the western Church accepted it with some reservations. By the eighteenth century in Pennsylvania, where banking was rudimentary, money making was 'considered the essence of moral conduct, even commanded in the name of duty'.[6]

Weber argued that a number of seventeenth-century Reformed churches subscribed to a common code of conduct which governed the daily lives of believers. The main religious groups were the neo-Calvinist churches of North America and western Europe, Anabaptism, Continental Pietism and Anglo-American Methodism (the latter from the eighteenth century). Many of these groups overlapped in different ways, and Weber believed that, despite doctrinal differences (e.g. on predestination, or the Eucharist), there was a common ethical teaching. A fuller description of Luther's understanding of vocation is given later in this chapter. What is important at this stage is to note that Weber began his argument with the Reformation rejection of ethical dualism. The Church until the Reformation had divided its ethical teaching on the Christian life into praecepta and consilia. Praecepta were for all Christians, but consilia were for the minority of Christians who were in religious orders, ordained or both. This was because of their theology of the atonement, whereby they interceded for sinful humanity on their behalf. Luther, and other Reformers, not only discarded this distinction, but also placed the Christian life in the world.

Calvinists proved their election by identifying the fruits of faith in daily life, which also glorified God. Daily life produced good works, but these did not earn salvation. Rather they demonstrated it, and eliminated the fear of damnation. There was, for Weber, deep loneliness in the identity of the Calvinist striving to be worthy of eternal salvation. No priest or sacrament could ensure the eternal destiny of the individual, but only a trust in the mercy of God through faith in Christ's saving grace. This trust could develop into a doctrine of assurance. Later Calvinist theologians taught that it was an absolute Christian duty to be sure of faith. Such self-assurance could be earned in a way that faith, which was an unmerited gift from God, could not be. Intense worldly activity, which was living the godly life, could produce that assurance. Again the doctrine of the atonement was central.

There were three ethical maxims which Weber described as the Protestant Work Ethic. All three were interrelated. These were diligence in lawful callings, asceticism with regard to consumption, and constructive utilization of one's time. What was commanded was spiritual diligence, hard work and the avoidance of pleasure. Pleasure summed up all that was wrong in the godly life. It was easily attained, time wasting and centred on the self. Such things including social drinking and eating, luxury, sexual activity and material comfort. Weber realized that some medieval theology had argued in a similar way, but as part of the heightening of the *consilia evangelica*, so that monks, nuns and clergy could intercede more fruitfully for the souls of the faithful, living and departed. What had changed was that the asceticism of the Christian life was part of daily life for all Christians, and a psychological assurance was given that the Christian was predestined to salvation. Here, Weber felt, was the answer to Sombart's arguments.

Weber also realized that Pietists, Methodists and Baptists were often Arminian: that is, they believed, in principle, that all of humanity could be saved. His answer was that the emotional, subjective commitment to a true faith tended to undermine the searching for assurance of predestined election in these other religious groups. Nevertheless, they did accept that 'signs of grace' could be manifested in the life of the believer. At the same time, the life of the sect led to discipline the daily conduct of the individual in ways that proved that one was regenerated and holy.

Weber agreed that capitalism was boosted in two ways. On the one hand there was the creation of 'modern' profit-maximizing capitalists. On the other hand, the Protestant Work Ethic produced these early capitalists with a godly, disciplined and sober workforce. The motivation of the workers in the work ethic feeds into the profit ethic of the employer. Calvin's commentary on the parable of the labourers in the vineyard makes the point explicitly: 'Man was created for activity . . . Each has his own divinely appointed station . . . Our whole life is useless, and we are justly condemned of laziness, until we frame our life to the command and calling of God.'[7]

There has been much debate on the Weber thesis, and a long running historical controversy. Nevertheless, there does seem to be empirical evidence that the behaviour of merchants, employers and laborurers did change. In traditional economic life, labour had held a consistent preference for increased leisure over increased income on the one hand, and, on the other, labour had grasped at the opportunity for windfall gains as they presented themselves. The Calvinist emphasis on stewardship gave labourers an interest in increasing the return on their labour. Above all, it created a workforce which was willing to adapt to new time and work disciplines. Marshall writes: 'Voluntary under-employment in medieval and late medieval Europe manifested itself in such phenomena as the spontaneous taking of holidays, long hours spent socializing in the home and the tavern, the unhurried pace of life, the discontinuous pattern of work caused by frequent stoppages for recreation, the late arrivals for work, and the early departures from it, and so forth.'[8] In place of this two developments took place. One is the hard-working, reliable and pliable labour force that filled the factories of the eighteenth-century Industrial Revolution as they were built. The other is the high degree of discipline which factory employers imposed anyway, but especially on non-Calvinist, traditional workforces.

There is, however, one fatal flaw in the Protestant Work Ethic. Quite apart from a decline in religious faith, and especially in a belief in predestination, in western civilization, capitalism has produced enormous wealth. Both Michael Lessnoff, in his study of *The Spirit of Calvinism and the Protestant Ethic*, and Peter Stubley in his study of a nineteenth-century Protestant English merchant city make the same point. Lessnoff argues that the Protestant Work Ethic should not lead to self-indulgence, but to ascetisism and to altruism for those in need. The development of capitalist wealth corrupts the soul by its indulgence. So Brian Griffiths, banker, political adviser to Mrs Thatcher in the 1980s, and Christian apologist for capitalism in *The Creation of Wealth*, distinguishes between prosperity and luxury. The problem is how to distinguish between them. In another of his books, *Morality and the Marketplace*, he argues that wealth creation is the discharge of a divine commission, a divine 'mandate'. God intends his world not to be poor but prosperous. This is not the same as luxury.[9]

Peter Stubley's study of nineteenth-century Hull, *A House Divided: Evangelicals and the Establishment in Hull 1790–1914*, shows that the problem faced by Lord Griffiths in the 1980s was there in the 1790s. Joseph Milner, son of a poor weaver in Leeds became headmaster of Hull Grammar School for thirty years in the eighteenth century. He also preached regularly at Holy Trinity Church, Hull, and expounded scripture in a deeply Evangelical manner. Milner feared 'the awful progress of gross wickedness and vice, of lewdness and impiety' which came from 'the rapid increase in commerce, in wealth in population, in building and in luxury'.[10] All this was the result of Hull's growth as a seaport. 'The Puritan ethic of success in business as a sign of God's approval was of little avail in a society increasingly absorbed by Evangelical values. Christ's warning against the perils of riches and his precepts on the superiority of poverty set the huge money-making enterprises of the age against its intense religious feelings.' Milner epitomized both the old Puritan ethic (he could preach on the godly man being useful and redeeming the time) and the new Evangelical one ('the excessive love of gain eating out the love of Christ'). Milner was strongly supported by William Wilberforce, MP. for Hull, but Milner died before he could become vicar of Holy Trinity, Hull. Many of the city merchants, while deeply pious, found Milner's consistant attacks on them very trying, and Wilberforce had to struggle to promote his candidate for the living of Holy Trinity – only to be thwarted by his death from a chill at the age of 52, in 1797.[11]

In this small vignette of eighteenth-century Hull, the central argument of chapter 2 meets the argument from this chapter. Consumerism was advancing, and displacing the work ethic. Milner saw this, and was horrified at its impiety, although most merchants were devout Protestants. Protestants were not necessarily affected by the Evangelical Revival, as Milner was. They could still articulate the Protestant Work Ethic, and see their wealth as blessed by God. The arguments for consumerism given in chapter 2 could be held within a Christian framework. Milner was not persuaded by this that Protestant merchants had a right to enjoy consumption and wealth.[12]

The Protestant Work Ethic was eventually absorbed into a secular work ethic (outlined below) and a consumer ethic. This left a theology of work in a difficult position. Even more it left the questions of Christian vocation, identity and an ethic of the workplace (commutative justice) split apart. It is the purpose of this chapter to reunite them.

PSYCHOLOGICAL AND SOCIOLOGICAL STUDIES OF THE WORK ETHIC

Furnham is a social psychologist, with an interest in theology. His study entitled *The Protestant Work Ethic* gives a complete survey of the debate about PWE. The initial chapters of his book look at psychological components of the PWE, methods of measurement and the way in which young people are socialized into it. He then examines its prevalence in paid employment and worklessness (which includes unemployment, illness and retirement), before exploring its future. There have been many alternative ethics suggested in recent decades, especially from what have been called post-industrial values.[13]

Furnham believes that the PWE has certainly lasted during the nineteenth and twentieth centuries, even if the religious motivation to behave in this way is now minute for many people. This work ethic has spanned the old heavy industries of coal, steel and shipbuilding, and the new industries of the mid twentieth century such as the car industry.

1. People have a normal (and previously religious) obligation to fill their lives with heavy physical toil. Hard work and effort are to be valued for their own sake, and an ascetic existence is the only way to live. Physical pleasures are to be shunned.
2. Men and women are expected to spend long hours at work, with little time for personal recreation.
3. A worker should have a dependable attendance record, with low absenteeism.

4. Workers should be highly productive.
5. Workers should take pride in their work, and do their jobs well.
6. Employees should have feelings of commitment and loyalty to their work group and company.
7. Workers should be achievement-oriented and strive for promotion. High-status jobs, with prestige, are marks of a 'good' person.
8. Frugality and thrift are desirable. Wealth should be acquired through honest labour. Extravagance and waste are to be avoided.

Other definitions may be mentioned, especially those of Oates and of Maccoby and Terzi. Oates wrote:[14] 'A universal taboo is placed on idleness, and industriousness is considered a religious ideal; waste is a vice, and frugality a virtue; complacency and failure are outlawed, and ambition and success are taken as sure signs of God's favour; the universal sign of sin is poverty, and the crowning sign of God's favour is wealth.' Maccoby and Terzi[15] found that the term PWE was being used very loosely. Inside the term there were several overlapping ethics:

1. the Puritan Ethic, which supports individualism, self-discipline, saving, and is hostile to sensuality;
2. the craft ethic stresses independence, pride in work, self-reliance, mobility and thrift;
3. the entrepreneurial ethic emphasizes risk-taking, exploiting opportunities, growth and the desire to succeed;
4. the career ethic implies ambition, talent, hard work and success. It leads to promotion and meritocracy.

Maccoby and Terzi focus most of their research on America, and believe that each of these four ethics developed into the succeeding ethic, although alternative ethical values now threaten the work ethic itself.

Furnham himself is a psychologist, and he therefore translates the PWE into psychological terms. Although Weber defined it as a theological and sociological variable, the PWE overlaps with several psychological variables, which also interrelate. It is not clear, as Furnham says, whether the variables which he mentions are the only psychological variables which overlap with the PWE, nor has he evaluated the relative importance of them. Finally, if all these variables do overlap with the PWE, does the concept have a unique variance? Does the concept have any importance psychologically, or is it redundant? It may still be retained as a useful summary which contains important variables. Furnham cites many empirical, psychological studies which show the links between psychological constructs and PWE beliefs.

The psychological constructs which are most important can be described simply. Achievement motivation;[16] belief in internal, personal control;[17] attitudes to time management;[18] and finally a belief in the productive use of leisure[19] are all features of those who espouse the PWE. The desire to accomplish something difficult, and to rival others in as independent a way as possible is a typical example of achievement motivation. Belief that events in one's life are the result of one's own behaviour, ability, personality and effort illustrate an expectancy of internal control. The converse is that one believes that events in one's life will be a function of chance, luck, divine agency or powers beyond one's control. Furnham notes that many forms of leisure pursuits, such as education, health and fitness, and crafts embody the PWE virtues precisely. Above all, time is seen as a valuable commodity which should be used as productively as possible. As McGrath and Kelly put it:[20]

To a large extent, time and money are not interchangeable as the phrase 'time is money' would imply. Rather they are exchangeable. Time is not money, but it can be turned into money. Money can bring time. Money increases in value over time. Time can be invested now to yield money later. Time, like money, can be counted, spent, saved . . . and valued.'

Weber conceived the PWE as a self-imposed willingness of the individual to co-operate with the ethic of industrialization (in the twentieth century), growth and social conformity. Work was only done for its own value, since it was an intrinsic ethic. There were no external, extrinsic characteristics which determined job satisfaction. Rather, this was an aspect of the strength of belief in the PWE. If belief in the PWE is now correlated with psychological traits, as mentioned above, the importance of the work ethic has to include psychological as well as moral aspects. It is important however that the moral dimension is not ignored, for the psychological aspects of the PWE always remain conformed to the moral dimension. As Weber noted, Calvin and his followers saw work as methodical, disciplined, rational and uniform. Casual, occasional work was not sufficient.

Furnham's analysis thus combines PWE beliefs (including moral beliefs) and psychological traits in the work place. A sharper picture begins to emerge. On the one hand, there can be a PWE corporate culture, or, indeed, an entire society, such as Reformation Scotland or Geneva. On the other hand, there are PWE individual beliefs which relate to vocational choice, job enrichment, competitiveness, and endurance. These beliefs are part of a psychological construct which sustains people in personal achievement against adversity. If Furnham's pyschological explanation is correct, then we can go on to look at how people experience work from a sociological and psychological viewpoint.

One of the best-known theorists of work and unemployment is another psychologist, Maria Jahoda, who also has carried out research in England. Jahoda argues from a theory of deprivation, although her critics[21] argue that she underplays individual choice and personal control. Based on research going back nearly fifty years, including the unemployment experienced by many workers in the 1930s, Jahoda believes that psychological distress is caused when the unemployed are deprived of the latent functions of work. There are five latent functions of work. These are the structuring of time, which results in depression, lack of purpose and lack of organization among some of the unemployed. Secondly, there is regular shared experience with those who are not immediate members of the family. Social support from family and friends increases coping ability, reduces illness and gives the means to manage stress. Social isolation is related to disturbed mental states, so unemployment both causes stress and reduces the means to cope with it. Thirdly, work provides the experience of creativity, mastery and purpose. Much of this can be expressed in terms of a sense of service, and a contribution to society. Fourth, work is a source of personal status and identity. This status can also be passed on to a person's family. Unemployment removes both status and identity. Finally, work is a source of activity, physical and mental effort.[22]

A much more extensive analysis is given by Lane.[23] He recognizes that any definition of work will be normative. Designating work in contrast to play suggests that work is not enjoyable. Each contrast provides a norm, but each norm itself can be challenged. If the norm is that work is not enjoyable, this is neither logical nor necessary. If the contrast is with idleness, work is given a virtuous connotation; if the contrast is with unremunerated activity, the importance of extrinsic rewards are exaggerated. Work has its own intrinsic value. A contrast with leisure, especially if leisure is defined as psychological free time, places obligation or time pressure at the centre. Even the definition of the economist, which sees labour as a disutility, because it involves the sacrifice of a desirable alternative use of time and strength, has the disadvantage of applying to any activity. Every activity has an opportunity cost, and so every activity becomes labour. Lane therefore adopts a non-normative definition: 'Work is the effort or activity an individual performs for the purpose of providing goods or services of value to others or the self and it is also considered to be work by the individual so involved.'

Work is disengaged from the concepts of pain and disutility. Work differs from play because of the product involved, and not because of pain or disutility. Lane's argument is crucial for this book, since he offers a definition of human identity which is related to work. He argues that the market economist who sees the person as human capital has an inadequate concept of human personality, with its intrinsic values. Theodore Schultz's book *Investment in Human Capital* is the classic statement in recent times which sees a person as a valuable economic commodity.[24] Schultz offers three reasons for investing in people, in addition to investment in physical capital resources. First, the return on human capital can be greater than the return on physical capital. Secondly, the return on human capital has a social as well as an individual aspect: societies perform better, and are more harmonious. This is an argument for public investment in people, such as, of course, more education. Thirdly, the market is, as we have seen in the previous chapter, concerned with novelty as well as efficiency. Economic growth is primarily a consequence of improved quality of human resources and increased knowledge. The market is increasingly aware that knowledge is the most powerful engine of production. There is also a feedback mechanism, where economic growth enables affluence which creates the conditions for cognitive development, which then creates further economic growth. Economic growth also leads to a feeling of well-being from affluence, which again affects behaviour, economic productivity and economic growth. This double feedback means that there are good economic reasons for 'investing in people' through training, education and better working conditions.

Lane is, however, aware of the powerful counter arguments. There are the traditional Marxist arguments of capital reducing wages to the level of the unskilled, which is cheaper, by eliminating the skills of the workforce through machinery. This is, almost certainly, the correct reading of labour history in Britain and America during the Industrial Revolution, and more recently the experience of women in typing pools and basic factory work.[25] Secondly, Lane points to economists from Marshall onwards who see human personality as simply one factor in the market economy. It may be productive to invest in people, and develop their skills, but 'mental states' are not inherently valuable to an economist. They merely allow greater productivity, create consumer demand or accept levels of wages. Indeed, the indifference of the market to individuals (especially low-skilled individuals) is so great that it almost discounts them.[26]

It is true that the market once promoted homogeneity, as Reich's book *The Work of Nations* makes clear, with his powerful evocation of vast American factories churning out enormous numbers of the same goods from machines manned by men who accepted orders in a quasi-military fashion. That was the United States half a century ago. Now the market values individuality, and product variation, following Durkheim in his argument in *The Division of Labour in Society*. Although written in 1893, it remains true that specialization enriches society. Increasing the wealth of the market requires more differentiated people. Variations are valued as creating greater opportunity for specialized manufacture, product niche development and more employment of 'problem-solvers' in Reich's terminology. Yet none of this means that individuals are valued, but only individuality. Indeed, the market can positively winnow out the weak and set them aside by a process of ruthless competition.[27]

Lane nevertheless believes that work does enhance personal development and human identity, even if not on the lines of the 'human development/human capital argument'. A person's sense of worth can be affected by two factors. One is her participation in the labour market, where a person is hired or fired. The other is her experience, once hired in the labour market, at work itself. These two are not the same, but they interact strongly.

In terms of the labour market, on average a person only enters it twelve times in a working lifetime. This lifetime itself is shrinking. Once it ran from 14 to 65, or even, if health allowed and energy permitted, until 70. That was over fifty years. Now, for graduates, it may be as low as forty years, from 21 to 60, with some retiring even earlier. However, Lane points out that even these few entries into the labour market can affect a person's personality all their life. Their sense of independence or dependency, their feelings of alienation and economic anxiety, their sense of self-respect and self-reliance all depend far more on the labour market than the consumer market. It is the profound effect of selling oneself, with your labour, talents and commitment to the firm, which influences self-perception. The consumer market interacts with the labour market. People may spend more to compensate for insecurity and anxiety in the past, or they may (as in Japan throughout the 1990s) be very thrifty despite their personal savings because of the anticipated economic insecurity in the labour market. Alternatively, they may simply have been fortunate in the labour market, earned a high salary and spent it on conspicuous consumption. Either way, the labour market and the consumer market affect the sense of identity at a deep personal (often unconscious) level very profoundly indeed.

Ballard in *In and Out of Work: A Pastoral Perspective* describes prolonged bad experiences in the labour market as being like the destructive effects of a divorce. Unemployment, and repeated rejections in the labour market, cause a crisis in the sense of personal identity: 'The sense of guilt and frustration or its opposite, sullen indifference, the alternative of frenetic activity and total inertia, the manic swing from high hopes to black despair, all block the ability to assess the situation with any sense of objectivity. Rational decision making is inhibited, about what one can and should do, given the choices available, and the hard reality of the historical situation is obscured.'[28]

Lane has an extensive study of a person's experience in paid employment, where he emphasizes the importance of work in leading to cognitive development and self-esteem. The sustantive complexity of job content[29] had a great effect on cognitive complexity. It is a symbiotic relationship. Complex jobs attract people with more flexible and sharper minds, which, in turn, is developed further by their job. So, too, self-directedness is also symbiotic. It is striking that 'prior work history is one of the most powerful predictors of recovery from schizophrenia, from drug addition, from delinquency, and from alcoholism . . . At least statistically, if not in every case, capacity to work correlates highly with both mental health and capacity to love. Job satisfaction, job stability . . . employment and income all appear highly associated with mental health.'[30]

What is significant is that this study did not distinguish between alienating and non-alienating work. It is certainly true that a sixteen year old finds work chores at home, and part-time jobs which are paid, equally alienating. Nevertheless, the psychological benefits remain, even if there are strong ethical reasons to criticize such dead-end jobs. (The report *Unemployment and the Future of Work* by the British Churches in 1997 drew attention to the growth in 'bad work', or unfulfilling jobs.) Even such jobs, while they will not develop self-direction or cognitive skills, do teach perseverance and a belief in one's ability to overcome problems. The number of part-time jobs taken by school and college students is increasing. All this makes long-term unemployment, especially youth unemployment, even more detrimental to psychological health than was supposed in the past.[31]

Lane contrasts his arguments with those of John Stuart Mill. Mill wrote in *Representative Government*: 'It is not sufficiently considered how little there is in most men's ordinary life to give any largeness either to their conceptions or to their sentiments.'[32] Mill felt that politics would widen the horizons of the workers. Instead, Lane argues, it is far more likely to be the workplace where a person has their mind challenged and enlarged. The person learns through vicarious experience by seeing other people work and learning from them. Cognitive complexity, a sense of personal control and self-esteem on the job do not disappear when a person leaves the place of employment, or leave the job altogether.

Such learning experiences draw, of course, on family background, parental values, early socialization and education. Work reinforces these experiences, although alienated labour may in the end cause deep resentment. Despite the study cited above, years of lack of fulfilment at work can lead to a general hostility. Where management treats workers with respect, workers will treat each other with respect. As Adam Smith said, in *The Wealth of Nations*, the 'understandings of the greater part of men are necessarily formed by their ordinary employments'.[33] Smith knew very well that a person engaged in repetitive industrial work 'becomes as stupid and ignorant as it is possible for a human creature to become'. Even if the division of labour created high gains in efficiency in the market, it also tended to brutalize labour:

The man whose life is spent performing a few simple operations, of which the effects are, perhaps, always the same or very nearly the same, has no occasion to exert his understanding, or to exercise his invention in finding expedients for removing difficulties which never occur. The torpor of his mind renders him not only incapable of relishing or bearing a part in any rational conversation, but of conceiving any generous, noble or tender sentiment.[34]

The problem with increasing workplace learning is that firms have to succeed in the market. Put another way, a consumer economy has priority over an economy that gives priority to workplace achievements and satisfactions. This means that the benefits of learning at work are sacrificed so that a firm can produce goods as cheaply as possible. The contrast between the workplace and the consumer market is once again heightened. Yet people remain human beings who want to work, even if they do not want alienation and degradation of their skills at the work place. Lane distinguishes between transcendent values in the work place, and immanent ones. Transcendent values include the Protestant work ethic, the Marxist emphasis on the victory of the proletariat, or other such national and imperial values. Immanent values include the value of work in itself as a learning or socializing process, where we value ourselves, become more skilled and meet others. Work can also be intrinsically good because it serves other people. This could be seen as a transcendent purpose if one was a Christian. For secular writers, there is no ulterior purpose except for the benefits which socially useful work provides. This could be called transcendent, in that work serves a society which transcends it, or intrinsic, in that the labour market and paid employment is part of society. The classic new way is expressed by R. H. Tawney in *The Acquisitive Society* in 1920: 'Degradation follows inevitably from the refusal of men to give the purpose of industry the first place in their thought about it . . . when the criterion of function is forgotten, the only criterion which remains is wealth.'[35]

THE FUTURE OF THE WORK ETHIC

What of the future of the work ethic? There has been discussion of this in the last three decades, but it is striking that in the 1970s with the welfare state appearing dominant and the growth of large companies and less work incentives there was a belief that the work ethic was in decline. However, even then a number of studies doubted this, and there has been increasing evidence in the last two decades that, in fact, the work ethic has been increasing.[36] What is changing are values in the work place. There are a striking number of changes that are apparent. Women were working much more, while men were no longer prepared to put up with bad jobs for the sake of economic security. Loyalty to particular organizations especially large industrial companies, and the achievement of identity through organizations were all in the decline. By the end of the 1970s, work was no longer seen as a paid activity that provided steady full-time employment over a lifetime, and the internal relationships within a company could no longer be guaranteed simply by appealing to money and status. Old signs of success were replaced by theories of self-development and a change from materialistic to psychological incentives which were both more diverse and more equitable.[37] In short, people saw their personalities as integrated with their work place and their role at work, in a way which echoed Habermas' analysis described in chapter 1. This is a two-edged sword. It could lead to the humanization of work, and the refusal of people to let their personalities and needs be subordinated to their role in the corporate organization. It is the end of the 'company man' of the 1950s. People stop being submissive. On the other hand, paid employment can also be seen as a way of protecting and fulfilling a person's personality, so that the ability to change the activities of people at work in ways which seem psychologically fulfilling can lead to the manipulation of the personality itself. It is reminiscent of Habermas' warning about the fragility of ego-identity in a society driven by technology and the achievement of personal goals. Put bluntly, even if people no longer agree with their boss, or have to agree, they still invest a great deal of their personal identity and self-image with how they succeed at work.

This finding has gradually proved itself to be accurate.[38] The future of work and leisure now become inextricably combined. Both depend on three factors: personal values, individual personality and the structure of society. People express themselves both at work and in their leisure: leisure as achievement.

Leisure and work will become increasingly integrated among the affluent workers of the West, and increasingly this will become a global phenomenon. At the same time, those who are less affluent will still be influenced by the dominant role models of those who can enjoy the life style portrayed in the media as desirable. So a classical work ethic, which is about working long hours, satisfying those in authority and being oriented to achievement, is gradually being supplemented by a 'work and leisure ethic' combined together:

The work ethic which has been strong for the last two centuries, but now shows signs of weakening, places work at the centre of the meaning and purpose in life with leisure as its servant. A leisure ethic would seek to reverse these priorities and make leisure the central area of meaning, fulfilment and personal identity with work as a means to these ends.[39]

This quotation from Parker sees work as being replaced by a leisure ethic. Others would be far more cautious, and see work and leisure being far more intertwined in the ethic which governs a person's motivation.

Parker argues for a redefinition of the work ethic which would allow it to become creative, and imbue it with choice and pleasurable activity. The reality has not borne out his expectations under the constraints of the global economy.

Handy, in his well-known writings, has also charted the future of work. What is of interest, however, is the implication of his writings for the work ethic. The changes in work can be briefly noted, for they are all fully described in many books, since Handy has been a highly influential writer. A full employment society is changing into one with part employment. Manual skills are being replaced by knowledge as the basis of work. Industry is declining and services growing. Hierarchies and bureaucracies are being replaced by networks and partnerships. One-organization careers are changing into job mobility and career change. Gender roles at work and home are no longer rigid. Life after employment is growing in importance. This will lead to fewer large corporations; more small businesses; more requirement for specialists and professionals; more people not working for an organization; more importance for the informal (or 'black') economy; a smaller manufacturing sector, with greater output; a smaller earning population, with a greater percentage of the population dependent on them; more demand for education; and new forms of social organization. But what will this mean for the work ethic? It will change as work changes, especially in its meaning and its pattern across weeks, years and lives. Above all the work ethic will be subsumed into education and training, both inside companies and outside, during the working career, before it and alongside it. Flexibility, variety and participation are all crucial here. He writes:

We are fixated, both as a nation and as individuals, by the employment organization. Work is defined as employment. Money is distributed through employment. Status and identity stem from employment. We therefore hang on to employment as long as we can; we measure our success in terms of it; we expect great things from it, for the country and for ourselves; and we cannot conceive of a future without it. And yet, ironically, we are very bad at it because there is an individualistic streak in all of us which agrees with Marx that it is alienating to sell ourselves or our time to another. Break through that constraint, and all sorts of things become possible, even if they are hard to visualize before they exist.[40]

Here it is not a combination of work and leisure, but of work and education, which governs the new work ethic. Handy opts for choice, responsibility and entrepreneurship as the redefinition of the work ethic. Education is the catalyst to make this happen. Indeed, another study by Yankelovich and Immerwahr argues that the work ethic is actually increasing as people become better educated. They suggest that:

As jobs become more challenging and more autonomous, and as people become better educated and focus more on personal growth, employees are also likely to see work as having a positive and central place in their lives. They are also much more likely to bring greater demands to their jobs. The degree to which these demands are met will have a great deal to do with whether the work ethic is harnessed and channelled into more productive work.[41]

What this means is that education, work and leisure can become far more integrated. There are great dangers in this. Csikszentmihaly describes this in relation to sport:

The attitudinal changes we are witnessing in mountaineering reflect in a nutshell many changes taking place in the rest of society. A game activity which until a generation ago was performed leisurely, within a complex logico-meaningful framework of experiences, is now becoming a calculated, precise, expert enterprise within a much narrower framework of experience . . . The value-system of the culture modifies the values of the game.[42]

Robert Reich has pointed out that what is most important to realize is that work is no longer a single entity. There are four clear categories. In place of the old divisions of worker, manager and self-employed, or manufacturing versus service, he proposes the three categories of routine producer, in-person server and symbolic analyst. A fourth category is that of Government employee. Up to the 1950s, the old categories still made sense, but since then the impact of new technologies and globalization have revolutionized the way in which people work. Routine producers are factory workers and clerks, who perform standard tasks. Data processors enter vast amounts of information into computer terminals, just as assembly line workers and, before them, textile workers processed raw materials. Such work includes routine supervisory jobs, performed by junior managers with the enforcement of standard operating procedures. Typically such workers do their tasks alongside others in large enclosed spaces. The essence of the job is that standard procedures are followed. Much of the tasks are repetitive and tedious, and pay is regarded as the source of motivation. It is striking, however, that the secularized work ethic varies strongly across cultures. The 'strong inner need to do the very best I can regardless of pay' was reported in a 1984 study as being true for 17% of British workers, 51% of American and 57% of Israeli.[43] It is also the case that those whose jobs allow them most discretion also will express views. It is, therefore, the case that the work ethic is strongest among employees who have the greatest skill and independence on the job. The important factor is that job experience should not be substantially routinized. Substantive complexity of work is less important than lack of routine. Feelings of competence arise from the experience of variety at work. The danger in this attitude is that, as well as building up feelings of initiative and self-worth, it can also cause individuals to look down on the poor and unemployed and ascribe their position as being due to their own fault.[44]

Reich is insistent that the old routine jobs in manufacturing are declining fast, both in the United States and in Europe. By 1990 traditional production work had fallen to one-quarter of American jobs, and was declining. The virtues which were expected of them were reliability, loyalty and the ability to obey orders. It is no surprise, therefore, at the ease of transition from factory-line production into the armed services for American and European workers during the Second World War. Equally, many of the senior management jobs were held by those whose formative experiences were during wartime right up to the 1960s:

America's corporate bureaucracies were organized like military bureaucracies, for the efficient implementation of preconceived plans. It is perhaps no accident that the war veterans who manned the core American corporations of the 1950s accommodated so naturally to the military like hierarchies inside them. They were described in much the same terms as military hierarchies – featuring chains of command, spans of control, job classifications, divisions and division heads, and standard operating procedures to guide every decision . . . As in the military, great emphasis was placed upon the maintenance of control – upon a superior's ability to inspire loyalty, discipline, and unquestioning obedience, and upon a subordinate's capacity to be so inspired.[45]

This world was destroyed in the 1970s, and ensuing decades, perhaps even earlier. First, manufactured goods began to be produced for cheaper cost in Asian factories, principally Japanese. The reaction of American and European companies was to appeal for protectionism, to cut the workforce and to engage in financial dexterity. In the 1970s, there was the conglomerate merger across Europe and North America, and then, in the 1980s, the takeover or the leveraged buyout. Corporate income tax was reduced, since interest on debt which financed such activities was tax deductible. Wall Street grew rich, but the underlying system of production did not change. Instead, a global web of producers, and problem-solvers, made the transition from mass production to high value activities. Mass production moved decisively away from Europe and North America in the 1970s and 1980s, taking with it the hierarchical and consensual nature of big business. Routine factory jobs were decimated in the 1980s in Europe and North America. To some extent they were replaced by data inputting in information technology, but not to the same extent. The crisis for routine production workers was that in Europe and North America their whole rationale disappeared.[46]

Two other types of employment remain. The second type of work is also routine, highly supervised and repetitive, but it works with people, and cannot be sold worldwide.[47] Included in this category are shop workers, waiters and waitresses, taxi drivers, secretaries, nursing-home aides and cleaners. What matters is that such people should be courteous, polite and helpful, as well as being reliable, punctual and obedient. It is no surprise that the cultural stereotype of women as caring should mean that in-person service jobs are largely done by women. By 1990, one third of American jobs were in this category, more than the number of routine factory jobs, and they were growing rapidly. Reich uses the illustration of a nursing-home chain, Beverly Enterprises, which employed 115,000 people. Chrysler Corporation employed 1,000 more making cars and trucks, and was far better known, but its numbers were declining steadily. By 1998, it was taken over by Daimler Benz of Germany, the maker of Mercedes cars, and its numbers employed had fallen further. Indeed, the entire American workforce in 1990 in textiles, steel and automobiles stood at under 3 million. The total number of new jobs alone created in the 1980s in bars, fast-food chains and restaurants was more than that. Of course, many such jobs were badly paid, part-time and had little skills. But they were growing rapidly. The challenge was to find ways of retraining such people, and to increase their skills.

A third category (apart from farmers and miners, who have now declined to less than 5 per cent of American workers) is that of government employees. They made up about 20 per cent of employment, and include teachers, doctors, and local government workers. What is distinctive is that they are not in a competitive market, although this has not prevented enormous redundancies in the 1980s and 1990s. This is because the decline of a consensual labour force led to a polarized political climate, where tax cuts for the fourth group (yet to be described) became a priority. At the same time, higher unemployment costs in benefit payments from the displaced routine production workers led to greater government costs. A combination of desire for tax cuts (related to monetarist economic policies) and a need to get government spending under control led to savage cuts in the workforce of public employees. Britain and the United States led the way in the 1980s, and a decline in public investment became common across the western industrialized world. Privatization of many aspects of government only tightened the screw further, since this invariably led to even more job cuts for efficiency gains. The cost in all this was twofold. On the one hand, what had distinguished this group of workers was a public service ethos. Here especially Tawney's dictum of work being to serve others held true. It became problematic to see how this sense of public vocation could be sustained. Many studies pointed to a lack of investment, especially in primary education.[48] Those that had entered public employment out of a sense of vocation or duty were often told that they were part of a self-justifying system, as Peter Berger has consistently argued. The second cost of the reduction in public employment was less of a sense of community. Where once there were public workers in public places (janitors or caretakers, park attendants, ticket collectors on public transport) now there was either nobody there at all, or an automated system supervising the area through electronic surveillance. The sense of insecurity fed on itself, and for those who could afford them, private security guards became the norm. They were among the fastest growing category of in-person servers in the United States. Andrew Adonis describes the change in values at Oxford University over the past twenty-five years. Describing the university as 'probably the single most important institution for shaping elite mentalities in modern Britain', he describes how the past 25 years have seen a wholesale switch from public sector careers (especially teaching) towards a narrow range of financial careers. Between 1971 and 1994 the number of Oxford graduates entering state school teaching collapsed by 60 per cent in numerical terms, and, as a proportion of graduate careers fell from 9.7 to 3.3 per cent, the number going into City occupations increased nearly four times. Adonis points to money, social esteem and responsibility as the reason for this collapse.[49]

It is not simply that the public sector ethos is under increasing strain among those who work there. It is also that the failings of the markets, including poverty, gross inequality and the loss of community, can only be remedied by investment in the public sector. Although private sector employment may take up some of the unemployed, it is also the case that without enormous investment in education for young people and retraining for older people there will be no possibility of work without skills. Equally, those who are affluent can afford to buy out of public transport, health and housing, living in the privileged areas so graphically described by Reich. Not only does this destroy a sense of community, and impoverish the national benefit of having universal, good public health and transport, it also leaves the poor and unemployed in declining areas of poor health care, housing, transport etc. The case for reviving a public sector ethos to deal with the failure of the market could hardly be stronger. The final group of workers is the one whom Reich spends most of his time on. These are the symbolic analysts. Indeed, his whole book is a description of how they came into being, their values and their future. They are the people who problem-identify, problem-solve and broker between the identification of the problem and its solution. Their work can be traded worldwide, but they do not sell standardized products – their value lies in being precisely the opposite of the standard products made by the routine producers. The list of jobs included in this category is lengthy. It includes research scientists, lawyers, bankers, financial and management consultants, journalists, entertainers, architects and university teachers. They analyse reality into abstract images which are rearranged, transformed and communicated back to other analysts. Like routine producers, analysts rarely come into contact with the ultimate beneficiaries of their work. But that is about all which they have in common.

Analysts rarely work in hierarchies, and are not paid by the volume of work which they produce, nor by hours worked. Instead, it is the originality and quality of work which matters, and the way in which they approach problems. Nor are their careers well defined. While some analysts in banking or universities may follow a traditional path upwards to the most senior positions in the institution, others may take on great responsibility and earn enormous wealth at a young age. Nor is their wealth and expertise related to their position in what is left of the traditional hierarchy. Quite 'junior' posts may, in fact, be critical for the exploration of new areas of research, and others may work in small teams. The international labour market joins together such teams in global webs, as flows of knowledge, finance and tangible products move rapidly across national boundaries. What matters is whether a company can add value in the global economy, and this is done by individuals or teams of analysts working together. Hence, there is a familiar comment that people working in the scientific community in Cambridge, England know far more about their colleagues in Cambridge, Massachusetts in the United States than about an industrial town in the same part of England as Cambridge. The vast majority of analysts are university graduates, although the degree of creative thinking required can draw on especially creative persons who did not have an extended formal education. The number of such analysts is growing because there is no finite limit to their number in the global economy. In the past, their size was restricted to the number needed to be in overall command of the routine producers, or factory workers, with a few others specializing in the media, architecture or law. That number was fairly small. If the analyst now earns her living (the number of white female analysts is growing, although it is still a minority) by solving problems in the global economy, then there is no limit to their numbers. What is striking is that this remains largely a racial divide. There is a small but slowly increasing, number of blacks and Hispanic analysts in the United States which make up the black middle class there. That has grown steadily since the 1960s. In Britain, the numbers remain small, except for an Asian group of business people, doctors and lawyers, and this is largely true of western Europe. It remains to be seen whether rapid industrialization of India will affect the position of those from South Asia in Britain. Racial prejudice remains high, especially in the less skilled sectors of the population and is expressed especially in employment discrimination.

Reich points out that symbolic analysts are getting richer, while the wages (in real terms) of the other main groups are slowly falling. Analysts now make up 20 per cent of the working American population, and have risen from 8 per cent at mid century. Above all, they are increasingly leading a social existence which is separate from other workers, with their own houses, schools and health care. Perhaps the more close-knit, and less mobile, European societies will resist this trend, although there are worrying signs to the contrary. Work, leisure and consumption come together for this group. Here the work ethic is at its strongest. As Reich says:

One of the best-kept secrets among symbolic analysts is that so many of them enjoy their work. In fact, so much of it does not count as work at all, in the traditional sense. The work of routine producers and in-person servers is typically monotonous; it causes muscles to tire or weaken and involves little independence or discretion. The 'work' of symbolic analysts, by contrast, often involves puzzles, experiments, games, a significant amount of chatter and substantial discretion over what to do next. Few routine producers or in-person servers would 'work' if they did not need to earn the money. Many symbolic analysts would 'work' even if money were no object.[50]

The future of the work ethic, then, depends on which group one is talking about. A summary of the argument so far may be helpful. Once there was a Protestant Work Ethic, which disciplined its workers and drove forward the rise of capitalism. This gradually collapsed partly because of affluence, and partly because of a decline in religious faith. What remained was a strong belief in the work ethic among some workers, and the continuing awareness of the benefits of work for those whose jobs were varied, complex and challenging.

In the last thirty years in the West the picture has changed even more dramatically. There really is no common experience of work anymore, although the psychological studies which show the benefit of the experience in the past of any paid work as a therapy to help recovery from mental illness or drugs are very telling. What the work of Reich and Lane shows is that western civilization now has very different experiences of work, and very different work ethics. For some work is hard to find, alienating, poorly paid and insecure. For others it is plentiful, highly paid, and highly rewarding – even if it is also insecure, for the global economy allows no passengers. The former group works in the declining world of mass production. The latter group employs its creative brilliance (call it work if you must) across the global economy, which grows apace. In between are two very different groups. One works with people, and what matters is whether the inter-personal skills required genuinely affirm both parties in the relationship, or whether there is a fake consciousness induced by the market's demand for friendly, and helpful staff. The other works in the public sector, and has been battered by the fierce winds of privatization and the distrust of government in much political debate. What is of the greatest importance is whether this spirit of public service can be revived, especially as European governments move back from the right.

This leaves the task of a Christian theology of vocation and of an ethic at work with a very considerable task. Once again Habermas' analysis remains very apposite. The world of human interaction and its social norms is increasingly dominated by the market: the 'colonization of the lifeworld', as Habemas calls it. How human identity is preserved in this domain is a crucial question. Put simply, work confers an identity, but it is a very insecure one. Even for those for whom work is most fulfilling, the question is whether it is all absorbing and destroys any human autonomy apart from that. The previous chapter has already described the pressures of the consumer market. Now the screw tightens further, with the same people who are most excluded from the consumer market and in debt who are also most likely to be in alienating and declining mass-production jobs. For some people, especially those who are the target of racial prejudice, there may be greater exclusion from work altogether. Those who most consume are also the highest paid in the global economy.

How, then, can a Christian understanding of work be developed? In the final part of this chapter I turn back to the medieval and Reformation debate, focusing this time, not on Calvin, but on Luther's reply to Thomas Aquinas. After this a contemporary theology of vocation will be given, which pays attention to the intrinsic benefits of creative work, the need for a public service ethic and theology of justice for jobs which are least rewarding and most insecure. This is not a single ethic, such as the Protestant Work Ethic was, for there is no single reality of work to be addressed. What there can be is a Christian ethic which combines creativity, compassion, justice and public service, in the world of paid employment.

A THEOLOGY OF VOCATION IN PAID EMPLOYMENT

Protestant theology has wrestled with the question of work, and its meaning, throughout the twentieth century. The theologians of the 1940s, such as Emil Brunner and J. H. Oldham, did so because they were dissatisfied with the understanding of vocation found in Lutheran and Protestant theology. Later theologians, sometimes working with Industrial Mission, such as Margaret Kane, David Jenkins, John Atherton and Paul Ballard, built on this critique of vocation, and attempted to express a theology of modern employment. Just as the theological debate has now moved from the understanding of vocation to one which is also concerned with poverty, dehumanization and the meaning of employment, so the nature of paid work has changed. There is a church building in South London which captured the nature of work in London in the 1950s through a series of stained-glass windows. Today they still are very moving, but they appear like museum pieces in their own right. A different dimension was that of mission, and how the Church could reach out to the industrial worker who was often alienated from the Christian faith. The missiological aspect of Brunner and Oldham's writings was very clear.

The understanding of vocation offered by Luther was, of course, closely connected with the Protestant Work Ethic analysed both in the previous chapter, and earlier in this one, which was closely associated with Calvinism by Max Weber. Habermas' critique of Weber has been given in chapter 1, and the argument has been made in chapter 2 that the Protestant Work Ethic became an ethic of consumption through the Romantic movement, and its previous eras of sensibility and sentimentalism. In a similar way, Habermas has claimed that the crucial feature of modernity was not the capitalist work ethic identified by Weber, but the fragmentation of knowledge and culture into different spheres of meaning. The psychological displacement of the Protestant Work Ethic (PWE) has also been charted by Furnham, earlier in this chapter, and the way in which it remains a residual but powerful influence in society.

However, Luther's understanding of vocation and its subsequent influence in Protestant theology is not to be equated with the Calvinist work ethic, as though the one was a synonym for the other. Luther developed his doctrine as an argument against Thomas Aquinas. In particular, Luther was concerned with the nature of manual labour, whether in employment or not, and the meaning which physical activity might have. This activity was placed in the context of a feudal society, and the role which a person might perform. The hierarchical nature of feudal society was such that each person had their place, through an occupation which carried duties. These duties were performed by the activity of physical labour. Luther's doctrine of vocation thus should be seen as a fulcrum, or turning-point, in the history of theological reflection on society. On the one hand, it stands at the end of several centuries of theological debate on the nature of social obligation and the meaning of work. On the other hand, it casts a long shadow down Lutheran theology into the twentieth century, which faithfully reflected for good or ill his reformulated ideas about vocation. Luther's opponents were largely the medieval theologians influenced by Thomas. His audience was the many generations of theologians until the twentieth century, both Lutheran but also more generally Protestant. This included many from the Church of England in the sixteenth to the nineteenth centuries. It is this rich, but also ambiguous, heritage which Brunner, Oldham and later Nordic, German and British theologians challenged in the twentieth century. Twentieth-century theologians writing about work often expressed a desire to break out of the tradition which they had inherited. It has also been pointed out, by R. H. Preston and others, that Calvin's work ethic (whether in the form understood by Weber, or in its more pristine form) was far more dynamic and future oriented. It did not look back to medieval theology nor to medieval society, and hence it was taken up by the emerging merchants and gentry who were challenging feudal society. The interplay of a Lutheran doctrine of vocation, and a Calvinist work ethic, across the centuries in theology would extend this study too far afield. No doubt, too, they were often indistinguishable in practice, especially among the middle-class traders and industrialists of the Industrial Revolution and the nineteenth century. Nevertheless, Luther's doctrine of vocation is not the same as Calvin's, and in this chapter Luther's theology will be spelled out.

Thomas followed Aristotle in maintaining that the contemplative life takes priority. He cites Luke 10:24, where Jesus praises Mary over Martha, who symbolizes the contemplative life. There are also a series of reasons why Thomas prefers the contemplative life to the active one. Action involves a lower form of reasoning than the intellect, which is displayed in contemplation, and is distinctive to human beings. Animals can act, but they do so from passions and without deliberation. Contemplative life may have to be set aside when material welfare is threatened, but on other occasions the contemplative life is to be preferred.[51] It is more constant, enduring, gives greater pleasure and satisfaction. Above all the value of its activity is intrinsic to it, and is not done as a means to an end. Physical labour is done so that a person might be warm, sheltered or fed, but the life of contemplation has no end other than itself. Within its activity there is peace, wholeness and harmony, which are the attributes of God's own life. Thus the contemplative life leads into both the search for God, and an indwelling of the qualities of the divine life. Speculative reason is focused on God, and the love of God. Practical reason is focused on humanity, and the love of neighbour. The universal good (*universale bonum*) has priority over the general good (*commune bonum*) for the former is the performance of duties towards God. There are duties towards the neighbour, which is the general good, but they flow into the universal good. This teleological ethic, where the value of all actions is determined by their goal or end, means that Thomas always gives priority to the contemplative life. In fulfilling the universal good, human beings fulfil also their nature, which is rational, and made in the image of God. The intellect is the chief part of the soul. Therefore the first part of the Ten Commandments (the Decalogue) always has priority in its command to love God over the duties to one's neighbour.

What is the implication of this argument for manual labour? Thomas defines 'manual labour' as 'all human activities by means of which a human being can earn his living in a justified way, whether it is carried out with the hand, the feet or the tongue'.[52] Thomas refers to the command which Paul lays on Christians in 1 Thessalonians 4:11, but the duty of manual labour is also part of natural law, which binds society. It is a collective requirement, and Thomas is clear that each person cannot fulfil this command individually. The ideal of a pre-social individual, who binds herself by a social contract as Locke was later to argue, is not only a political fiction (as Locke admitted), but also makes no sense whatsoever. The division of labour dates from the origin of society, which is as old (and as intrinsic to) as humanity itself. Augustine argued that the members of a monastic order were free to carry out manual labour if they wished to do so, but were not obliged. Thomas claimed that his view was in accordance with Augustine, but the emphasis lies in fact elsewhere.

Augustine and Ongen, in fact, developed a theology of manual labour, with Augustine providing a sophisticated defence of manual work which is not reached again until Luther. Augustine's defence of manual labour is highly unusual. When the subject occurs again in Thomas, the influence of Aristotle has become evident. Augustine's *De Opere Monachorum* argued that labour was not a hardship, but a means of self-expression. The Garden of Eden was both a place of delight and of work. The two do not contradict one another. Adam was created as a gardener, for manual work is not a consequence of Adam's sin at the Fall. As in his commentary on Genesis, Augustine argued that work was related to the human spirit, not the necessary satisfaction of the needs of the body. It was from manual work that culture springs, created by the interplay of reason and physical strength. In Eden, body, instincts, will and intellect were all in harmony. Even after the Fall, the corruption of work is that it becomes selfish. Private gain is put before the common good. Selfishness, not ardousness, is the sign that we live in a fallen world. Manual work has dignity, and if done for the good of the community it can be transformed. Looking at the farmers in the fields in North Africa, Augustine notes their toil, hardship and struggle, but also their joy (jubilation) as they sing in the fields at harvest time.[53]

Thomas argues for the division of labour, so that some in society may be rulers, judges or teachers, while others engage in manual labour, pastoral care or trade. The same is true of monastic orders. While they are bound by the natural law which commands laity and clergy, not all members of the order have to perform those duties. Manual labour has four aims for Thomas.

First, it provides for the existence of human life, and thus is part of the commandment of practical necessity. If subsistence cannot be achieved without manual labour, then one must work, but, if one can gain a living in another way and pay others to work manually on one's behalf, this is acceptable.[54] It follows that, in practice, manual labour is an option only for those who have no other choice.

The second and third aims of manual labour are again practices which are not obligatory for all. Idleness and mortification of the flesh are the two enemies of the soul. Work removes idleness, and restrains desires and passions. Unlike subsistence, these two aims can be achieved without manual labour, so there is no practical necessity about these aims. In effect, Thomas argues that it may be useful for the majority of society, but it is not an intrinsic part of self-discipline.

Finally, work allows one to share one's products with the poor in the form of alms. Again this is only a conditional argument. If there is a need, and the only way which it can be met is through manual labour, then this is necessary. However, alms can be given out of wealth, and so again Thomas denies that religious orders must labour.

A final argument which Thomas uses is that the public devotion to spiritual activities is different from private religious practice. Public, and constant, religious activity is something which requires complete attention, and it is for the good of society. Both these reasons mean that material support should be given to those who serve God. In terms of the doctrine of merit, Thomas holds that manual labour (external toil) increases wages which are strictly transitory. Divine service increases the merit of blessedness, which is greater than the merit of active life.[55]

Thomas gives great importance to the preservation of social cohesion, and in no way denies the value of manual work. Nevertheless, the challenge which Martin Luther made was profound. His doctrine of vocation embodied co-creation with God, as well as the service of neighbour and imitation of Christ. The idea of co-creation meant that God's creation was still continuous, and in this act of creation God continued to provide what was necessary for the preservation of life. God creates through the work of human beings, which becomes an act of co-creation. Each person in human society contributes to the maintenance of society, and in their work enables the gifts of God (food, warmth, social order) to be provided. As well as the doctrine of *'cooperator Dei'*, there is also the idea of the 'mask of God' or *'larva Dei'*.[56] Human beings enable God to appear on earth as a Creator hidden behind many masks, offering his gifts, and seeking the respect of human beings for each office and function. It is intrinsic to this theology that the recognition of divine authority and action is mediated through the different social orders, positions and functions.[57]

Luther's theology has a deep coherence. In the second table of the Decalogue the primary commandment is that of obedience to father and mother (the fourth commandment). It has the chief place in the list of duties to our neighbour, taking priority over all others. Although we are all equal before God, God has not created society to embody equality. In the social hierarchy, we continually encounter the duties of obedience and of respect. Obedience is the means of respect, while those who are put in authority must care for and protect those who are subordinate. What is of crucial significance is that the doctrines of co-operation with God, and the masks of God, in the spheres of daily work are combined with the commandments of obedience and respect in the Decalogue. The two form a seamless whole, so that God is co-operated with, found and respected in the continual practice of social order and hierarchy. Each person performs a job, or office, which has its role in the social hierarchy. This is further strengthened by his distinction between individual and social ethics. Whatever my obligations as a Christian to another individual, where a person should follow the Sermon on the Mount and give as generously as one can, as an office-holder one must perform the duties of one's office.[58]

Vocation for Luther is the living-out of this co-creation, and respect for others in obedience, wherein we allow God to put on a mask through our work. It follows that work must have great social value. Work which is to do with producing luxuries, or is essentially frivolous (such as forms of entertainment by which people earn a living), becomes highly suspect. Love of neighbour is fulfilled through daily work. It is a divine ordinance that human beings are to live in the world, and fulfil their Christian calling as members of a family, a state, an employer and a church. These are the four orders of creation where God expresses his will and appears on earth as a hidden, but gracious, Creator. Any form of work can act as a means by which God gives graciously to his creation, hides himself and commands both obedience to a superior and love of neighbour – so long as the labour is of social and Christian benefit. Neither intellectual employment nor ecclessiastical duties become more important than manual labour in this world view. The government of this social order is by the law, and not by the Gospel. Vocation lives according to the law, and does not win righteousness, but it is nevertheless a form of co-creation and existence with God.

There is no single work by Luther which examines the meaning of work in itself. Like Thomas, he refers to the mortification of the flesh, and the service of others. The emphasis on sin means that Luther was highly aware of the possibilities which existed for a body which was not disciplined by activity. However, what is distinctive in Luther is the vision of work as co-creative with God, and the realization of our social duties. There is little in Luther on self-realization or purposive action, whereby work becomes a form of self-expression, either for the species as a whole as in Marx, or for the individual in psychological self-fulfilment (as above, in Lane). What matters is that Thomas' vision of social order, where work enables the preservation of society but largely becomes a task done out of necessity, is transformed into an expression of divine action. The temporal kingdom of this world, where sin is kept at bay, assumes that human beings recognize through their social existence what it means to do good and avoid evil. Vocation (*'Beruf'*) can be a dual, or even multiple, obligation laid by God on a person through natural morality. There is no need of revelation to know what deeds are good: practical reason is sufficient. A vocation can be multiple, because *'beruf'* can refer to a position in the family, such as son or mother, and to social employment, such as farmer, soldier or ruler. Luther also uses it at times to refer to the exhortation to be converted to the Gospel, and to enter the Kingdom of God, and to become a minister of the Gospel. But the social form is what shapes his theology of work.[59]

The rural society of early sixteenth-century Germany was still feudal, made up of small states, each with their own nobility, and a few merchant cities, such as the Hanseatic League on the north German coast. The predominant activity was agriculture, with some trading, interspersed by periods of war and sickness, sometimes at the same time. None of this allowed much distinction between 'home' and 'place of work', since they were often synonymous, nor between work and leisure, since at harvest the work continued as long as light and weather allowed. Nor, finally, was the distinction between paid employment and employment especially meaningful in a rural society where trade was either carried on through barter, or social duties were performed because of feudal obligations. Grain might be traded for wool, and military service might be provided alongside the payment of rent. What mattered was the social order which was where Christian existence was lived out through vocation. Vocation was realized by social occupation.

This is a deeply conservative view of society, and it answered the social needs of many of the German states profoundly. Thomas' social theology had ceased to speak to this society, and Luther enabled social order to be preserved while keeping the religious expression of daily life. It is a patriarchal, hierarchical social order, which Luther saw as the expression of divine will. The great value of his reformulation of the doctrine of vocation was that it enabled manual labour to be valued as much as intellectual activity.[60] It also enabled the duty of compassionate social care to be preached by the Reformation Church, which led to a long tradition of social welfare in Protestant Christianity. Its difficulties in time became equally apparent. One is that the social order is now far more diffuse, in ways which resist a portrayal of social life as organic and ordered. Habermas' analysis of social legitimation, and the difficulties of holding together social coherence, show this clearly. The other is how Luther's idea of vocation could be adapted to a society in which the transcendent purpose of work was problematic, to say the least. The twentieth century has seen a great interest in the theology of vocation, which is now detached from the seventeenth-century debates in English Puritanism about providence and predestination. English theology in the present century has been heavily influenced both by German–Swiss theology (Brunner, Bonhoeffer and Barth) and by the writings of theologians who have worked with Industrial Mission (Jenkins, Kane, Atherton, Ballard, Preston and Suggate). More recent writing has shown a dichotomy inside theology between theologians who are deeply critical of the market and capitalism (Gorringe would be one) and those who have attempted to reformulate a theology of paid employment within the existing economic order, but open to a dialogue with a Spirit-based theology (Volf, following the influence of Moltmann).[61]

Finally, there are those who continue to write in the English tradition, while accepting capitalism, even if being highly critical of it. Such authors would include Malcolm Brown at Manchester, who works with the Work and Economy Network of the European Churches, and Stephen Pattison, who has written a very interesting book on the cult of the new managerialism. There are also those women who have taken up the experience of women in the economy, especially those who are low paid. Elaine Graham, Margaret Halsey and Ann Borrowdale have written extensively in this area. There has been much less written on the growing minority of women in managerial positions. Equally there is a well-developed theology of race relations, especially from Ken Leech, but much less on the experience at work of ethnic minorities.[62]

A theology of work today draws on three traditions. First, there is the mid-twentieth century articulation of the vocation of the lay Christian at work, which drew on Temple, the Swiss–German theologians and theologians linked with Industrial Mission. This is the attempt to bring Luther's writings into the twentieth century. Secondly, there are those writing at the moment who take up particular experiences of work, which are often destructive of human worth with a sense of identity. This is a theology of justice, and it calls for much greater attention to be given by the churches to the failures of the market place and work place. Thirdly, there are those who realize that the enormous changes of the last three decades described by Reich and others mean that a theology of paid employment must begin anew. John Atherton and Malcolm Brown in Manchester have especially tried to rethink what a theology of work might mean. The report in 1997 entitled *Unemployment and the Future of Work*, from the Council of Churches in Britain and Ireland, was a valuable attempt to draw attention to the injustice of long-term unemployment and of the experience of dehumanizing work.[63] It also attempts to sketch out what a theology of vocation might mean at the end of this century, now that the stable world of corporate employers and mass-labour forces has increasingly disappeared. The report was written by Andrew Britton, a lay economist and Anglican lay reader.

The understanding of vocation in Brunner is not very different from Luther. Like Luther, Brunner holds that human beings are co-workers in creation with God, and serve their fellow human beings at work. Unlike Luther, Brunner does not maintain that work is a cross, causing suffering in imitation of Christ. Instead, work has a conscious purpose, which brings fulfilment to those who engage in it. Human beings are social, and carry out their work in co-operation with others. Work is not a necessary evil, but is the will of God, by which we create the civilization in which we live. Through this civilization, human beings can transform nature into the purposes of human life. Manual labour is not of lower value than intellectual labour, but both contribute to the service of others. At the same time, Brunner also builds restraints into his theology. There is no explicit argument that work is a means of dealing with human self-realization, but he does say that work is an intrinsic part of human nature. Work is part of the fundamental conditions of human life, and so Brunner feels that it needs to be revalued. In effect, although he does not say so directly, work is one of the activities by which we become more fully human. Nevertheless, work is not intrinsically good. The Sabbath rest partially means that leisure is also important, and partially acts as a symbol that work is not an end in itself. It is there to serve others and to serve God. When work is abused, and becomes a curse, then human beings have lost sight of the purpose of work. Pride, and the worship of material wealth, destroys the value of work. Work becomes a form of slavery, dehumanizing the worker. Brunner fears that the European and American civilizations of the 1930s have become overmaterialistic, and the meaning of work is lost in the struggle for greater wealth.[64]

In many ways Brunner marked a great advance on Luther's theology. By allying civilization as closely as he did to the nature of work, he drew on the Marxist theory of production and the underlying dependence of values and beliefs on the central reality of work. He also emphasized, far more than Luther, the sheer value and meaning which can be found in work, even if he did not commit himself to a theory of self-realization, through work.

Brunner steered a middle way in the 1930s between state socialism and free-market capitalism. The problem with capitalism is that labour was degraded into the status of a commodity. This was a common criticism of capitalism at this time, and is found in Reinhold Neibuhr's writings in America as well as in those of J. H. Oldham in England. This was the period when Henry Ford, and other major industrialists, were attempting to break the power of the trade unions in industrial life by violent and dangerous means. For thirty years a precarious consensus developed, from the 1940s to the 1970s, in industrial life. Reich describes the period very clearly, but the consensus has now disappeared. Brunner fears that the worker is treated as a means to an end. Equally, capitalism fails to regulate the individual factory owner or business-person enough, and also does not combine work for the common good with individual ownership of social capital. Production is to satisfy human needs, for the economic order is not an end in itself but only a means to that end. In itself, the economic system is ethically indifferent, but it becomes important ethically in terms of the way it is used. State socialism, or communism, is considered by Brunner as an alternative to capitalism. However, the dangers are the power of the state and the denial of individual responsibility – dangers well demonstrated this century. Brunner proposes instead to keep the right of private property, but to regulate it much more closely. In keeping with the hopes of the 1930s, Brunner placed much faith in economic planning, which could steer the economy to enhancing the common good in collaboration with private enterprise. What should be regulated was the treatment of employees, and the free and unhindered right of the capitalist to dispose of his wealth in ways that suited his own needs. Capitalism should be reformed so that private ownership of employment became more like a trust held by some on behalf of others.[65]

Brunner develops strongly the doctrine of creation in his account of vocation. It is both the divine will, and part of human nature, that we have to work. Our nature is fulfilled as we work, and work becomes an instrument of God's continuous act of creation. Unlike animal behaviour, which is instinctive, human labour is conscious and purposeful. The human being as worker is certainly one strand of Brunner's thought which connects him to Marx, even if Brunner would want to stress the transcendent dimension as well. Brunner would also be critical of the utopianism found in Marx, believing that the search for a perfect society is an illusion. The will of God is expressed in the divine order of creation, with a natural morality, which is then amplified by the revelation of human nature and the Kingdom of God found in scripture. A social order which embodies interdependence through the world of work is Brunner's objective, which is not the same as a classless, harmonious society. Instead, the destructiveness of the present highly materialist and conflictual social order is to be challenged by the divine order, so that work can be humanized. Justice should take account of the fact that human beings differ in function even if they all have the same value under God. This allows Brunner to justify hierarchy, while also respecting the intrinsic worth of each person. There should be consultation with the workforce on managerial decision-making, but not the participation of the workers in the decisions themselves. Brunner held that a just distribution of economic power should allow managerial autonomy, even if this was exercised in consultation with subordinates.[66]

Brunner's theology was highly influential in the Protestant churches of Continental Europe as well as in Britain, and he shaped much of the thinking about work in the post-war period by the churches. It was a mixture of conservatism, which did not seek to change the existing social hierarchies very much, and social concern. At its heart, Brunner's theology saw in the twentieth-century human being someone who was fundamentally an industrial worker. They should find fulfilment in their work as a person, be treated fairly and justly, and know that they served God's will as they worked in everyday life. This is a theology which finds the presence of God in the industrial world as part of God's creation. Although Brunner distinguished sharply between a Christian ethic of love and a humanist ethic, he brought a Christian social ethic into line with much secular German thought in the middle of the twentieth century. His advocacy of economic planning, work consultation and restrictions on private ownership was a dramatic advance on earlier Lutheran theology, but the danger is that he did not press his challenge to the industrial order far enough. Nor was it entirely clear how a person found fulfilment at work. Nevertheless, Brunner is noteworthy for being the first theologian to reshape the Lutheran theology of vocation in the industrial era.

Atherton, Kane and Ballard were more critical than Brunner. Atherton's book, *Faith in the Nation: A Christian Vision for Britain* rethinks the Christian view of work as vocation. He is critical of the Protestant Work Ethic, and denies that the benefits of life, including social rights, are to be regarded as a reward for effort. Calvin, argues Atherton, did not seek an ethic which was about rewards and punishments. Our examination of Calvin, in the earlier section on Weber's interpretation of him, shows this to be the case. Setting aside the concern with predestination, Calvin was committed to the good of the community. God's love could not be earned, but only responded to. A theology of vocation today should be about our contribution to society, which is wider than paid employment. At the same time, employment provides a true structure for daily living. It involves purposive and creative activity, it generates opportunities for socializing and interdependence, it creates personal status and identity in society, and it produces income and welfare benefits. In other words, employment is an integral part of the pursuit of human fulfilment in contemporary urban society. And it is this high estimate of the significance of work which is confirmed by much in the Scriptures and Christian tradition.[67]

Atherton argues in very concrete terms that society should attempt to provide a job for everyone who chooses to work. It would bring the debate about unemployment into 'the wider debate about a participatory and reciprocal society'.[68] Atherton writes at length and in great and informed detail about the scourge of unemployment in Britain in the late 1980s. There is great prosperity, caused by the arrival of global capitalism with its service based economy, but there is also great poverty.[69] Ballard and Kane in their books also outline the identity which is given in work, and the damage which is caused by bad employment practices. What is helpful about Ballard and Kane is that they also recognize the enormous differences at work now between the different categories of employment. In particular, both writers stress the reality of conflict at work, of stress and of dehumanization. Also, for the first time, the theological importance of trade unionism is developed in their writings. This can be a mark of personal responsibility in the workplace, although Christians in the past have considered that the reality of 'conflict is to be avoided at any cost'.[70] There is the dilemma of the collective against the individual, which worried Brunner. Trade union activity is about solidarity, which involves collective action, and which may be at odds with personal choice.[71] Brunner feared the overpowering force of the collective in political terms, but the reality of the collective is more likely to be encountered in a strike in the work place. Trade union membership has fallen dramatically in Britain in the 1980s after a series of government changes in union law. By 1994, Britain's strike record was one of the lowest in the industrialized world.[72] Irrespective of this, the great contribution of Ballard and Kane is that they illustrate the messy reality of industrial life, and the endemic nature of conflict at work. They also show how much people can rise above very difficult circumstances to create their own identity by political and economic struggle.

The structures of work are taken by Ballard as part of God's restraining power which enables imperfect societies to continue. Drawing on 2 Thessalonians 2:6, Ballard argues that the Kingdom of God is manifest among human beings as it is served by the creative striving of people, but it is also true that part of the creative work of God is that he 'does not let the abyss of chaos and destruction open up'.[73]

The first aspect of a theology of work is the reworking of the doctrine of vocation, found especially in Brunner, but also in the British writers described above. Ballard has spent much of his career teaching in Cardiff, South Wales, and the Scottish

Industrial Mission has produced a study entitled *New Patterns of Work*. The second is the question of justice, especially but by no means entirely among women, who are often working in low-paid, part-time and insecure jobs. Kane pioneered the question of a theology of justice in her three books, drawing on the exploitation of working people in north-east England. The writing of Margaret Halsey shows the poverty which is prevalent among contract cleaners. Halsey writes, in graphic terms:

> However, one of the most heartening aspects of my research and conversations was the way in which cleaners have maintained a sense of their own worth and value. There was a clear recognition amongst them that whilst their jobs had been devalued, the process was the result of a political and economic climate. This refusal to take responsibility for suffering and injustice – albeit in a less proactive way than would have been the case twenty years ago – has some parallels with the writing of feminist theologians about redemption.

Halsey has been influenced by the English feminist theologian Mary Grey, who argues that women have often been absorbed by the ethic of self-sacrifice and punishment. What is needed is the recovery of a sense of self-worth, and an awareness of being made in the image of God. This is a redemptive act. Halsey also turns back to Margaret Kane, and finds her experience of working with marginalized women workers a prophetic one. Salvation is both a personal and a corporate action.[74]

The second aspect of a theology of work is the reformulation needed in the light of both globalization and the changes in the perception of vocation in recent years. Volf points out that Luther's understanding of vocation is indifferent towards alienation at work. Equally, vocation can easily absorb the spiritual call of God, so that the structure in which one works can become consecrated in a dangerous way. Thirdly, vocational language about work which is dehumanizing can be misused, ideologically. Fourthly, the notion of vocation in Luther's theology equated the irrevocable and single call of God (one is only converted once) with a single occupation which lasts lifelong. In a mobile society, where people change jobs regularly, this makes no sense. Fifthly, and following from the above point, Luther argues that a person could have multiple vocations as father, son and farmer. Nevertheless, one could never be more than one employer or employee, and again the mobility of work makes this outmoded. The reality of several part-time jobs is well-established in some areas.[75]

In its place, Volf proposes a theology of work in the Spirit. The Spirit of God empowers Christians in their vocations. As in the Old Testament the Spirit fills God's workers with skill and ability (Exod. 35:2-3; 1 Chr. 28:11-12; 1 Sam. 16:13), so today a Spirit-based approach can allow for multiple vocations. It is true that the Old Testament understanding of empowerment by the Spirit refers to extraordinary tasks by specially gifted individuals. However, a Christian understanding of the Spirit could see the Christian community as gifted communally with the Spirit. Thus, in place of Calvin's understanding of the work ethic as the response to God's election of an individual, which provides assurance of salvation, Volf sees God as electing (or calling) his people, gifting them with the Spirit, and giving them tasks in the world. The emphasis has become different. Volf argues that 'elevating work to cooperation with God in the pneumatological understanding of work implies an obligation to overcome alienation because the individual gifts of the person need to be taken seriously'. Equally, just as the gifts of the Spirit can be given at different times for different tasks (1 Cor. 12:31, 14:1, 12), so people can work at different jobs at the same time, or for a while, and then move on.[76]

It is important to realize that Volf does not exclude non-Christians from his argument. The Spirit in the realm of grace is active as the first fruits of the whole creation.[77] The same Spirit is active in the Church and in creation. Equally, just as a person shapes their identity by their participation at work, so the gift of the Spirit is not something from 'outside' or 'above', but rather has to be internalized and received by the recipient.[78]

As well as this theological move, Volf ends his book with an interesting chapter on the humanization of work. Taking up the themes of liberation and justice (Luke 4:18; Jer. 22:13), and placing it alongside the value of human work (Gen. 2:15), Volf develops the ideas of worker participation. Here he goes far beyond Emil Brunner's cautious ideas, and affirms the end of vertical hierarchies in management as far as is possible.[79] There are some important reflections on autonomy, the relationship to technology, respect for creation and the environment, and community. Here his ideas chime in with the views of the management theorist Christian Schumacher in his book *To Live and Work*.[80]

Schumacher wishes to give individuals responsibility back for the 'whole work' process, enabling groups of individuals to carry out one complete transformation in the process of production. The structural deformation of work gives operators in automated sequences little opportunity to evaluate performance.[81] He uses his skill as a management consultant to incorporate workers into the planning process, drawing on analogies from the interdependence of members of the Church (Rom. 12:4-5, one body, many members and 1 Cor. 12:19-23).[82] There is, however, an important critique of more aggressive managerial approaches in Pattison's book. He argues that managerial techniques are value-laden, and that Christians should be wary. For Pattison, some (not all) modern management theory still reinforces the old hierarchical relationships, and the world exists for the benefit of organizational exploitation.[83] Equally, there are very worrying concerns which Pattison identifies in management theory: the exclusion of the past from our thinking; the exclusion of the possibility of failure; the denial of diversity and the intangible.[84] Selling the 'vision' and the message of the company having a 'mission' can become an aggressive occupation, drawing all too easily on past Christian understanding of mission as spiritual warfare and subordinating all peoples to the Gospel: 'Despite living in a secular society, religiously derived metaphors continue to be powerful. This is not surprising, because a main purpose of religious language is to be transformative and motivating.'[85] Pattison shows how the Protestant Work Ethic can retain its power, even when secularized, as the earlier discussion of it in this chapter showed very clearly.

The future of industry will continue to change: 'Life as we know it, with a dominant corporate state and penumbra of great industries and organizations, with all that meant for the distribution of work and income, has gone for ever.'[86] No one policy can address the complexity of the new realities of fast-changing work and unemployment: 'No wonder there is no feel good factor, because such change generates turbulences, insecurities, and marginalization.' Atherton argues that the key task for Christian theology is to understand the change. That task has certainly guided this chapter. Alongside the secular reality, of partnership between public and private, contracts at work and short-term alliances, there is also a need for a covenanting dimension. As in chapter 1, on the theological significance of religious language and the importance of the covenant as symbolic of transformation and faithfulness, so here the covenant speaks of obligations and rights which sustain the contract culture.[87]

A theology of work must reshape Luther's theology of vocation into a far more flexible concept of understanding any work (paid or not) as empowered by the gifts of the Spirit, which can humanize work and not accept alienating experiences as the norm. Secondly, it must constantly be aware of the dimensions of injustice at work, especially (but not only) among women, as the work of Margaret Halsey and others has shown. Thirdly, participation at work is a central Christian requirement. Here, the task for theology is to realize that in the 'emerging context of different faiths, genders and environments' Christian theology must struggle to hold together both stewardship and efficiency in an ultimate reconciliation in Christ.[88] Brown argues in the same way: 'How can communities and traditions be the location for moral and ethical practice. . . and be open to dialogue?'[89]

Christian identity remains in tension with the identity that is both given and challenged in paid work. Identity is given at work; that is the indisputable conclusion from Lane and Furnham. It is also challenged by the speed of change, by dehumanizing work, and by 'management as religion' (Pattison). The 'expression and realization of faith in the secular world' is never easy, but the dialogue of theology and the world of work turns on the question of salvation, reconciliation and the presence of the Spirit. It is both individual and collective, concerned with drawing work more into the dimension of Christ-likeness and with justice. Paul Bagshaw, writing on fifty years of Sheffield Industrial Mission in 1994, sums it up well.

The style of this discourse would be tentative, provisional and concerned with particularities. It would counter any attempt to construct and apply present theological certitude. It would rather seek to discover and further God's Kingdom within the complexities and ambiguities of the world. It would constantly struggle to hold together the paradoxical nature of salvation. Its central problem would be the discernment, in theory and in practice, of exactly how and where God may be glimpsed, and, which particular human actions further God's purposes. It would be expressed in practical struggle against all forms of oppression, violence, security and exploitation.[90]

CHAPTER 4

Globalization

This chapter considers the preceding two chapters, on consumption and the work ethic in the context of globalization. Habermas provides the conceptual analysis for examining the impact of capitalism and the world economic system on modernity. That is why he is considered first in this book. Nevertheless, he is not intrinsically concerned with globalization and particularity, especially not in his writings up to the mid 1980s when globalization was not a central political and philosophical concept. Instead, he concentrates on human beings as consumers, workers, political citizens and participants in the market. Hence this book progressed through a consideration of consumption and work. It is now time to examine how globalization has affected all of these concepts. The argument will be that it has done so profoundly. Human identity is increasingly constructed as consumer, worker and participator in the market, including the health-care and educational market. That is the argument so far. However, if globalization also affects our culture by its pattern both of consumption and of its impact on local culture, then human identity will be reshaped again. If the twentieth century has seen in the West the gradual dominance of the activities of consumption and work, in the context of the market, then what we now appear to be evolving into is a global society where consumption, culture and work are reshaped yet again. The implications for human identity are presumably equally profound, both for those who have access to the wealth of the global market and for those who do not.

For understandable and compelling reasons, Christians have pointed to the injustice and misery created by the global market for those deprived of basic needs by its inequities. In turn, this has given rise to arguments about the nature of the development economics being used by theologians and Christians when they speak about globalization. However, in some ways this is to narrow the focus too much when considering globalization, vital through questions of international poverty and debt undoubtedly are. This chapter attempts to widen the debate, while not denying the moral force with which some Christians have focused, with those of other faiths and none, on the issue of global poverty.

First, there is the question of the future of local cultures and societies in the face of globalization. This is an indirect way of taking up the question of consumption, while relating consumption to culture and particular identity. Three books especially seem to contribute to this debate. Some while ago, Michael Walzer mounted a defence of pluralism and distributive justice in the context of particular identity and local culture in his book *Spheres of Justice*. Walzer's argument was that our understanding of social need and consumption must be seen in the context of what it means to belong or to be a 'member'. If this argument is taken as the base line, then two more recent accounts show how much has changed since Walzer wrote his defence in the early 1980s. John Gray, the English political philosopher, has gradually evolved in the 1980s and 1990s from apologist for the New Right to sceptic, environmentalist and (increasingly) apocalyptic prophet of the end of western European and Asian civilization at the hands of American/Enlightenment free-market capitalism. (The reason for the dual description will be seen later.) In *False Dawn*, he offers an account of political economy that compliments his other recent works, *Enlightenment's Wake: Politics and Culture at the Close of the Modern Age* and *Endgames: Questions in Late Modern Political Thought*. A different, more elegiac note is struck by the third of the writers to be considered, who is Nicholas Boyle, a literary critic and Christian political philosopher. Unlike Gray and Walzer, Boyle seeks to bring a Christian perspective to bear on the issue of globalization. During the period 1987 to 1990, Boyle published a trenchant attack on the prevailing intellectual orthodoxy among supporters of the Conservative government in the journal of the English Dominicans, *New Blackfriars*. These essays have now been collected by Boyle in a recent volume entitled *Who Are We Now? Christian Humanism and the Global Market From Hegel to Heaney*, with an afterword written in 1997.

We come secondly to the failings of the global market. The literature here is enormous, and grows all the time. Particular mention might be made of two European theologians, who have written on the frontiers of systematic theology and Christian social ethics. Peter Selby, Anglican Bishop of Worcester in England and a former academic, has written of the way in which his belief in God (especially his belief in Jesus Christ) shapes and is shaped by the overwhelming importance of debt. Debt affects both the domestic economy of the United Kingdom and of the international world order. In his book *Grace and Mortgage*, Selby attempts to reformulate a Christian ethic which will take account of global and domestic debt. Peter Selby was involved also in the Lambeth Conference of Anglican Bishops, which meets every ten years worldwide, and chaired the section dealing with debt. A similar attack on global markets is mounted by Ulrich Düchrow. Düchrow was originally a German Lutheran theologian who was a specialist on the Lutheran doctrine of the two kingdoms of law and gospel which shaped Lutheran social ethics for the last four centuries. He became convinced of the demonic nature of the global market, and has written a series of books attacking it. He has worked especially with the World Council of Churches, and published a number of pamphlets on the relationship of Europe to the world system. However, at the same time, many political commentators have pointed to the weakness of the nation state in the world order, and the difficulty of establishing any control over the global market. Düchrow has also in turn been strongly criticized by Ronald Preston, an English social ethicist, who believes that the whole wcc approach has now become fundamentally utopian and flawed. The debate here is very intense.

However, this survey of globalization is not yet complete. Some theologians have sought to match the reality of the global market with the creation of a new global ethic which would encompass culture and consumption, work and the global market. The foremost writer in this area is Hans Küng, who has been involved in the Parliament of the World's Religions held in Chicago in 1993. This endorsed a Declaration Toward a Global Ethic, and Küng has developed this strategy. He edited *Yes to a Global Ethic* in 1996, and wrote *A Global Ethic for Global Politics and Economics* in 1997. How far such an approach is compatible with the local, and particular, approach of Walzer and Gray remains to be seen.

Consumption, and culture, is affected by globalization, as is the work ethic and the nature of the market. The exploration of globalization is only at the beginning, and it is an investigation which looks at an ever evolving subject. However, there is nothing new in this: political science emerged at the end of the nineteenth century to examine the growth of the newly industrialized nation states and their welfare bureaucracies. The focus of this chapter is not, however, globalization *per se*. It is rather the nature of human identity, as shaped by consumption, work and the market, and the way in which that shaping is now carried on in a global dimension with often unforseen possibilities of homogeneity and employment. In response to this chapter, the penultimate chapter of the book will study the churches as they have wrestled with the issues of consumption, globalization and the market. They themselves are part of a global community of the universal Church across time and space, as expressed in the doctrine of catholicity and *oikoumene* (loosely translated unity, but a unity of the whole created world). How far the churches can offer a vision of a fulfilled human identity, that embraces consumption, work and the market as the means of its fulfilment, but also transcends it by fulfilment through religious faith and relationships within a local culture, is one of the most pressing questions which the churches face today.

CULTURE AND CONSUMPTION

Unlike Habermas, Walzer believes that the social location of an individual action matters a great deal. Habermas abstracted the discussion of modern society, and of communication, from any particular society, arguing that the formal logic of his position gave it its strength. Walzer disagrees profoundly. He states that the idea of distributive justice 'presupposes a bounded world within which distributions take place: a group of people committed to dividing, exchanging, and sharing social goods, first of all among themselves . . . We think about independent cities or countries capable of arranging their own patterns of division and exchange, justly or unjustly. We assume an established group and a fixed population.'[1] Walzer argues that the concept of membership of a group or society is prior to the understanding of a need or of welfare. All need, he appears to argue, is ultimately a social need (or at least expressed through society) and this means that the question of society must be prior to that of need or desire. 'Membership as a social good is constituted by our understanding, its value is fixed by our work and conversation; and then we are in charge (who else could be in charge) of its distribution.'[2]

The alternatives are to accept that we are all strangers to one another, or that global identity will prevail over local or national identity. Walzer uses the arguments of the Victorian English moral philosopher Henry Sidgwick to criticize the latter claim. In the *Elements of Politics*,[3] an argument is put forward that social welfare and human culture would be defeated by an ever-changing, heterogeneous population. This appears a utilitarian argument, but (as Walzer shows) the ultimate foundation of the argument is non-utilitarian. Communal cohesion creates obligation and shared meaning, so that there are not strangers but members of a community. The intrinsic moral consideration in communal cohesion is what Sidgwick calls the value of 'patriotic sentiments'. Walzer agrees with Sidgwick: 'The distinctiveness of cultures and groups depend upon closure and, without it, cannot be conceived as a stable feature of human life. If this distinctiveness is a value . . . then closure must be permitted somewhere.' A global state that overwhelmed local communities would create 'a world of radically deracinated men and women'.[4]

Furthermore, Walzer doubts how successful globalization

will be. An open state, with cosmopolitan cities and multi-national institutions, or a multinational empire, produces closed and parochial communities. 'Neighbourhoods can be open only if countries are at least potentially closed. Only if the state makes a selection among would-be members and guarantees the loyalty, security, and welfare of the individuals it selects, can local communities take shape as 'indifferent' associations, determined solely by personal preference and market capacity.'[5] A truly global society would overwhelm this. While cohesive culture could be maintained for a few generations in local neighbourhoods on a voluntary basis, the cohesion would evaporate given continual population movement. Walzer does not wish to exclude refugees or immigrants, but merely to suggest that some control is necessary. The danger, which applies directly to the issue of globalization, is that of accepting guest workers. Walzer recognizes that if naturalization is controlled strictly, and immigration only loosely, then immigrants become resident aliens. Human identity for the dominant group is enhanced by the preservation of a culture, but the price is unacceptable. The issue of guest workers goes back not just to slavery but to the 'metics' of Athens in ancient Greece. These were not slaves, who also existed, but residents who did the city's work yet who never had any hope of becoming citizens. Some were very wealthy in fourth-century Athens BCE, but they had no welfare rights nor political rights. Equally, Athenian society treated them with contempt. Walzer considers the dilemma carefully. He argues for some social closure against globalization, but also sees that social exclusion demeans those who are excluded. Hence he regrets Aristotle's argument that co-residence and labour is insufficient to make one a citizen, for citizenship is an 'excellence' not available to all. The irony, as Walzer points out, is that Aristotle was himself a metic, and eventually died living away from Athens to guard himself against anti-Macedonian feeling.

Walzer considers the issue of guest workers in modern capitalist countries. He considers the issue not simply for its own sake, but because it illustrates the difficulty of arguing for some form of political or cultural closure to a society:

Defenders of the guest-worker system claim that the country is now a neighbourhood economically, but politically still a club or a family. As a place to live, it is open to anyone who can find work; as a forum or assembly, as a nation or a people, it is closed except to those who meet the requirements set by the present members. The system is a perfect synthesis of labour mobility and patriotic solidarity.[6]

Walzer, however, does not believe that the system is as innocent as this. There is a denial of rights and civil liberties. For, unlike ancient Athens (and even that was a denial of participation), there is no comprehensible place for outsiders, and no metic system with protected areas of work. This leads Walzer to an interesting, and controversial point. He will accept constraints on immigration but not on naturalization. Once admitted to a territory, an immigrant must be offered the opportunities to citizenship. So Walzer is prepared to argue that 'the distribution of membership is not pervasively subject to the constraints of justice'.[7]

At stake here is the shape of the community that acts in the world, exercises sovereignty, and so on. Admission and exclusion are at the core of communal independence. They suggest the deepest meaning of self-determination. Without them, there could not be communities of character, historically stable, ongoing associations of men and women with some special commitment to one another and some special sense of their common life.[8]

Walzer also anticipates a further part of our argument. Within these communities there can be market systems of exchange which can include or exclude its members. Without, for the moment, anticipating Peter Selby's argument that debt and economic failure exclude people from citizenship, it is important to notice that commodities within a particular culture 'carry meanings far beyond their obvious use, and that we need them for the sake of standing and identity . . . Commodities are symbols of belonging; standing and identity are distributed through the market'.[9] Walzer thus advances one of the most thoughtful accounts of relativism in relation to justice, and stands at the opposite extreme to Habermas. Justice is relative, he claims, to social meanings, and the nature of a society is infinitely varied: 'There are an infinite number of possible lives, shaped by an infinite number of possible cultures . . . A given life is just if its substantive life is lived in a certain way – that is, in a way faithful to the shared understandings of its members.'[10] Consumption is part of that way of life.

It is intrinsic to Walzer's argument that what he calls 'shared conceptions of social goods . . . local and particular in character'[11] are the origins of rights beyond the basic, elementary rights of life and liberty. Rights in society, which are distributive, are for Walzer not derived from our common humanity but from the particularity of local culture and society. Distributive justice depends on the recognition that rights are pluralist, heterogeneous and relativist, in Walzer's argument. It follows that the preservation of local cultures, local identity and communal existence is not an accidental matter. What this implies for globalization is that an imposed uniformity by the power (and tyranny) of money is something to be resisted strongly. Walzer himself sees the tyranny of money as a threat to egalitarianism, but fifteen years after the publication of *Spheres of Justice* the global argument looms as large.[12]

Boyle and Gray show how much the global market has swept over human civilization in the last few decades.

The world-historical movement we call globalization has momentum that is inexorable. We are not the masters of the technologies that drove the global economy: they condition us in many ways we have not begun to understand. Institutions that could monitor or counteract their dangerous side-effects are lacking. It is more than doubtful now whether any late modern society can restrain technological development even if its consequences are injurious to vital human needs. Such societies are too uncertain of their values, and too wedded to an understanding of the earth as a resource to be consumed in the service of unlimited human wants, to attempt such a heroic task.[13]

Gray feels that the American model of aggressive free market capitalism will drive social democracy out of Europe, although he agrees with Reich that the majority of American workers are themselves deeply insecure economically.[14] Social market economies are being progressively dismantled, and he foresees a period of deep and traumatic reform for German social

democracy in the next two decades.[15] Boyle offers a far more
optimistic understanding of Germany, but his analysis globally
of what is taking place is equally trenchant.[16] The political
world is 'shrivelled' up into a series of managerially run institutions, with the non-economic spheres (judiciary, media, church)
relegated to one side.[17] 'We are at best the series of consumer
choices we have made' he feels, and 'the concept of a vocation
. . . loses its value and is actively persecuted'.[18] Globalization
threatens the identities of national life, and as nation states
become obsolescent, so our identities are no longer shaped by
national institutions. 'The old transcendent certainties fade and
are replaced by the harsh realities and tangible rewards of the
global marketplace in the global village.'[19] Boyle feels that there
is a deep correspondence between the question of personal
identity, so much speculated about in post-modernist thought,
and the establishment of the global market. The institutions
which gave us our identity are failing, and the continuity of jobs
for life becomes a nostalgic dream.

Boyle recognizes that the only morally defensible and conceptually consistent answer to the question 'Who are we now?'
is 'future citizens of the world'. The problem is how we relate
that answer to local and regional responsibilities, in theory or in
practice, individually or together. 'Too much in contemporary
thinking is an obstacle to understanding that relation between
the global and the particular in which the contradictions within
the world-system are being played out, and in which our
identity ultimately resides.'[20]

Others are not so despairing, although they do not under-
estimate the difficulty of the task. The publications of the
German Evangelical and Roman Catholic Churches show that
it is still possible to attempt an answer. They write: 'Changes of
this magnitude enhance the importance of joint responsibility
on the part of the international community. Globalisation is not
a force of nature but calls for political regulation and control.'[21]
It is the task of the church to engage in the task of shaping the
world. The German document draws on the fundamental
biblical narrative. On the one hand, there are the stories of
chaos and disorder, such as Cain and Abel, the Tower of Babel

and the Flood: 'It portrays the human condition, defined by sin and guilt, human pride and selfishness, and structural injustice.' Human beings are already redeemed in Christ, so 'they do not need to save themselves as they run their lives and the affairs of the world. That liberates them to act without care for themselves and concern for security through power.'[22]

The concept of social justice is expressed through the twin concepts of solidarity and subsidiarity. Solidarity can be a global ethic, committing the industrialized nations to reduce protectionism and enable the poor to help themselves.[23] In a similar way they argue that the question of human identity must be rethought. Identity is seen as a far more plural concept, where male/female, paid/voluntary work, personal freedom/ political commitment and family/job all come together. What was seen as exclusive is no longer the case. The spread of new values has become widespread. 'What many of these new values have in common is an expansion of the concept of solidarity. Threats and risks, which have become limitless in extent and effect, fundamentally concern everyone and so promote an awareness of being globally connected.'[24] This echoes John Atherton's idea of partnership and reconciliation in the previous chapter when he discussed the changing concept of a theology of work. This leads the German churches to emphasize the importance of action groups, new social movements, and other forms of social solidarity that complement the reduced power of national institutions. Equally the document strongly emphasizes the importance of human rights, the European union and the various international organizations.[25]

Walzer, Boyle and Grey show the importance of the local and particular for human identity. However Grey expresses deep pessimism about the future of social democracy and national culture, which Boyle echoes. The statement of the German churches does not share this pessimism, and it is significant that it has been discussed very widely at local, regional and national levels. The question of globalization and human identity remains unresolved, and it is an open question whether Grey (who received mixed reviews of his book) will prove to be correct. Certainly the German Church document is a magnificent theological response to the issue, and embodies very deeply the ecumenical commitment to common action together by the churches.

THE FAILINGS OF THE GLOBAL MARKET

For the first time in history, the vast majority of the world's population is bound together in a global capitalist system. This development compels a re-examination of the market system and the world economy. In the past, different regions of the world had entirely different economic systems. In seventeenth- and eighteenth-century Europe, different states, such as Prussia, France and England could develop alternative economic strategies, some of which were mercantilist, some oriented to military power, some to world trade. Other parts of the world, such as China, were virtually unknown even though there were sophisticated economic systems, now charted by historians in the great intellectual enterprise itself begun this century by Joseph Needham of mapping the intellectual, social and economic history of China. Even this century there were radically incompatible economic systems, especially in the 1930s with German fascism, Russian Communism, American freetrade (though increasingly circumscribed by the depression and relations with Japan) and the British combination of freetrade and imperial protection. Only in the last few decades has the world begun to adopt a single economic system, even if we are not fully there yet. In the past, different economic policies produced vast differences in economic performance, even allowing for natural resources, social development and degrees of industrialization. In the future, policies and economic performance will slowly become more equal. However, economic policy can only go so far. There are other reasons why countries will have different standards of living.

Adam Smith understood the limits of economic convergence, which partly depends on geography. Even today sea-based trade is less expensive than land trade, which was a point which Smith emphasized: 'So it is upon the seacoast and along the banks of navigable rivers, that industry . . . naturally begins to subdivide and improve itself, and it is frequently not till a long time after that these improvements extend themselves to the inland parts of the country.'[26] Smith believed that England's prosperity was due to the interplay of geography and national policy. Geography was responsible for fertile soil, many navigable rivers and a long coastline. National policy gave the rule of law, secure property rights and an economic policy comparatively free from state interference. However, what Smith did not appreciate, and which later economists such as Jeffrey Sachs at Harvard have pointed out, is that policy and geography interact.[27] It is not as though variable human intelligence is employed upon the passive geographical conditions of a state. Policy can influence geography, such as through investment in geography and communications. Geography can also influence policy. Coastal states have over history been supportive of market institutions. Landlocked states have tended to have hierarchical, sometimes militarised, societies. Temperate climates support generally higher densities of population, with a more intensive division of labour than tropical regions. Until this century, disease, landlocked regions and low agricultural productivity kept the density in sub-Saharan Africa among the lowest in the world, except in coastal trading areas and a few mountainous areas such as in Ethiopia. Low agricultural productivity can itself be determined by geography, for torrential rain in tropical regions leach the soil of nutrients and specific diseases are found in tropical or sub-tropical regions. These do not simply affect human beings, but also crops and livestock.

This inequality of geographical endowment was reinforced by economic policies throughout the nineteenth and twentieth centuries. On the one hand the economic policies of the Great Powers was designed to encourage the 'mother country' in industrialization, while the colonies produced cheap raw materials, which were exported back to the colonial power. On the other hand the colonial powers had more productive economic systems. The interaction of nature (geography) and nurture (social and economic policy) has continued to the present day. In 1913 western Europe, North America and Australia/New

Zealand had only 17 per cent of the world's population, but produced 48 per cent of global income.

This sets the argument about globalization in a different context. In this chapter, I will sketch out briefly what is the central feature of globalization. This is not the enormous increase in financial transactions across the world, nor the ability of multinational companies to invest anywhere at will. It is instead the adoption of a broadly similar set of economic and social policies across the globe, and the way in which the adoption of these policies has led to a rapid increase in economic productivity. This development of industrialization, and the service economy, leads to a crucial feature of globalization, which is the interaction of geography and policy on a global scale.

The implications for a social ethic are enormous, for what specialists in international relations have begun to chart is the reduction in the power of states to set policy. Instead, the economic reality of the power of the market, with a variety of institutions competing for power within the market, such as cartels, multinationals, nation states, regional institutions (such as the European Union) and pressure groups with non-government organizations (NGOs), leads to a development in policy which leaves governments with far less power than earlier this century. Yet, at the same time, the rapid advances in communications technology make it far more difficult for governments to hold onto power and information except by the crudest and harshest forms of social control. Therefore, it is the question of cultural and social homogeneity, along with the ability of governments to influence the transition to a global economy which excludes no geographical region, which is posed by the stark reality of global change. In the middle of the twentieth century, a group of German theologians and social theorists (the Paulos Gesselschaft) imagined a global development in which semi-planned economic growth gradually encompassed the globe through the efforts of national states. This version of soft Marxism, or a particular form of western European socialism, was enthusiastically embraced by such theologians as Rahner and Moltmann. It envisaged a high degree of commitment to social egalitarianism, cultural diversity and (rather less emphatically) environmental protection. If the work of such analysts as Susan Strange is correct, and the growth of the global market has far outstripped the ability of national governments to plan the future, this theological–political vision lies in ruins. The alternative, developed by liberation theology, has increasingly been to focus on the most vulnerable groups in geographical regions, and to seek to protect them from the regions of global change. This has been taken up by the wcc, especially by the theologian Ulrich Düchrow in a series of sharp exchanges with the English social ethicist Ronald Preston. The position held by Düchrow is also held by Tim Gorringe in Exeter in his book *Capital and the Kingdom*, and by the Lutheran South African economist Klaus Nürnberger.

It is, however, important to return to the argument about nature and nurture, geography and policy. Otherwise the argument about globalization loses its force. During 1965–1990 global patterns of growth depended on four factors: initial conditions; physical geography; government policy and demographic change. Initial conditions matter because, other things being equal, poorer countries tend to grow 'faster than rich ones'. Physical geography affects the rate of growth. Landlocked countries can grow at least 0.7 per cent slower than coastal ones, and tropical ones 1.3 per cent slower than temperate, even allowing for other factors. This reflects the cost of poor health and unproductive farming. However, richer urban states such as Hong Kong and Singapore overcome this by technology. Air-conditioning is the greater equalizer in labour productivity. However, low productivity and tropical farming serves as a kind of poverty trap. Economic policies are crucial in three different ways. Allowing for all other factors, open economies grew 1.2 per cent faster per annum than closed ones. Secondly, good government helps economic growth. Good government can be defined by an absence of certain factors. These are corruption, government breach of contract, expropriation of property and inefficiency of public administration. There are also positive factors: investment in public resources such as education, health and infrastructure. This is neither simply a moral argument, nor a basis for political legitimacy, as Habermas argued in *Legitimation Crisis*. It allows faster economic growth. Finally, there is the demographic factor. In developing countries, there is a standard, invariant pattern. Medical care prolongs adult lives and reduces infant mortality. However fertility rates do not decline for a while, and population growth increases. Then households adjust to lower infant mortality, as mothers' time in the labour market rises in value. Longer life expectancy also eventually coincides with a fall in birth-rates. Families tend to have fewer children. In sub-Saharan Africa and South Asia, with lower levels of development and less economic value for mothers' participation in the labour force, birth-rates have continued to remain high. This leads to a bulge in the number of dependent children, without an increase in the number of productive workers. In East Asia, rapid population growth is decreasing, and more of the population is now of working age. Again, during 1965–1990, the difference due to demography between East Asia and South Asia or sub-Saharan Africa was as much as 0.6 per cent (per annum) in economic growth. Since the increase is exponential, the difference in 25 years was great.

There remains the enormous problem of global poverty. Later in this chapter the responses of Düchrow, the WCC and others will be explored. It is important, however, that the reasons for this poverty are set out. It would be wrong to adopt a geographical determination. Tropical Africa is affected by being landlocked for fourteen countries, and by climate with disease. This is also exacerbated by the spread of AIDS. At the same time, the rise in population growth means that the tropical regions already have one third of the world's population at two billion people. This share will rise sharply, for these regions have the fastest population growth in the world. However, economic and social policies can change the economic possibilities even for regions with difficult climates, poor soils and physical isolation. South Asia is now adopting market-based policies after decades of controlled economic strategies, and the demographic transition is now becoming more favourable. The percentage of workers in the population will slowly increase.

China is largely a temperate country, with life expectancy already at seventy years. Disease is beginning to be controlled. It is the coastal regions which are dynamic. Inland there is a vast population with poor transport, low agricultural productivity and social-economic policies which hark back to the decades of state communism. Slowly China will change into a more dynamic nation as a whole, with greater population change from the hinterland to the coast. India, likewise, is evolving, especially around the great parts of the southern coastline. It is here that export-oriented manufacturers will spread along the trade routes.

Parts of Asia, and above all sub-Saharan Africa, face difficult problems. Diseases such as malaria are still prevalent, and the developed world spends vastly more on research for temperate-zone diseases than tropical ones. (Malaria kills 1 million people per annum, and affects between 200 and 400 million others, and 90 per cent of the deaths are in sub-Saharan Africa. Yet research on malaria vaccine by public-health bodies is very low. Private pharmaceutical companies invest little in research for the poorer, tropical regions.) AIDS remains a great scourge of Africa and Asia.

Secondly, research is needed to overcome the long-term difficulties of tropical agriculture, even allowing for the 'green revolution' in productivity in recent decades. Writing about sub-Saharan Africa in 1986 Charles Elliott write that: 'for these physical constraints to be overcome, a quantum leap in agricultural technology is required such as occurred in the Punjab in the 1970s. Such a quantum leap – particularly one that protected the interests of the rural poor – will take a long time and a lot of resources to bring about.'[28] In 1997, Jeffrey Sachs could write: 'Much of the world's tropical population is still engaged in farming. This has long suggested to development economists that agriculture-led growth should play a key role in tropical development. At the very least, the evidence on growth in the tropics calls this view into question. Nowhere has tropical agriculture led the escape from poverty.'[29] Vastly greater research on tropical agriculture is needed, and much enhanced access to information technology. This could overcome the difficulties of landlocked regions and allow them to participate in the global economy.

Thirdly, there is the issue of global migration. Many poor nations rely on the money sent back by their workers overseas, although there are increasing signs that the western nations are seeking to restrict migration. Nations in the Caribbean, South America, Africa and the Philippines are all involved in this struggle to survive. At the same time civil wars and regional conflicts have now persisted over decades rather than years. In nations such as Angola, the struggle for colonial independence has turned into a long-running civil war. Other nations are plagued by civil unrest, corruption and large numbers of refugees. Migration is a feature of sub-Saharan Africa itself, as refugees seek to escape persecution and violence.

Finally there is the issue of world debt and the regulation of global trade. Sachs' view of this is trenchant: 'The current pattern of the rich countries – to provide financial aid to tropical Africa while blocking Africa's chances to export textiles, footwear, leather goods, and other labour-intensive products – may be worse than cynical. It may in fact fundamentally undermine Africa's chances for economic development.'[30] His concern is also that agriculture may be harmed by disease, poor soil, and unreliable rainfall. In a surprising comment, he suggests that temperate-zone food (from Australia, the United States or Argentina) may supply sub-Saharan Africa with its needs. This would require a major change in African development. Some African nations do benefit from market-based economies, and perhaps a dozen countries have recently begun to grow at 5 per cent per annum. However, the great deterrent to growth, apart from disease, climate and population growth, is world debt. There have been many studies of the debt crisis, and the churches have been heavily involved in lobbying for change. The Jubilee 2000 initiative is perhaps the best known.

It is now clear that there is a 'substantial shift of power from territorial states to world markets' and indirectly on to the transnational firms. However, Strange and McRae both show the enormous limitations which operate on global firms. As the economy has moved further into the service sector, developing countries have become far more dependent on the financial services provided by large firms in the developed countries. Transnational Corporations (TNCS) increasingly exercise a parallel authority alongside governments in economic issues such as technological innovation, the management of labour relations, the fiscal extraction of surplus value, and the location of industry and investment.[31] At the same time, the enormous competition between them means that they do not have great freedom to manœuvre either. They also operate in a highly unstable global financial context, which currently lacks any overall authority and control.[32] This means that the local nation state can no longer control TNCS. On the other hand, there has been enormous growth in industrialization in Latin America and Asia in the last three decades – 'beyond the wildest dreams of the 1960s', in Strange's words. Brandt assumed in his 1970s Commission that industrialization would only come there by massive state aid. He was wrong, for most of the industrialization came by the migration of industry and capital.[33]

The OECD, before the international financial crisis of August 1998 which engulfed Russia and further destabilized East Asia, was gradually rediscovering the 'capable state'. The great challenges are to sustain the environment and to avert global poverty, in areas where industrialization has failed to take place. Yet this optimistic scenario does not take account of the great suffering and poverty in Africa and Asia, which is the criticism made by the WCC.[34]

There is a deep disagreement between those like Deepak Lal and his critics. Lal sees poverty as mainly rural, and feels that in time 'a large increase in the demand for rural labour relative to its supply will raise the earnings of all classes of the poor'.[35] However the question turns on the length of time which Lal is concerned with. He admits that growth in population will drive up the labour force in many densely populated countries for the next fifty years, and this will need much greater efforts at industrialization to employ them.[36] Lal feels that rapid economic development can take place across the developing world, if governments cease to influence the market.[37]

Others would be far more critical. Van Drimmelin shows how the gap between rich and poor is widening even in the South. Brazil has the most unequal distribution of income. The richest 20 per cent of the population earn 26 times the income of the poorest 20 per cent. Throughout the South, life expectancy has fallen in many nations which have not industrialized, especially in Africa.[38] Africa as a whole has 33 of the worlds 50 poorest countries, and the debt issue hangs over them like a sword.

It is the main contention of Selby's book that the world debt has become out of control: 'the continued worsening of the international debt crisis', where debts must be repaid and the consequences for the poorest of the world are ignored.[39] Every aid agency makes the same point, and yet progress is painfully slow: 'Providing effective debt relief to the 20 worst affected countries would cost . . . roughly equivalent to building the Euro-Disney theme park in France.'[40] This terrible contrast of consumerism and starvation shows the way in which priorities can be distorted by the effect of consumerism.

What Selby argues at the end of his book is that the extent of indebtedness forces the Church to reassess the condition which this imposes on those who want to belong to the global economy. Put more simply, debt imposes conditions. If you want to belong to us, you must pay your debts. If you do not do this, you will feel guilty, and the desire for truth and love is transformed into a debt. In other words, debt has become an idol which the Church must unmask. Our identity is threatened by the injustice with which we collude, for we see in this debt a symbol of 'our constant tendency to erect barriers, conditions for belonging' and our past history of discrimination.[41]

Many companies have responded to sustained criticism, and adopted far more open and responsible policies as a result. The Churches have mounted major criticisms of such companies over many years. Shell, for instance, now issues an annual *Health, Safety and Environment* report. What is taking place is a slow convergence between two very different camps. Van Drimmlen can accept the usefulness of the market,[42] while McRae argues that the industrialized world must take responsibility for global poverty, especially in Africa.[43]

Nevertheless the barriers of debt, protectionism and trade remain very strong. The outlook for the global economy remains difficult. Küng, in his book on *A Global Ethic for Global Politics and Economics*, describes the attempts to construct an ideal politics, through Woodrow Wilson and the international forum.[44] What is needed is a realistic politics. This means that the religions must address the clash between their own civilizations, such as fundamentalism. He sees Yugoslavia as the great warning of a future breakdown of states into warring groups of ethnic and religious forces. Globalization and religion must be addressed at the same time. The problem is one of motivating and convincing both business and political leaders, and local grass-roots communities.

Küng lays most of his stress on a responsible moral ethic which allows interreligious dialogue. He feels that the religious ethic can keep its force and engage in dialogue with governments. Küng's global theology lays great stress on interfaith dialogue, ethical responsibility and awareness of the need for each religious tradition to reinterpret its own teachings in the light of the global context in which all theology is now done.

The alternative, for more grass-roots approach, is the painful re-evaluation which liberation theology has engaged in over the last decade. It is clear that in South America the fastest growing churches have been the Pentecostal ones, who find in their spirit-based theology an alternative to the rootlessness induced by global capitalism. For a while, liberation theology was deeply critical of this development, finding it socially quite complacent, and often linked to American conservative evangelicalism which blessed the global capitalism so dominant in South America. Ian Linden notes that, between 1990 and 1992, 710 new churches were founded in San Paolo, Brazil; 90 per cent of these were Pentecostal. These churches represent a reaction to the secular, urban world that dehumanizes the poor. The issue is whether such pentecostalism will be a half-way house to consumerism and secularism.[45]

Equally, liberation theology has learnt much from feminism, with its emphasis on empowerment and accompanying the poor. At the same time, eco-feminism has pointed out the environmental concerns which poverty has to wrestle with, caused by the destruction of the environment by the command economies and by unbridled global capitalism.[46]

What can the response be to the global economy? On the one hand, the outright opposition of liberation theology to the principalities and powers of international, global capitalism is now far more nuanced. Some are in dialogue with evangelical groups, some with feminist, while Küng's theology is a far more liberal approach of discussion with major employers. Even as this more nuanced approach develops, political theorists such as Boyle and Gray wonder if local culture and indigenous peoples can survive at all. Here the debate is about the possibility of identity at all. It would be tragic and ironic if liberation theology's recent emphasis on local indigenous culture came about as it was most under threat. It is obviously the case that pentecostalism provides such an identity for the dispossessed, although it remains open how socially critical this theology will be.

Equally, there is no resolution, as the second response to global capitalism, about the debate on the market. It goes without saying that debt needs to be rescheduled and trading barriers made more open. Without this, life expectancy will fall further in Africa. Reich, in 1991, pointed out that 20 per cent of the world's population lived in North America, East Asia (Japan, Taiwan, Hong Kong, South Korea) and western Europe, but 75 per cent of gross world trade took place between them. Putting it another way, 60 per cent of the 12,000 children born every hour join families whose annual income (in 1991) was less than $350 per annum. Many sub-Saharan African countries are threatened by AIDS, environmental degradation, civil war and the withdrawal of international investment. As a result, several African nations had much larger populations in the 1990s than the 1970s, but a lower per caput income.[47]

Some, such as Paul Vallely, have argued for ethical trading as a response to global capitalism. While arguing that debt must be cancelled, he is critical of the development economies of Peter Selby. He is prepared to work with transnational corporations, carrying out social auditing which monitors the impact a firm has on the environment, local community, staff, customers and suppliers. Several large corporations, including Shell and British Telecom, have now taken up this idea, as has the new British Government, in its development ministry. Equally, the distinction between the European Union and the other trading blocs (North American; South American – Mercosur – and South East Asia) is that only the former is a governmental transnational structure. The latter trading blocs are only for economic liberalization. The influence of the EU. in regulating the market outside Europe by codes of conduct on transnational corporations, and dialogue with the World Bank, World Trade Organization and the IMF is all important.[48]

There is no agreement here. McRae, Strange and others believe that eventually the benefits of world trade will spread worldwide, although sub-Saharan Africa remains dire. Others, such as Düchrow and Gomnge, believe that capitalism is in crisis. Düchrow argues that 'the global system' provides a life-or-death struggle. Düchrow's earlier work on Luther and the Two Kingdoms means that he believes that the very integrity of the Church is at stake in this struggle. Düchrow argues that the churches must oppose international capitalism in the same way that they opposed Hitler and Nazism in the 1930s. Equally, Düchrow has been subjected to stringent criticism by Ronald Preston for naïvety. Atherton supports Preston, and attacks Düchrow, in the same way as he criticized Meeks in an earlier chapter.[49]

There is one point of convergence. The World Bank Development Report now argues for a more internationalist state, where increased economic efficiency goes alongside the provision of social welfare and education. Here, the challenge of the market, which John Atherton sees as the most fundamental political challenge at the end of this century world-wide, can be met and transcended. What is needed is co-operation with transnational corporations, and greater monitoring of their behaviour. The global economy has provided enormous benefits, but it also needs regulation.[50]

CHAPTER 5

The response of the churches

In November 1986, the American Roman Catholic Bishops issued the final draft of their pastoral letter entitled *Economic Justice for All*, which was their text on the morality of the United States economy. It is worth examining this text in detail as an example of how a church responded to issues of work and consumerism of work. What is significant about this report is that it represented a process, in which the publication of the report was only one stage. Before the publication there were hearings, and, in the case of the American report, there were also draft versions of it. After the publication, in each case, there were conferences and discussions with government.

All of this is an attempt to educate Christians about some of the basic realities of their lives: conditions at work, consumerism and the relations set up by the market. If Habermas' work represents a philosophical overview of the nature of social existence in contemporary western culture, the response of the churches represents the attempt to integrate the conditions of social life into the life of faith. The work of Habermas, and the response of the churches, frame this book's discussion of the realities of economic life. What these responses suggest is that it matters that there is an ecclesial response and not simply an individual one to economic life.[1]

What did the Catholic Bishops say? They set out their report in five chapters, and built a cumulative case. In the first chapter, there is a brief sketch of the United States economy, followed by a substantial chapter on ethical norms. This includes biblical perspectives, and a lengthy analysis of the relationships between persons and institutions, as well as ethical norms themselves.

They then turn to selected economic policy issues. What is interesting, as will be seen when the chapter is examined in more detail, is that it is primarily about exclusion rather than about economic life *per se*. Thus, employment becomes a matter of unemployment, and poverty is an underlying issue. As a pastoral letter concerned with the stresses on ordinary citizens this is perfectly appropriate, but it does deflect some of the issues which might have been addressed, such as labour relations, credit and debt, and the market. Two final chapters set out their vision for the future. One is entitled 'A New American Experiment: Partnership for the Public Good'. It emphasizes co-operation within firms, locally, regionally and internationally. The other chapter is more individual and ecclesial, spelling out the Christian vocation, the challenge to the Church, and a commitment to what is called 'A Kingdom of Love and Justice'.

This is an overarching vision of participation within an advanced industrial economy on the basis of Catholic moral theology. What is significant is that it remains the most sustained attempt to examine economic justice in Roman Catholic official publications. It stands in contrast (though not contradiction) to the emphasis on liberation theology in South America, which has been reported far more widely in Britain. There is one response to it by liberation theologians in Britain, including Austin Smith, who are sympathetic but also critical at times.[2] What is interesting is that such journals as *New Blackfriars*, or the weekly magazine *The Tablet*, never published any articles on it in Britain. Roman Catholic debate appears to have concentrated in the 1980s either on methods of moral theology or on liberation theology. This is in marked contrast to the United States.

The pastoral letter 'is not a blueprint for the American economy. It does not embrace any particular theory of how the economy works, nor does it attempt to resolve the disputes between different schools of economic thought'.[3] Instead it is a pastoral letter resting on 'basic moral principles'. A pastoral letter is a particular way of addressing an issue. Two Anglican moral theologians, writing in the United States (Timothy Sedgwick and Philip Turner), point out the difference between a pastoral letter and a report, resolution or canon.[4] Reports are ways of marshalling large amounts of information, and present different opinions on an issue. They cite the Church of England's Board for Social Responsibility as a good example of one body which produces reports. A canon, which features in the life of Roman Catholic and Anglican churches, has not been used in the Anglican communion to educate the conscience of Anglicans. In the past, canons were only used rarely, on such matters as rebellion, regicide and treason, or the grave matter (certainly in past centuries) of divorce. Turner writes that, for Anglicans, canon law 'limits the pastoral practice of the church and inadvisedly entangles the church in the discipline of the lives of its individual members'.[5] Roman Catholic canon law was much more specific, especially in medieval times on the practice of usury. Recent revision of canon law has, however, left much more scope on individual matters of moral choice in the economic or social sphere.

This leaves the resolution and the pastoral letter. Resolutions can express a majority opinion from ecclesial delegates at a synod or convention. The problem lies with the instruction of the individual conscience of church members. The assent of conscience must require free acceptance, based on conviction. This conviction can only come from justifying arguments, which resolutions cannot provide. Resolutions can identify issues, and announce a conclusion, but in the absence of the debate which led to the resolution there is little instruction.

It is this ecclesial digression which shows the importance of the method of a pastoral letter. As Turner says, the American Catholic Bishops have had 'a significant impact on public debate'. The letter on the economy, and the one on nuclear war entitled *The Challenge of Peace*, have made a reasoned appeal to conscience: 'Personal commitment, clear statement, and careful justification are characteristics that serve at the same time to convey the authority of those who undertake to instruct the mind of the churches, to respect the liberty of those reading the letter, and to recommend the teaching of the churches both to mind and heart.'[6] In the light of Turner's analysis, we can understand better the 'basic moral principles' of the letter. First,

'Every economic decision and institution must be judged in the light of whether it protects or undermines the dignity of the human person.'[7] The letter speaks of the person as sacred, and to be the 'clearest reflection of God amongst us'. Human dignity is a divine gift, and the purpose of any economic system is how it treats people. The question of participation is crucial, and this will lead on in other chapters to the question of social exclusion. Secondly, 'Human dignity can be realized and protected only in community.'[8] The organization of society affects human dignity directly, and the capacity of individuals to grow in community. The Christian vision of economic life is not primarily concerned with GNP or per caput income, but the health of the community. Economic life is never neutral. It can enhance or threaten community, or 'commitment to the common good'. Love of neighbour has this social dimension as well as an individual one. Thirdly, 'All people have a right to participate in the economic life of society.'[9] Participation is 'vital to human development'. A double justification is offered. On the one hand, most individuals use their employment to 'meet their material needs, exercise their talents, and have an opportunity to contribute to the larger community'. On the other hand, it is a means 'by which we join in carrying forward God's creative activity'.

Unemployment leads to the deprivation of the participation vital to this development. The Bishops therefore call for a minimum level of economic participation. Fourth, 'all members of society have a special obligation to the poor and vulnerable'.[10] The justification here is different from the second and third principles. After claiming that human dignity was sacred and reflects the presence of God amongst us, the letter then argued for community, and participation in community. These moral arguments could be justified without reference to theology, although as noted above there is a reference to co-creation with God. The fourth principle is, however, entirely biblical and ecclesial. Based on the divine covenant with Israel, justice was the sign of this covenant. This justice was measured by the treatment of the poor and unprotected. At the time of Jesus' ministry, the poor are seen by him as agents of God's transformation. The first public utterance by Jesus in Luke's gospel (Luke 4:18) speaks of being anointed by the 'Spirit of the Lord' to bring glad tidings 'to the poor'. The Last Judgement described in Matthew's gospel turns on the treatment of those in need. The letter also refers to 'early church teaching', although it does not specify a source. The 'option for the poor' is what is required of Christ's followers, which means speaking for those without a voice, and assessing all institutions in terms of their impact on the poor. Jesus proclaimed a Kingdom in word and ministry which 'excluded no one'. The shift of tone is noticeable in this exposition of the fourth principle. However, the fifth and sixth principles revert to a morality which need not have theistic justification. Although Pope John XXIII is cited as an example of Catholic social teaching in the fifth principle, neither of the final two principles need be justified theologically. The fifth one states that: 'Human rights are the minimum conditions for life in community.'[11] The sixth says that: 'Society as a whole, acting through public and private institutions has the moral responsibility to enhance human dignity and protect human rights.'[12] Human rights are widened to include not only civil and political rights, but also economic ones. This is defined by Pope John as including employment: as the pastoral letter puts it, the 'chance to earn a living'. Society is the body which must protect those rights. The role of government is to be the agent of society. It is neither the primary nor the exclusive role, but it does have a 'positive' or 'essential' responsibility morally. Human rights must be safeguarded, and minimum conditions of human dignity met for all. There is an appeal also to democracy. In a democracy, government is one means by which common action can be achieved to protect and promote common values.

These six principles can all be justified by Christian social teaching, but it is striking how some are much more specifically theological than others. The sacredness of the human person and the special status of the poor within the divine covenant are the two central tenets of the argument. Human dignity is sacred because it is revelatory of God, and poverty matters because the needs of human beings are not met in a society where the divine covenant requires a response of justice to the poor. Again the poor act as agents of divine transformation. If human dignity gives the 'clearest reflection' of God, and the poor are God's agents of 'transforming power', the remaining principles spell out a vision of a society where there is healthy participation. The importance of community, participation, the minimum conditions for life in community (a definition of human rights) and the responsibility of society to protect community are a series of descriptions of social anthropology: this is how human life is lived at its fullest and richest. Social ethics becomes an interpersonal ethic.

If these are the principles on which the Bishops argue, then what follows is an exposition of these principles. They point to the 'signs of the times', following the Second Vatican Council. In *Gaudium Et Spes* (*The Pastoral Constitution on the Church in the Modern World*) there are references to the joys and hopes of 'the people of this age'. These joys, along with griefs and anxieties, are shared by the followers of Christ. The joys and griefs are marked by signs of the times. The concern of the Bishops is clear. The culture of the United States is marked by an emphasis on material display and self-gratification. There is poverty, homelessness and unemployment among the young and the middle-aged. 'The system of Enterprise' helped create jobs, but there is a fear that it might destroy jobs and communities tomorrow. The nature of the economic system confronts families with major new challenges. There is dwindling social support for family stability, and economic pressures that force both parents of young children to work. If one is successful, there is 'a driven pace of life' which can 'sap love and commitment'. If one is less successful, there is a lack of hope. Above all, there is world-wide poverty and malnourishment.

The perspective with which the Bishops approach the American economy is bleak. Although they recognize that the economy has created productive work for millions of immigrants, which improved their families' quality of life and improved their freedoms, nevertheless the price has been high. Many immigrants were Christians and often saw their new lives in the light of biblical faith. The United States was portrayed as

'a promised land of political freedom and economic opportunity'.[13] Their response was one of hard work, self-sacrifice,
co-operation and the harnessing of vast natural resources. The
cost was injustice to native Americans, slavery and a violent
civil war which ended slavery. It took a further sustained
struggle to establish the protection of industrial workers, and to
overcome the Great Depression in the 1930s. Women's suffrage
and civil rights legislation were equally hard fought.

At the centre of their analysis (chapter 1, paragraph 18) is the
dichotomy between family life and economic life. The economic
and cultural strength of the nation is linked to the stability and
health of family life. They cite Pope John Paul II's *Familiaris
Consortio*.[14] A thriving family gives children the chance to
develop a sense of their own worth and their responsibility to
serve others. However, the Bishops find 'the lack of a mutually
supportive relationship' between family life and economic life is
'one of the most serious problems' in the United States today.[15]

Harsh poverty and unemployment are one manifestation of
this threat to the family. Children are the largest single group
among the poor. A rising number of families rely on the wages
of several of their members to survive at all. At the heart of the
letter is a lengthy section on unemployment and poverty,
covering thirty-seven pages out of a text of one hundred and
eighty pages, which is nearly a quarter of the text. When the
theological exposition of human dignity is included, it is clear
that the bulk of the letter is devoted to the casualties of the
United States economy, and a theological rationale for their
pastoral care by the Bishops. It is not primarily a document
about capitalism, as one American journalist pointed out: it was
intended to be that initially, but it changed its focus. However,
Archbishop Rembert Weakland of Milwaukee has mounted a
strong defence of the Commission which drafted the letter. Both
this letter, and the one on war and peace, were attempts to deal
with secular liberalism and the Enlightenment in Weakland's
view. Roman Catholic neo-Conservatives, such as Michael
Novak and George Weigel, have in Weakland's view sought to
reclaim 'the enlightenment into a Catholic framework'. What is
problematic for Weakland is how they achieve this.

The letter is explicitly pragmatic: 'Our approach in analyzing the United States economic is pragmatic and evolutionary in nature. We live in a "mixed" economic system which is the product of a long history of reform and adjustment. It is in the spirit of this American pragmatic tradition of reform that we seek to continue the search for a more just economy.'[16] There is also a slightly defensive, or apologetic, tone following this declaration of pragmatism. It raises a series of moral issues about the values which the economic system expresses. However, it pleads that this document does not allow exploration of these issues in a comprehensive way, and urges others to do so. The issues raised are certainly far-reaching. There is the relationship of the maximizing of profits to the meeting of human needs and dignity. There is the question of whether benefits are distributed equitably or whether power and resources are concentrated in the hands of a few. 'Does it promote excessive materialism and individualism? Does it adequately protect the environment and the nation's natural resources? Does it direct too many scarce resources to military purposes?'[17] Instead the document must be taken on its own terms. In conclusion, there are four aspects of the nature of work and the economy which are worth analysing in depth from the document. These are first the nature of work, employment and unemployment, or (to use the language of the document) participation in the economic system. Secondly, there is the issue of poverty, especially in relation to race and gender. Thirdly, there is the question of co-operation, planning and alternatives to competition and a free market. Finally, there is the issue of globalization, which is raised especially in relation to the 'developing nations'. We turn to an analysis of the treatment of work, or employment.

Work is evaluated through commutative and social justice, and a reference is made to David Hollenbach's writings on justice.[18] Commutative justice includes fairness in economic contracts, such as wages, work conditions and treatment of workers. Social justice is also called contributive, since it stresses the duty to create the goods and services, with the nonmaterial values, necessary for the welfare of the community. Again this contribution must respect the freedom and dignity of labour. Discrimination on any arbitrary basis is condemned.

The understanding of work follows the papal encyclical *On Human Work* (*Laborens Exercens*). Work has a threefold moral significance. First, it is a principal way that people express the 'distinctive human capacity for self-expression and self-realiza-tion. Second, it is the ordinary way for human beings to fulfil their material needs. Finally, work enables people to contribute to the well-being of the larger community.'[19] This significance applies whether the person works for a small business or a multinational, or whether the person works in the private or public sphere.

Again, following *On Human Work*, there is also an analysis of trade (labour) unions. The dignity of labour means that all who can work must do so. This obligation is both from a divine command and from a responsibility to humanity and the common good. Industriousness is also a virtue which expresses dignity and solidarity. There is a call to excellence in production and service from those who work, for this is a contribution to the common good.

Work is therefore spoken of as a right: 'a right to employ-ment'. This is not elaborated, but what is spelled out is the way in which power is unequally distributed between employers and employees. This results in inadequate wages and poor benefits, such as health care, pensions, holidays and security against arbitrary dismissal. Unions are part of the response of workers, and the right to form unions is a more specific application of the general right to associate. Attempts to break unions are 'firmly opposed'. Migrant agricultural workers in the United States are especially in need of protection, but attacks on the right to organize are common across the world. The Bishops describe this as 'an intolerable attack on social solidarity'. At the same time, workers should not abuse their position by pressing demands 'whose fulfilment would damage the common good and the rights of more vulnerable members of society'.[20] As the twentieth century comes to an end, the letter recognizes the ambiguous position which trade unions hold in American society. The dynamism of the unions that led to their rapid growth in the middle decades of the twentieth century has faded. There is a decline in the percentage of United States workers who are in trade unions. Falling wage costs outside the United States, often because of a denial of the right to organize, threaten American jobs. The temptation is for reactive or defensive strategies to take place, rather than imaginative vision. However, some labour (union) leaders react differently. Education and training can keep workers employable. At the same time, links can be built with developing countries: 'A vital labour movement will be one that looks to the future with a deepened sense of global interdependence.'[21]

It is, however, unemployment which receives most attention in the letter. There are references to unemployment and psychological harm, as well as oral histories of the unemployed: 'Unemployment takes a terrible toll on the health and stability of both individuals and families. It gives rise to family quarrels, greater consumption of alcohol, child abuse, spouse abuse, divorce, and higher rates of infant mortality.'[22] Unemployment at the time of the letter (1986) was 7 per cent, or higher, and had been so since 1979. Except for periodic recessions, unemployment from 1950 to 1980 was as low as 3–4 per cent. Black teenagers have a rate of 33 per cent unemployed (which the letter describes as 'scandalous'), ethnic minorities have almost double the white rate of unemployment, and for female heads of households the rate is over 10 per cent. Since work is so central to the freedom and well-being of people in American culture, unemployment can make people feel rejected and worthless. Because of the individual and social costs to society, such as crime, increased government expenditure, and lost revenue, the Bishops conclude that there is 'a moral obligation to work for policies that will reduce joblessness'. The analysis of unemployment is familiar. The labour market has expanded due to population growth, and large numbers of women have been forced to work. Immigrants have also joined the labour force. Unemployment has risen because of automation, globalization, and the arms race. Referring to the other pastoral letter, *The Challenge of Peace*, the Bishops note the economic distortions caused by the arms race and its use of high technology. The cost of developing new weapons, and the 60 per cent of the federal research budget which goes to defence, prevents full employment.

Nevertheless, the letter recognizes that 20 million jobs have been created since 1970. What has failed to happen is sufficient investment in industries and regions; inadequate education and retraining; and insufficient help for the unemployed. The letter pleads for the level of unemployment to be regarded as intolerable, as it would have been in earlier decades. There is a call to federal government to co-ordinate its fiscal and monetary policies to achieve the goal of full employment. It also asks for a job-creation programme, both through subsidies to private industry and through a direct job programme. In particular, jobs in education, welfare and public works could be greatly expanded. Less should be spent on defence, and the question of job sharing should be explored. The issue of taxation is not specifically addressed at any length.

There is very little analysis of how jobs are changing, of the significance of the much greater participation of women in the economy, nor of the value of leisure and recreation. The role of the owner, or of the manager, is praised as 'dynamic' (again following Pope John Paul II, this time not in *On Human Work* but in an address in Milan to managers in 1983). Freedom of entrepreneurship, business and finance should be protected, within the overall accountability to the common good. Private ownership is defended, both as a right first articulated in *Rerum Novarum* in 1981, and as enlarging 'our capacity for creativity and initiative'. So entrepreneurial activity is something which should be highly valued, as should be businesses as a whole. What this analysis of work reveals is a great deal of concern for the unemployed, and considerable awareness of their condition. This reflects the daily pastoral contact which the Roman Catholic Church has in the United States with immigrants, often from Catholic nations such as those in South America, and with poor ethnic minorities, especially women. As the introduction puts it graphically:

In our letter, we write as pastors, not public officials . . . We feel the hurts and hopes of our people. We feel the pain of our sisters and brothers who are poor, unemployed, homeless, living on the edge. The poor and vulnerable are on our doorsteps, in our parishes, in our service agencies and in our shelters . . . As pastors, we also see the decency, generosity and vulnerability of our people.[23]

This is not a message opposed to business people: 'We know the desire of managers, professionals, and business people to shape what they do by what they believe.' It is a letter inspired by 'the faith, good will, and generosity of our people'.

The second issue which is discussed at length is poverty, which again is a deeply pastoral issue. Poverty affects one in seven of the nation's population by the government's official definition. It is evaluated in terms of distributive justice, which requires that the allocation of income, wealth and power in society be evaluated in the light of its effects on persons whose basic material needs are unmet. *Gaudium et Spes* put the doctrine clearly at the Second Vatican Council: 'The right to have a share of earthly goods sufficient for oneself and for one's family belongs to everyone. The fathers and doctors of the Church held this view, teaching that we are obliged to come to the relief of the poor and to do so not merely out of our superfluous goods.'[24] The only reason why need should not be relieved is if an absolute scarcity of resources exists, which is not the case in the United States. Human beings have minimum material needs. If they are not met, persons are not recognized as members of the human community.

There is a sustained discussion of the biblical meaning of poverty. The treatment in the Gospel of Luke is especially relevant, with the Magnificat referring to the raising up of the poor (Luke 1:53). Jesus' first public utterance is about his anointing by the Spirit to preach good news to the poor (Luke 4:18, cf. Isaiah 61:1–2). The poor are blessed, and the rich warned at Luke 6:24. The parable of the man who relies on the security of his wealth (Luke 12:13–21) is reinforced by the parable which is found only in Luke, which is that of the poor Lazarus at the gate of the rich man (Luke 16:19–31). When Lazarus is finally 'seen' by the rich man, it is too late for a change of heart. Jesus lives as a poor man in the Gospel of Luke, and takes the side of the poor as the prophets did.

Material poverty is a cause of sadness in Isaiah, Zephaniah and Proverbs. Riches are a source of danger, since they blind those who have them (Proverbs, Amos, James). The poor are called 'blessed', not because it is a good condition, but because they are open to God. Since the poor can receive God more easily, they are seen in scripture as the transforming agents of God's power. Equally, God has a special concern for them, and this concern was continued in the early Church. Acts 4 suggests a mutual sharing of goods, and friendship and concern. Such a perspective provides the basis for the 'preferential option for the poor'. Following the example of Jesus, the Church has a particular concern for those in poverty. There are four challenges which the example of Jesus poses. First, there is the prophetic mandate to speak for those who are defenceless, who in biblical terms are the poor. Secondly, there is a compassionate vision to see things from the side of the poor and powerless, assessing policies, life styles and institutions in terms of their impact on the poor. Thirdly, the Church must be an instrument of liberation, so that they can respond to the Gospel in freedom and dignity. The practical implications of this are not worked out, nor are the final claims on the Church. This calls 'for an emptying of self, both individually and corporately, that allows the Church to experience the power of God in the midst of poverty and powerlessness'.[25] Human rights are seen as bestowed on human beings by God, and grounded in the nature and dignity of persons. They are not created by society. The letter sees a strong support for the United Nations Universal Declaration of Human Rights in the papal encylical *Peace on Earth* (or *Pacem in Terris*). This encylical refers to 'the right to work', which the letter interprets as the right to useful employment for all who are able and willing to work. It also includes the right to wages, and to economic security in sickness, unemployment and old age. This is the minimum condition for social institutions in the economic sphere that respects human dignity, solidarity and justice.

Economic empowerment is an expression of the right to employment, which calls for positive action by individuals and society. Just as civil and political rights were secured by a long history of creating the institutions of constitutional government, so a similar effort is needed to shape new economic arrangements. The first step is the development of a new cultural consensus on the essential nature of basic economic conditions to human dignity. Securing these rights is the second step, which makes demands on private institutions and government. This leads the letter to specific moral priorities. If fulfilling basic human needs of the poor is the priority, it must apply not only to decisions of private institutions and government, but also to personal decisions and power relationships.

Poverty, argue the Bishops, has increased dramatically in the last decade. In this period, the numbers affected have gone up by a third. The Bishops describe a situation where social security fails to cope with the homeless, who are often former mental patients, and with children suffering malnourishment. Poverty is defined by the government's official definition, which means that it is not an isolated problem. Instead, it is a condition affecting many people at different times of their lives. It is significant that there are many who work and are still poor: indeed, this is one of the fastest-growing groups. Women especially suffer wage discrimination, with jobs that have low status, little security and few fringe benefits. Poverty is rife among women who head minority ethnic families, for poverty is far more likely to be present among black communities, and there is strong condemnation by the Bishops of racial discrimination. The report also emphasizes the enormous disparity of economic capital in the United States. The top 10% of families hold 57% of total net wealth, although, if homes and other buildings are excluded and financial assets alone are included, 86% of these assets are held by that 10%. In a similar way, the top 20% of American families received 42.9% of total pre-tax income, which was the highest share since 1948. In contrast, the bottom 40% received only 15.7%, the lowest share on record in US history. The worst disparity was found among the bottom 20% of families who earned only 4.7% of total income (1984 US government figures). The United States is one of the more unequal industrialized nations, and the disparity between rich and poor is widening.

Catholic social teaching, in the view of the Bishops, accepts inequality for pragmatic reasons, such as the need for incentives and the reward for taking risks. Nevertheless, the moral principles listed by the Bishops, such as the relief of basic material needs and the importance of increasing participation in the life of society, means that the extreme inequality and poverty described in the report are very disturbing and 'unacceptable': 'These norms establish a strong presumption against extreme inequality of income and wealth so long as there are poor, hungry and homeless people in our midst. They also suggest that extreme inequalities are detrimental to the development of social solidarity and community.'[26] The answer to poverty is to give the poor the power to control their own lives. Poverty involves powerlessness about decisions that affect one's life, and this assaults human dignity. The solution lies in programmes of self-help, such as employment, even if the alleviation of poverty also requires personal charity. The report points to the success of government anti-poverty strategies in the 1960s and 1970s, especially among the elderly. It is also critical of ideas of a permanent 'underclass' who do not want to work, and have not worked for years. In fact, poverty is more like water flowing through a pipe: people move in and out of welfare quite regularly, and punitive social attitudes are deeply misguided. Job creation, just wages, and an attack on barriers to equal employment for women and ethnic minorities are the best way forward. There is a need for congressional action to raise the minimum wage, but the main emphasis is on self-help. Small-scale, local programmes of training, seed money and organizational support are what is necessary. Self-help can operate in 'Low-income housing, credit unions, worker cooperatives, legal assistance and neighbourhood and community organizations. Efforts that enable the poor to participate in the ownership and control of economic resources are especially important.'[27]

Much of the discussion of poverty is detailed, including tax programmes, education and welfare provision. The strength of the analysis lies in its rootedness in the life of the Catholic Church: thus, Catholic inner city schools can provide an alternative for many families, and Catholic social institutions work with lone mothers. One of the basic moral principles is the support of the family. Here the Bishops are uncompromising, following the lead set by Pope John Paul II, in *Laborens Exercens* and *Familiaris Consortio*:

Society's institutions and policies should be structured so that mothers of young children are not forced by economic necessity to leave their children for jobs outside the home. The nation's social welfare and tax policies should support parents' decision to care for their own children and should recognize the work of parents in the home because of its value for the family and for society.[28]

At the same time, the breakdown of traditional family values, shown in the high divorce and teenage pregnancy rates, has more damaging economic consequences among the poor. There is a call for a '[r]evived sense of personal responsibility, and commitment to family values'.

How far does the discussion of poverty reflect economic realities? The report is detailed in its analysis of poverty, especially in low-paid wages and the disparity in state welfare payments. The significance of greater participation by women in the economy is seen as a pastoral issue:

Most new jobs for women are in areas with low pay and limited chances of advancement. Many women suffer discrimination in wages, salaries, job classifications, promotions, and other areas. As a result, they find themselves in jobs that have low status, little security, weak unionization, and few fringe benefits. Such discrimination is immoral and efforts must be made to overcome the effects of sexism in our society.[29]

The strongest analysis of economic life is found in the discussion of co-operation and planning. The Bishops set out an appeal to the history of the United States. This is seen as 'a bold experiment in democracy'. The founders of the nation sought to establish justice, welfare and liberty for all. However, this 'great venture' remains incomplete, for many lack a 'fair share in the general welfare'. Competition and initiative are not enough, for they damage the environment, the economically vulnerable and family life. Among theorists who are appealed to in a footnote are Etzioni, Lindblom, Sturm and Thurow.[30] This is an early recognition of communitarianism, including institutional arrangements that support the virtues of a commitment to the common good, the recognition of obligations and the wish to participate in the 'commonwealth'. This appeal is linked to the papal encyclical *Octogesima Adveniens*. The report draws a parallel with the American Revolution. Politically that era took 'daring steps to create structures of participation, mutual accountability and widely distributed power to ensure the political rights and freedoms of all'.[31] Today the Bishops call for the broadening of the sharing of economic power, making economic decisions more accountable and expanding economic participation. In Catholic terms, this is the working out of the principle of subsidiarity in economic justice.

The section of the report concerned with co-operation covers industrial life, as well as regional, national and international co-operation. The principle is that of stakeholding. Workers, managers, owners or shareholders, suppliers, customers, creditors, the local community and the wider society all have a stake in the enterprise. What is needed is the development of 'New institutional mechanisms' for accountability, while preserving the flexibility needed to respond in a business environment. Adversarial employment patterns damage both sides, and the report calls for the development of new patterns of work. The aim is both to support family life for employees, and to benefit business enterprise.

There are a number of means by which such co-operation might be built. Profit sharing by workers, greater shareholding and worker participation are all mentioned. So, too, is co-operative ownership. A large number of case studies are cited, although the Bishops are also cautious ('none of these approaches provides a panacea, and all have certain drawbacks'). There is also a strong emphasis on the continuity in Catholic social teaching on this theme. The 1919 statement of the US Catholic Bishops entitled *Program of Social Reconstruction* observed: 'The full possibilities of increased production will not be realized so long as the majority of workers remain wage earners. The majority must somehow become owners, at least in part, of the instruments of production.'[32] The report argues that this approach remains 'generally valid'. Other Catholic social ethicists who are cited to support this approach are the American John Cronin (*Catholic Social Principles*, 1950), the Austrian Jesuit Oswald von Nell-Breuning (*Reorganization of Social Economy*, 1936) and the French Jean-Yves Calvez (*The Church and Social Justice*, 1961). At the same time, the Bishops support the role of unions in economic participation. The closure of plants or the movement of capital should involve collaborative decisions, with the burden not simply falling on the workers themselves. Quoting *Laborens Exercens*, they argue that the 'Capital at the disposal of management is in part the product of the labour of those who have toiled in the company over the years, including currently employed workers.'[33] Minimal rights for workers should be being informed in advance of possible decisions; the right to negotiate about possible alternatives, the right to fair compensation, and assistance with retraining and relocation expenses. Even the minimal rights are jeopardized without collective negotiation, which depend on trade (labour) unions and their strong role. At the same time, unions are also challenged to change. Cronin is cited for explanation, as is the United States union(AFL–CIO) report in 1983, called *The Future of Work*.

Cronin argued that the place of unions transcends the existence of injustice and exploitation. Unions were legitimate, for they are '[t]he normal voice of labour, necessary to organize social life for the common good'.[34] Order and harmony in society and the economy are 'the fruit of conscious and organized effort'. Abuses brought unions into existence, which they had to tackle. However, Cronin hopes that the long-term future of unions will go beyond these 'unpleasant, even though temporarily necessary, tasks'. They can 'devote all their time and efforts to a better organization of social life'. This strongly corporatist strategy is picked up by the Bishops, who see unions as both defending existing wages and conditions, and making creative contributions to the firm, the community and the larger society. The report recognizes that only a fraction of workers are unionized, but looks for a future of organized co-operation. This is not, however, developed in detail: instead there is a call for 'experiments' in union life.

Equally, there is a general approach to stakeholding, which at no point becomes specific, unlike the discussion of welfare reform. The report recognizes the legal responsibility of managers to '[e]xercise prudent business judgement in the interest of a profitable return to investors'.[35] Morally however there are the interests of other stakeholders. Corporate mergers and hostile takeovers may bring benefits to shareholders, but they can bring 'decreased concern for the well-being of local communities' and greater vulnerability to decisions taken far away. Shareholders need to have their rights and responsibilities related to the interests of stakeholders affected by corporate decisions. As the report argues, this question is 'complex and insufficiently understood'. Most shareholders see return on investment as the governing criterion in the relation between them and management, although they have the power to vote on the appointment of directors, policy and investment. Few however do this, and exercise relatively little power in corporate governance. Shareholders 'exercise relatively little power in corporate governance'. The report urges serious, long-term research and experimentation in this area to enable firms to serve the common good.

The report then turns to examine the local neighbourhood. It is clearly the case that it is at this point that the principle of solidarity becomes of importance. Mediating institutions, such as community groups, business and civic organizations, and public pressure groups as well as special interest groups are all included in the concept of a 'mediating structure'. So are the familiar ones of family and neighbourhood. Their role is to link the individual to society in ways that enable people to have greater freedom and power to act, thus exercising moral responsibility. Once again the task is to create partnerships for the common good, especially in creating employment in depressed areas. Yet it is not only a moral argument which is developed here, but also a pragmatic one. The 'vicious cycle' of a deteriorating social environment puts off new investment. The cycle is made up of 'lack of financial resources, limited entrepreneurial skill, blighted and unsafe environments, and a deteriorating infrastructure'.[36]

Communal co-operation can break this cycle in a number of ways. Community development can focus efforts on the greatest needs. Entrepreneurial innovators can work with business, union, financial and academic institutions. Co-operative, local ownership will create a symbiotic relationship, in which the local community and business feel that they have a mutual share in each other's welfare. The role of government, at all levels, is seen as that of funding environmental and infra-structure improvements, while encouraging investment in poor areas by tax structures. The role of the Church is as a facilitator, in encouraging co-operation across the community. There are three resources which the churches have: a first-hand know-ledge of community needs; a membership drawn from different parts of the community, enabling mediation between groups who might otherwise regard each other with suspicion; and a commitment to the protection of the dignity of all. This should encourage church leaders in their sustaining of a strategy of co-operation.

The most controversial sections of the report undoubtedly came in the seven pages on national and international partner-ships. Again citing a papal encyclical, Pope John XXIII's *Mater et Magistra*, there is a call for an increased role for government in the complexity of social relationships. They also cite John Paul II's *Laborens Exercens* in arguing that 'society make provision for overall planning' in economic life. Planning does not mean simply 'one-sided centralization by the public authorities', but rather 'a just and rational coordination' which safeguards individuals, groups and industries. Planning is to protect justice and ensure basic rights and freedoms. The report becomes highly defensive at this point: 'The Pope's words should not be construed as an endorsement of a highly centralized form of economic planning, much less a totalitarian one.'[37] They say that 'we are well aware' of the 'strong negative reaction' in US society to the idea of planning: 'images of centralized planning boards, command economies and inefficient bureaucracies'.

Again there is a general call for 'creative new partnerships and forms of participation' in planning. The report defends itself by pointing to planning in management, and in cities, as

well as in private life, claiming that congressional legislation is
'a form of public planning'. The footnotes, however, refer to
studies in the 1960s and 1970s of planning in France (the most
highly developed system of national planning in the western
capitalist world) and in development economies. What did the
report seek at this point? They wished for greater partnership
between public and private agencies, developing government
intervention and regulation, without denying the contribution
of non-governmental agencies. There is a plea for greater
consensus in society, with a particular focus on the needs of the
vulnerable: 'the poor, the unemployed, the homeless, the displaced'. At the same time, the report calls for attention to
'massive national spending on defence'. The effect is that the
poor, both in the United States and worldwide, have suffered
from spending so much of the national budget on military
purposes. It is also the case that the government, the economy
and the military are closely intertwined through military
research and defence contracts: 'Defence-related industries
make up a major part of the U.S. economy and have intimate
links with both the military and civilian government; they often
depart from the competitive model of free-market capitalism.'[38]

   The report accepts that there is no detailed agenda, nor is
there any discussion of how goals might be arrived at in a
democratic society. What they call for is a greater 'level of
commitment to the common good, and the virtues of citizenship'. This will increase the ability to achieve the goals which
are agreed as a nation. Yet the challenge of the report goes
beyond the nation. The world has limited material resources,
and international co-operation is required. In the years after
1945, the United States took a lead in establishing multilateral
bodies, which has not been the case in recent years. Again
quoting John XXIII in *On the Development of Peoples*, the report
speaks of an 'structural defect' in the international order. There
lacks any co-ordination and regulation by an overall international institution. GATT, the IMF and the World Bank do not
possess the requisite authority, nor does the UN. Poverty and
injustice are the result worldwide. What is needed is 'positive
and often difficult action by corporations, banks, labour unions,

governments, and other major actors on the international stage'.[39] This is yet one more step in the 'unfinished business of the American experiment'. This refers to the fact that 'the cause of democracy is closely tied to the cause of economic justice'. This justice is worldwide, for our responsibility is to the common good of all people. Relationships with the developing countries must be ones of partnership, including 'mutual respect, co-operation, and a dedication to fundamental justice'.

This attention to the need for greater global co-operation is, however, only part of the report's interest in global issues. The other aspect is that of 'developing nations'. Again, the report is primarily pastoral. It outlines the 'scandal of the shocking inequality between the rich and the poor' (quoting the Vatican's encyclical *Instruction in Certain Aspects of The Theology of Liberation*).[40] The absolute poverty of 800 million people, the hunger of many of them, and the high rate of infant mortality across much of the developing world are all explained. At this point the report does become specific in its economic considerations. There is detailed discussion of the international debt crisis, the unfair patterns of trade in commodity goods, American investment and the world food problem. Once again, there is an attack on the military expenditure of the United States: in 1985, the US budgeted more than twenty times as much for defence as for foreign aid, but two-thirds of that aid was either for military assistance or went to countries with perceived strategic value for the US.

It is the question of trade, commodity prices, investment and interest rates with the developing countries which is central to the critique of US policy. The 'global economy' primarily refers to this rich/poor divide. There are a complex set of actors, including private relief and development agencies, trade unions, popular movements, banks, transnational corporations, multilateral institutions and, of course, nations. Many of these agents also are supported by domestic constituencies in America, and domestic American political decisions now have important consequences for other nations. Globalization in this context means the increasingly recognized link of domestic and foreign issues, and the effects on world poverty of the major industrialized nations. As the report puts it, many economic factors 'are essentially determined by the industrialized world. Moreover, their traditional cultures are increasingly susceptible to the aggressive cultural penetration of Northern (especially U.S.) Advertising and media programming. The developing countries are junior partners at best.'[41]

This analysis of globalization is not focused on the trade and investment patterns of the world economic blocs, nor on financial circulation in currency speculation. There is an account of the developments after the 1944 Bretton Woods Conference which set up the IMF, World Bank and GATT, but the focus is on the debt crisis. There is nothing on the growth of Asian capitalism, and the question of overseas investment is very much addressed in terms of American investment in poor countries. The analysis of investment and development is done with some care, and the well-known pitfalls of overseas investment are set out. These would include the aggravation of social inequality in the recipient nation, the increase of food dependency by encouraging cash cropping for export, the displacement of labour by capital-intensive agriculture and the exploitation of workers. Nevertheless, the report is not simply hostile to transnational corporations, for it says that they can 'contribute to development by attracting and training high-caliber managers and other personnel, by helping organize effective marketing systems, by generating additional capital, by introducing or reinforcing financial accountability, and by sharing the knowledge gained from their own research and development activities'. The report urges an international effort 'to develop a code of conduct for foreign corporations that recognizes their quasi-public character and encourages both development and the equitable distribution of their benefits. Trans national corporations should be required to adopt such a code, and to conform their behaviour to its provisions.'[42]

The analysis of the agricultural sector in the report, while of great interest, is not central to our investigation of the report's contents. What is striking is how much the report concentrates on poverty, unemployment and global poverty. As a pastoral report, this cannot be faulted, but the problem is that the correlation promised in the title of the report does not fully come about. The report is called *Economic Justice for All*, with the sub-title *Pastoral Letter on Catholic Social Teaching and the U.S. Economy*. It is clear that this is a selective reading of the US economy, and in particular the effects of the economy. Since unemployment and poverty cause such harm to families, in ways which are well documented in the report, there is a controlled sense of anger at what is happening to ethnic minorities, women and children. Perhaps the most striking comment is where the report expresses the pain which its authors feel as pastors. American society is highly unequal, and the poor are increasingly marginalized in their capacity to control their own lives. World poverty only makes this worse. Much of the protest which the report represents is expressed in terms of a hope for co-operation, planning and partnership.

The debate on the report was very intense. As Ronald Preston pointed out, the debate was a novel experience. There was a rumour that the Vatican was not happy with a national conference of Bishops issuing teaching in an elaborate way. Certainly, there were many references to Vatican documents. Paul VI in *Octogesima Adveniens* had made the point that it was difficult for Rome to issue 'solutions' with universal validity. Instead, it was up to local Christian communities to analyse their own situation, and to combine this analysis with the teaching of the whole Church. Indeed, paragraph 26 of the report speaks of making 'the legacy of Christian social thought a living, growing resource that can inspire hope and help share the future'.[43] They seek 'the co-operation and support of those who do not share our faith or tradition'. What they rest their argument on is 'the common bond of humanity' and the search for 'a renewed public vision'. As they acknowledge, 'the answers are often elusive'.

Critics from the Right were numerous, including an unofficial lay commission which published its own report one day before the Bishop's Letter. Many writers idealized the free market. As Preston says:

Economic efficiency, in the sense of maximizing the output of relatively scarce resources, is set up as the supreme value, and then it is maintained that any modification of the structure which prevents each citizen of working age from individually following the haggling of the market will produce less than maximum efficiency. Hence it is alleged that any such interference is inherently contradictory. Moreover it will end in a totally centralized economy.[44]

A more sophisticated approach does not idealize the free market economy, but instead questions the concept of 'economic rights'. Positive economic rights is a notion which is central to the document, and it enables expression of moral urgency and the legitimacy of government action. The counter-attack is found in several quarters, but most cogently from the report *Liberty and Justice for All*.[45] This report was written by the 'Lay Commission on Catholic Social Teaching and the U.S. Economy'. It was chaired by William Simon, the former Secretary of the Treasury, and Michael Novak, the Catholic theologian and author of *The Spirit of Democratic Capitalism*,[46] who is based at the American Enterprise Unit. Their report was issued on 5 November 1986, just before the American Catholic Bishops were due to meet to revise the third draft of the pastoral (June 1986) into the final draft. The final draft was published later that month.

Liberty and Justice for All distinguishes between welfare rights and economic rights. Welfare rights are related to the right to life. Economic rights are there 'to protect citizens in their activism and in their active contributions to society'. They are kept separate in the encyclical of Pope John XXIII in 1961 entitled *Pacem in Terris*. The fear of the authors of *Liberty and Justice for All* is that a union of the two concepts will lead to paternalism by the state and a retreat from economic activism, by individuals. There is some truth in this charge, but the language of economic rights protects the needs of the poor in an affluent society. The challenge to economic rights in Catholic social thought is not new. In 1961, when *Pacem in Terris* was published, it was criticized by Reinhold Niebuhr and Paul Ramsey for its idealism.[47] The neo-conservative critique depends on the idea that redistribution of wealth, and the guarantee of economic activity, becomes seen as the moral equivalent of theft. The myth is that individuals create wealth by their individual efforts, which the state appropriates.

The problems with this approach have been outlined in an earlier chapter on the work ethic. The pure, abstract conception of the market is an artificial concept, which ignores human interdependence. Power is a central feature of capitalism, with the owners of capital seeking to affect the free market in their own interests.

Lisa Cahill has pointed out that the distinctive contribution of Roman Catholic moral theology to public-policy discourse has been its insistence that it is open to conversation partners representing diverse religious and philosophical traditions. There has been a development in Catholic theology towards economic justice, which draws heavily on the experience of Latin America in the 1960s. As early as 1961, Pope John XXIII's encyclical *Mater et Magistra* had begun to widen the term 'common good' to include the notion of just economic distribution internationally. There were conditions necessary 'to make accessible the goods and services for a better life to as many persons as possible'.[48] These were requirements of the common good.

The Second General Conference of Latin American Bishops in Bogota and Medellin, Colombia in 1968 was a turning-point. The Bishops refer to the collective 'misery' of their people: it was 'an injustice which cries to the heavens'. Paul VI's encyclical, *Populorum Progressio* (1967), spoke of 'the duty of human solidarity' and related it to economic rights and duties. At about the same time, the Synod of Bishops Second General Assembly in Rome (1971) published their statement, *Justice in the World*: 'Economic injustice and lack of social participation keep a man from attaining his basic human and civil rights.'

This introduces what has been called a normative principle of 'relative equality'. This principle implies a continued redistribution of resources, income and social advantages. Economic and class divisions should diminish, and 'the realization of full human life by all' is made possible. As 'the common good' is increasingly identified with 'human solidarity', so what is seen is the close connection between two sets of rights. For some time, Catholic documents have focused on civil–political rights, but now there is a link made with social–economic rights. Indeed, the two are seen as intrinsically linked. The dignity of persons requires, not only the establishment and protection of human freedoms, but also that conditions are created which allow for full participation in society. David Hollenbach has also drawn attention to the possibility of an empirical relationship between respect for economic and civil rights. Societies which are good at guaranteeing one sort of rights usually manage to guarantee the other sort at a level which is adequate. On the other hand, societies which place social and economic wealth in a narrow social group usually fail to deliver political and civil rights as well. What was distinctive about Latin American Catholic thought in the late 1960s and early 1970s was its embracing of Marxist categories into Roman Catholic theology. As Cahill has noticed above, this reformulation of thought is quite characteristic of Roman Catholic moral theology in its dialogue with diverse philosophical traditions. The language of 'rights of the working classes', 'solidarity with the oppressed', 'class struggle' and other Marxist terms are reformulated. They are not simply changed into doctrinal or ethical categories, for Roman Catholic moral theology has become heavily influenced by biblical theology in the last half-century. Hence, the reformulation is into biblically oriented terms such as 'Jesus' preferential option for the poor', 'defend the rights of the poor and oppressed', and 'liberation' from economic slavery. However, it is noticeable that Catholic documents do not press Marxist language to its logical conclusion. That would entail class victory, or else the continuation of conflict in some endless dialectic. Nevertheless, the emphasis on a participatory society does involve struggle and challenge. Cahill stresses the Christian language of charity, compassion and self-sacrifice. As mentioned in the analysis of *Economic Justice for All*, the Bishops repeatedly stress that they write as pastors, aware both of the cry of their people and of the value of those who are 'managers, professionals and business people'. The reference to the generosity and goodwill of 'our people' is far from Marxist rhetoric.

One of the most interesting dialogues on the pastoral is between the Jesuit moral theologian John Langan and another Washington academic, the Georgetown economist Henry

Briefs.[49] Briefs finds that the biblical basis of the pastoral leads to a particular emphasis on justice in a direct and unmediated way. This has the danger of turning the appeal to the common good in earlier Catholic social teaching into a subordinate instrument, thus disregarding the contribution of social philosophy and social economics. However, the pastoral also depends on what Briefs calls 'a solidaristic form of democratic syndicalism'. This emphasizes the social responsibilities of each economic agent and institution to their constituency. It also seeks to increase participation as far as possible. Briefs argues that 'the private property language remains, but its content and meaning are to be replaced by something very different'.

The difficulties in the pastoral are twofold. First, if a government were to guarantee effectively everyone's economic and social rights it would 'require a government of far and deep reaching powers'. Such a government would need active participation to ensure that government did not abuse its powers. This would give a different twist to the demand for full participation. It would not be participation which was intrinsically a good thing, but one that was also a necessary and defensive measure. A true Christian commonwealth, which accorded priority to basic (or biblically based) ideals of justice over a consensual society which appealed to the common good, would be a radical transformation of society in a utopian manner. Briefs argues that the Bishops have not realized the full extent of their commitment. A second difficulty in the pastoral is the ideal of full economic participation. This participatory ideal will have high transaction costs which will not be compatible with the constant drive to economic efficiency. This, in turn, leads to an economic downturn, with serious consequences for society, especially the poor and unemployed. Briefs prefers the traditional appeal to the common good found in Catholic social teaching, which is both an approach that encourages a pragmatic response and one which recognizes the complexity of contemporary economic life. He writes that 'only in idealized pastoral or craft-tending settings is full-dimensional sharing of daily life compatible with productive effectiveness'. Briefs urges a return to a consensus approach, with an emphasis on the common good, rather than an advocacy of the disadvantaged alone. Langan's response is to portray the pastoral letter not as a blueprint for a new economic order, but 'as a set of corrective norms for an imperfect order which will continue developing in terms of its own logic. This might be seen as a dilution of the Bishops' teaching but it would be in accord with the pragmatic element in their presentation of Catholic social teaching and in their policy recommendations.'[50]

In conclusion, it is both a prophetic and a pastoral document. Indeed, the chair of the committee which wrote the report, Archbishop Rembert Weakland OSB, presents it in these terms. It is a necessarily provisional and incomplete document, designed 'to serve a continuing process of reflection and social transformation'. Many Catholic commentators, who are summarized in a helpful way by Langan, welcomed the document. Its aims for transformation are large. It is both transformist and conservative at the same time. It seeks a society that 'will be egalitarian, participatory, non-discriminatory, less dependant on military force for its security, more respectful of the environment, and comparatively austere in its consumption patterns'. It is also conservative with regard to family preservation, forming local democracy, trade unions and local self-determination. It is critical of traditional restrictions on the role of women, the unregulated market economy and large corporate structures.

There have been further developments in Catholic social teaching since then, most especially the papal encyclicals *Sollicitudo Rei Socialis* (1987) and *Centesimus Annus* (1991). *Sollicitudo Rei Socialis*, written in 1988, is highly critical of poverty and deprivation. It was written for the twentieth anniversary of *Populorum Progressio*, which was the papal encyclical of Pope Paul VI on world development. This had argued that because producers and brokers influenced prices to suit the demands of the rich European and North American nations therefore 'the poor nations remain ever poorer while the rich ones become still richer'.[51]

The raw export market draws in more poor countries 'under the cloak of financial aid or technical assistance'.[52] The encyclical *Populorum Progressio* dismisses this as 'neo-colonialism', and says the outcome is 'complete dominance' by the rich nations over the poor 'in the form of political pressures and economic suzerainty'. Property ownership and financial investment are regarded critically as often being counterproductive to the interests of the poor who live in developing countries.[53] Indeed, it denounces industrialists 'who are not lacking in social sensitivity in their own country' but 'return to the inhuman principles of individualism when they operate in less developed countries'.[54]

Equally rapid industrial growth which takes no account of the immediate community is condemned, even if it is promoted by governments who wish to overcome economic weakness.[55] Above all the fundamental issue is inequity in global economic distribution: 'The very life of poor nations, civil peace in developing countries, is at stake.'[56] There is an attack on what is perceived to be free trade as in fact being very different: 'Prices which are "freely" set in the market can produce unfair results.'[57] So there is considerable scepticism about international relations: 'One must recognize that it is the fundamental principle of liberalism, as the rule for commercial exchange, which is questioned here.'

The satisfaction of legal contracts is not enough: 'If the positions of the contracting parties are too unequal, the consent of the parties does not suffice to guarantee the justice of their contact.'[58] Indeed, even the sanctity of private property, which has always had a high status in papal teaching from *Rerum Novarum* onwards, begins to be questioned. The encyclical accuses capitalists of defending 'private ownership of the means of production as an absolute right that has no limits and carries no corresponding social obligation'.[59] Therefore it legitimates state expropriation of 'extensive, unused or poorly used' land when such private property 'bring hardship to peoples or are detrimental to the interests of the country'.[60] Furthermore, tax increases are recommended on the wealthy to help the poor.[61] The aim may be long-term, but it nevertheless remains equality.[62]

Sollicitudo echoes many of these statements. Indeed, it felt that conditions had grown 'notably worse' in the twenty years since *Populorum Progressio* was published. It describes the failure of hopes for development,[63] with a widening gap between north and south.[64] Although *Sollicitudo* speaks of 'the right of economic initiative',[65] and the danger of overdependence on state bureaucracy, nevertheless it is critical of 'economic, financial and social mechanisms which . . . often function almost automatically' and create great worldwide divisions of rich and poor: 'In the end they suffocate or condition the economies of the less developed countries.'[66] This leads to shanty-towns with bad housing and severe unemployment in many poor countries.[67] It also speaks at length of international debt. Debtor nations are obliged to export the capital needed for maintaining a standard of living.[68] Perhaps the greatest criticism is focused on what it calls 'this blind submission to pure consumerism'; on people as 'slaves of "possession" and of immediate gratification . . . the so-called civilization of . . . "consumerism"'. The encyclical sees the civilization of 'crass materialism and at the same time a radical dissatisfaction' with consumerism.[69] What causes the dissatisfaction is the realization 'that the more one possesses the more one wants, while deeper aspirations remain unsatisfied and perhaps even stifled'.

The encyclical sees that the appeal of consumerism is promoted by a 'flood of publicity and the ceaseless and tempting offer of products'. This is called 'superdevelopment', or the 'excessive availability of every kind of material goods'. It leads to the discarding of goods which still work, or are valuable, 'with no thought of its possible lasting value in itself, nor of some other human being who is poorer'.

Underlying this distinction is a philosophy that distinguishes 'being' and 'having'. 'Being' is the realization of the human vocation, in which a person matures and enriches herself. 'Having' should mean that a person respects the quality and nature of the goods one owns. The encyclical uses Thomistic language in speaking of an 'ordered hierarchy' of goods which should be subordinate to a true vocation. There is a deep injustice in the fact that some cannot realize their human vocation because of poverty, while others are hindered by having too much wealth. However, the phrase 'hierarchy of goods' is not unpacked in the document.

This analysis of consumerism is also related to 'structures of sin'. Structures of sin are those institutions which 'introduce into the world influences and obstacles which go far beyond the actions and the brief lifespan of an individual. This also involves interference in the process of the development of peoples, the delay or slowness of which must be judged also in this light.'[70] However institutions, structures and societies are not themselves the subject of moral acts. All social sin is 'the result of the accumulation and concentration of many personal sins'. This is so even if it involves the collective behaviour of social groups, or whole nations and blocs of nations. Sin can be caused by 'secret complicity . . . indifference . . . fear . . . the conspiracy of silence' as well as the support of evil. 'The real responsibility lies with individuals.' Such structures are dominated by the desire for profit and for power.[71] Here the papal encyclical reflects the analysis offered by Habermas in the first chapter. There is an interdependent 'system, determining relationships in the contemporary world, in its economic, cultural, political and religious elements'. What hinders full development is the desire for profit and power. The appropriate response is that of solidarity, or a 'firm and persevering determination to commit oneself to the common good'.[72]

The encyclical spells out what are signs of hope in the contemporary world. Positive signs are 'the growing awareness of the solidarity of the poor among themselves, their efforts to support one another, and their public demonstrations on the social scene which, without recourse to violence, present their own needs and rights in the face of the inefficiency or corruption of the public authorities'.[73] The Church is placed alongside the poor in their search for justice. Equally international relations should be 'transformed into solidarity, based upon the principle that the goods of creation are meant for all'. Human industry must serve the good of all. Instead, what exists at the moment is the division of the world into opposing blocs, preoccupied with security and oppressing weaker nations. Solidarity is seen as the path to peace and world development, which requires 'the abandonment of the politics of blocs, the sacrifice of all forms of economic, military or political imperialism, and the transformation of mutual distrust into collaboration'. It is not simply a question of justice. Each country has its own 'treasures of humanity and culture'. If they cannot make a contribution to the common good, these treasures will be lost for ever. Economically weaker countries must be helped by the international community, and in particular stronger and richer countries, to develop. The goal is the establishment of an international system that 'will rest on the foundation of the equality of all peoples and on the necessary respect for their legitimate differences'. The task is both a human one ('human and natural bonds, already so close and strong') and a Christian one ('there is discerned in the light of faith a new model of the unity of the human race, which must ultimately inspire our solidarity').[74] There is no 'technical solution' on offer for world underdevelopment: the Church 'does not propose economic and political systems or programmes'.[75] It is not therefore a 'third way' between liberal capitalism and Marxist collectivism, for it is not ideology but moral theology. Nevertheless, the 'option for the poor' remains critical, since poverty increases in number both in the developing and in the developed world.

Paragraph 43 is worth examining in detail. Like *Economic Justice for All*, there is specific comment on the international trade system, the monetary and financial system, technological exchanges and the international juridical order. The analysis argues that there is discrimination against the products of young industries in the developing world, and this discourages the producers of raw materials. Equally, weak labour laws, or the failure to apply them, lead to an international division of labour. Low-cost products are sold elsewhere in the world by international companies. Fluctuating interest rates and exchange rates bear down on the debt situation and balance of payments of the poorer countries. Equally, technology transfer often denies these countries the resources which they need. Nor are international organizations always helpful: 'Their operating methods, operating costs and effectiveness need careful review and possible correction. Obviously, such a delicate process cannot be put into effect without the collaboration of all. This presupposes the overcoming of political rivalries and the renouncing of all desire to manipulate these organizations, which exist solely for the common good.'[76] There is also reference in the next paragraph to the need to achieve self-sufficiency in food, 'where starvation claims so many victims, especially among the very young'. Finally there is a strong commitment to human rights and the rule of law, and a condemnation of 'corrupt, dictatorial and authoritarian forms of government'. The emphasis is on the 'free and responsible participation of all citizens in public affairs', and on democracy.[77]

The encyclical marks twenty-five years of Roman Catholic involvement in the issues of development and international affairs. While it is possible to trace back continuity in papal teaching to *Rerum Novarum* in 1891, it is more convincing to see a sharp shift at the Second Vatican Council from 1962 to 1965. *Gaudium et Spes*, the encyclical on social change and the place of the Church in this, is the expression of the Council itself. Pope Paul VI added *Populorum Progressio* and *Octogesima Adveniens* (14 May 1971), while the American Bishops contributed *Economic Justice for All*. There was also the encyclical *Mater et Magistra*, published by Pope John XXIII in 1961, which introduced the idea of 'economic rights'.

The change at the Second Vatican Council, along with the liberation teaching of the South American Bishops at Medellin in 1968 and Puebla in 1979, are twofold. First, there is a greater concern with 'the signs of the times', which include increasing poverty, inequality, unrest and cultural damage as problems which need addressing, especially in the developing nations. Secondly, the concepts of economic rights and the option for the poor dominate the teaching from 1962 to 1988. For liberation theologians, the option for the poor is an epistemological principle, asserting that the world economic order can only be understood by the Christian faith from their perspective. In effect, it assimilates the idea of economic activity from the doctrine of creation to that of sin and redemption, by uncovering the contradictions in that order. Only so can the eschatological hope be preserved against the corruption of economic life, which exploits the poor and commodifies all human values into the market-place. For the papal encyclicals, and for the American Bishops, the option for the poor stems from Christian anthropology, and specifically the dignity of human nature. It is, therefore, an ethical principle. The American Bishops deliberately do not discuss capitalism as such. The biblical themes are creation in the divine image, the covenant and discipleship, and Christian vocation.[78]

Part of this corpus of documents now already looks dated. The strong emphasis on social and economic planning reflects the requirement of serving the common good. Barbara Hogan notes that there is a tension between centralization and decentralization, quoting Gregory Baum. However, the exegesis of the meaning of centralization and decentralization is revealing. Decentralization means cutting down the size of transnational corporations, fostering community organizations and workers' ownership of industry. Centralization means the role of the government in co-ordinating planning for the common good, including 'responsible and democratically controlled economic planning'. Neither the expectation of greater government planning, nor the search for worker's control, would reflect the emphasis of much social democracy in Europe in the 1990s. It may well be replied that Catholic social thought does not see itself as being confined to the ideas of the late twentieth-century social democracy.[79]

Yet *Sollicitudo* does mark a change on earlier encyclicals since Vatican II and Pope John XXIII. There is much greater emphasis on theology than ethics, and the idea of a world divided into ideological blocs gains prominence. Development is seen as a matter of social culture, as is education. However it also senses the changes that occurred a few years later: 'People do not always resign themselves to their fate.'[80] This certainly anticipates the collapse of the Soviet Union, described (in language that does not explicitly name it) as 'an economy stifled by military expenditure and by bureaucracy and intrinsic inefficiency'.[81] The response of the Church is to argue that 'our own history, marked by our personal and collective efforts to raise up the human condition and to overcome the obstacles' is a way of seeing the premises of the Kingdom of God.[82]

If this is what *Sollicitudo Rei Socialis* said, did John Paul II further develop his ideas in the four years between 1987 and 1991, when he published *Centesimus Annus*? As we shall see, *Centesimus Annus* certainly can be read as an attack on liberal culture, and this reading by Stanley Hauerwas and others is probably the correct interpretation of John Paul II. This confrontation between liberation and Catholic truth is discussed below. However, this is not to say that John Paul II changed his mind on liberal capitalism. The question is discussed by one of the most distinguished North American Catholic theologians, Gregory Baum, in an article in *Essays in Critical Theology*.[83]

Sollicitudo was critical of both Marxist collectivism and liberal capitalism. It deplored the division of Europe, North America and the Soviet Union into two superpowers bitterly opposed to each other. It saw this division as being ideological in nature: the principles of liberal capitalism against Marxist collectivism. These have now become armed blocs, 'each suspicious and fearful of the other's domination'.[84]

Centesimus Annus, the papal encyclical of 1991 which marked the centenary of *Rerum Novarum* published by Pope Leo XIII in 1891, marked a change in papal teaching. There is a greater stress on the business economy, with its focus on scientific knowledge, complex organizations and the free market. However, although the free market is seen as 'the most efficient instrument for utilizing resources and effectively responding to needs',[85] there are countervailling forces. Human dignity, and the possibility of making 'an active contribution to the common good of humanity' are prior to the forms of justice appropriate to capitalism. At the same time, the inefficiency of command economies in Central and Eastern Europe is seen as not simply a technical problem but 'a consequence of the violation of the human rights to private initiative, to ownership of property and to freedom in the "economic sphere".'[86] This strong language sees the right of private property as 'fundamental for the autonomy and development of the person'. There is a balance to be struck between the 'use' of goods, which should be marked by freedom, and their 'original common destination' as created goods.[87] This abstract language seeks to hold together private property and the needs of others. So the encyclical returns to the question of poverty. 'Aspects typical of the Third World also appear in developed countries, where the constant transformation of the methods of consumption devalues certain acquired skills and professional expertise, and thus requires a continual effort of retraining and updating. Those who fail to keep up with the times can easily be marginalized.'[88] The elderly, youth and women are especially vulnerable.

Centesimus Annus therefore defends what seems like a paradox, and is certainly a difficult argument to hold. There is a necessity and therefore a legitimacy about private ownership, but these goods should also be seen as common goods. It quotes from *Gaudium et Spes*, although the argument sets up the tension rather than showing any way of resolving it: 'In making use of the exterior things we lawfully possess, we ought to regard them not just as our own but also as common, in the sense that they can profit not only the owners but others too.'[89] Later it quotes from the same text: 'Private property or some ownership of external goods affords each person the scope needed for personal and family autonomy, and should be regarded as an extension of human freedom. . . Of its nature private property also has a social function which is based on the law of the common purpose of goods.'[90] Work is the origin of individual property, making 'part of the earth his own'.[91] In language which seems far removed from the environmental stewardship of creation, *Centesimus Annus* speaks of man, through work, using his intelligence, exercising his freedom, 'dominating the earth and making it a fitting home'.[92] It is true that later in section 37 there is a condemnation of a subjection of the earth without restraint, which leads to the 'senseless destruction of the natural environment'. Nevertheless, sections 31 and 32 speak of co-operation with others in the task of dominating the earth. Work now outstrips the natural fruitfulness of the earth as the primary factor in wealth creation, both in material and non-material production. Technology and skill magnify the wealth of human work and of the land.

Technology must be used by organized human work. Initiative and entrepreneural ability become decisive here:

Besides, many goods cannot be adequately produced through the work of an isolated individual, they require the co-operation of many people in working towards a common goal. Organizing such a productive effort, planning its duration in time, making sure that it corresponds in a positive way to the demands which it must satisfy and taking the necessary risks – all this too is a source of wealth in today's society. In this way, the role of disciplined and creative human work and, as an essential part of that work, initiative and entrepreneurial ability becomes increasingly evident and decisive.[93]

So there has been a transition from land as the decisive factor of production through capital seen as the total complex of the instruments of production to 'man itself, that is, his knowledge, especially his scientific knowledge, his capacity for interrelated and compact organization, as well as his ability to perceive the needs of others and to satisfy them'.[94] Nevertheless, the encyclical concedes that this process has 'risks and problems'. The majority, perhaps, do not have the means which would enable them to take a place in the productive system in 'an effective and humanly dignified way'. There is 'no possibility of acquiring the basic knowledge which would enable them to express their creativity and develop their potential. They have no way of entering the network of knowledge and intercommunication which would enable them to see their qualities appreciated and utilized.'[95] This lengthy quotation shows the appreciation in *Centesimus Annus* of the ambiguity of a modern, hi-tech market economy. It leads to a situation well described in the document: 'if not actually exploited they are to a great extent marginalized'.[96]

Economic development takes place over the heads of those who cannot manage the change to a new economic order. The old economic order was subsistent, at best. This already narrow way of life is reduced further. The ability of this form of life to compete against new forms of production becomes difficult, and needs which were met by traditional ways of production are supplied in radically different ways. The danger in areas of the Third World is that society disintegrates. Urban migration, rootlessness and violence are the common pattern of those drawn by necessity and 'allured by the dazzle of an opulence which is beyond their reach'.[97] Capitalism is described as humanly inadequate, for poverty and 'humiliating subjection' are the usual lot of those marginalized by economic advance. Nor is there any escape from the global economy. Countries which have tried this route have suffered 'stagnation and recession'. The document calls for 'fair access to the international market'.[98] The problem is that the defeat of socialism 'leaves capitalism as the only model of economic organization. It is necessary to break down the barriers and monopolies which leave so many countries on the margins of development.'[99] It is not revolutionary language which is in use here. Weaker nations must learn to respond to opportunities offered by stronger nations. The language is one of responsibility. Stronger nations must offer a partnership. Weaker nations must make 'the necessary efforts and sacrifices . . . by ensuring political and economic stability, the certainty of better prospects for the future, the improvement of workers' skills, and the training of competent business leaders who are conscious of their responsibilities'.[100]

There has been a sharp division in the assessment of *Centesimus Annus*. It was not primarily between Roman Catholics and other Christians, nor between the supporters of the free market and its critics. This was the case with *Economic Justice for All*, as has been described above. However, the conflict in the discussion of *Centesimus Annus* is between liberal theologians, such as the Anglican, English theologian Ronald Preston and those who criticize liberal theology and applaud its critics. One of the chief critics of liberalism in theology, and in secular humanism, is Pope John Paul II, and *Centesimus Annus* certainly bears his stamp. This is especially so in the sections on revolution in Eastern Europe, where the interest of a Polish Pope is self-evident. Stanley Hauerwas is an American, Methodist theologian who finds the papal argument against contemporary economic life very convincing. Preston and Hauerwas mounted diametrically opposed evaluations of *Centesimus Annus* in *Theology* a year after the publication of the papal encyclical. Another commentator on the debate, Michael Northcott from Scotland, says that the contrast between the two is so striking that one wonders if they have been reading the same document.[101]

The disagreement can be stated fairly succinctly, but the resolution is much more difficult. Preston points to the changes in Catholic social teaching in the last century, such as 'religious liberty, a greater stress on freedom and equality, and a new emphasis on participation'. However, the greatest weakness of *Centesimus Annus* is 'its absurdly utopian picture of a new world economic order'. In this respect it is like 'recent works from the World Council of Churches'. Preston's complaint is that what is needed is to work out more clearly 'the steps towards a more just and yet viable economic order, after the collapse of the Soviet-style economies, with particular reference to the Third World'. Preston especially objects to *Centesimus Annus*' analysis of socialism. Socialism (by which is meant Marxism) is caricatured, and is attributed to atheism and enlightenment rationalism. Atheism causes militarism and the class struggle, and there is no sense that Marxism has contributed to a new understanding of the modern world. Preston is not a Marxist, but he feels that this sweeping dismissal is unjustified.[102]

Preston points to a strange section in *Centesimus Annus*, where in section 48 the Welfare State is called the 'Social Assistance State'. It refers to state intervention which causes excesses and abuses. Malfunctions and defects are due to state intervention taking away responsibility in society. The result is 'a loss of human energies and an inordinate increase of public agencies, which are dominated more by bureaucratic ways of thinking than by concern for serving their clients, and which are accompanied by an enormous increase in spending'.[103] Preston responds that the grain of truth in this passage is far outweighed by its superficiality. He reflects that this passage may have been included to please some of the New Right, especially wealthy and important Catholics. It is out of keeping with the rest of *Centesimus Annus*, and seems to be written by someone else.

However, the real criticism which Preston makes is more acute. There is a constant temptation which the document falls into, which is to call for a more moral and different style of behaviour, which will solve human problems. Thus paragraph

58 calls for a 'change in life style, modes of production and consumption, and of the established structures of power which today govern societies'. This leads on to a demand that 'there be increased co-ordination among the more powerful countries, and that in international agencies the interests of the whole human family be equally represented'.

Preston complains (very much in the spirit of Reinhold Niebuhr fifty years ago) that there is no 'analysis of how international relations and structures of power actually work'.[104] Equally, *Centesimus Annus* does not spell out the challenge to the First World in its talk of 'fair access to the international market' by poorer countries. Nor does it explain its statement about democracy. It argues that democracy needs 'to situate particular interests within the framework of the common good. The latter is not simply the sum total of particular interests, rather it involves an assessment and integration of those interests on the basis of a balanced hierarchy of values'.[105]

Finally Preston notes the lack of ecumenical interest in all the papal encyclicals. Previous popes, the Fathers, the documents of the magisterium and even the occasional reference to the United Nations are all mentioned, but other churches are ignored. Nor is there any reference to the need for justice within the Church itself. Above all, Preston disagrees with the cardinal assumption of *Centesimus Annus*. The authoritative teaching of the Roman Catholic Church 'enters into dialogue with the various disciplines concerned with man'. The document does not use inclusive language: 'It assimilates what these disciplines have to contribute and helps them to open themselves to a broader horizon.'[106] Preston argues that the principles underlying this are not articulated in depth. What is mentioned in the document are references to 'the dignity of man' or 'the person', but again the argument passes lightly over the issue of structural sin, which is mentioned in passing but then ignored.[107] Nor is the principle of 'the common destination of material goods' argued out. It is not simply a theological debate which is raised here. Paragraph 60 expresses the hope that 'many people who profess no religion will also contribute to providing the social question with the necessary ethical foundation'.

Hauerwas' response to *Centesimus Annus* is very different. He praises the fact that this encyclical 'does not invite us to speculate about a "third way" between capitalism and socialism'.[108] Leo XIII and Pope John Paul II refused to underwrite the prevailing economic order. Hauerwas regrets that the Pope goes to great lengths to distinguish different types of market society, but does not do the same for socialism (a criticism which, Hauerwas says, was originally made to him by Herbert McCabe, OP, one of the most distinguished theologians from the Christian/Marxist dialogue of the 1960s).

Instead, Hauerwas presents a view of economics where the Church is an alternative to liberal society. Sin is a theological category, which we only know from Christ's revelation of what it means to live a human life. Only in the light of salvation in Christ is the Church concerned with 'the working class, the family and education, the duties of the state, the ordering of national and international society, economic life' and the other issues of society.[109] There is no independent anthropology that can be known by anyone. Instead, Hauerwas, following John Milbank closely in his *Theology and Social Theory*, attacks what he calls the liberal project. The social sciences 'train us to act as individuals in competition with other individuals for survival'.[110] These sciences 'pretend to predicative power', legitimate the liberal project and describe it in a way that makes the social world of modernity seem inevitable. Yet the social world of our day is not inevitable at all, in the eyes of Hauerwas and Milbank. It is a world built on the assumption that violence, and not love, is the basic characteristic of humanity. Violence and competition are the great signs of the fallen condition of modernity.

In the end, Hauerwas believes that Karl Marx and Leo XIII were friends: that is, they both were 'fundamentally conservative radicals challenging the presupposition behind the development of industrial capitalism which, they rightly saw, was destroying any form of community that can sustain a sense of human solidarity'.[111] It is the opposition to liberalism which

Hauerwas likes in the original 1891 encyclical *Rerum Novarum*. Later encyclicals make too much peace with liberalism. *Centesimus Annus* still takes more from the intervening encyclicals than Hauerwas would like, but nevertheless it marks a return to *Rerum Novarum*. (He does not discuss it in this article, but it may be assumed that Hauerwas would find the American Catholic Bishop's letter *Economic Justice for All* a sell-out to liberalism.)

Economics in liberalism, and economic life, is fundamentally wrong for Hauerwas. Liberalism seeks to make the economic realm an independent realm in Hauerwas' view. It has its own laws and processes. Therefore it is a science separable from politics and ethics. Indeed, Hauerwas feels that the encyclical inadvertently reflects a liberal theology that it is overall trying to challenge. *Centesimus Annus* says:

The economy in fact is only one aspect and one dimension of the whole human activity. If economic life is absolutized, if the production and consumption of goods become the centre of social life and society's only value, not subject to any other value, the reason is to be found not so much in the economic system itself as in the fact that the entire sociocultural system, by ignoring the ethical and religious dimension has weakened and ends by limiting itself to the production of goods and services alone.[112]

Hauerwas accepts that this passage, with its distinction between 'the economic' and 'the cultural' may intend to subordinate activities which are called economic to more determinative goods, such as family life. Hauerwas fears however that this may lead back into becoming an ideology for capitalism. His great concern is that efficiency becomes the creation of good business, for this is inimical to the growth of a society in which other values are central. *Rerum Novarum* challenged the autonomous market by arguing that the just wage is not that determined by the market but that which is required to sustain family life. *Centesimus Annus* echoes this challenge.

Hauerwas will not accept that the economic life of a nation is a separate sphere. What can be done is to look at the concrete nature of work. Instead of abstractions such as socialism and capitalism there is a focus on work. John Paul II focuses on work to explain the character of that society. Work is increasingly seen in a communal way, as *Centesimus Annus* illustrates in two passages:

It is becoming clearer how a person's work is naturally interrelated with the work of others. More than ever, work is work with others and work for others. It is a matter of doing something for someone else.[113]

By means of his work man commits himself not only for his own sake, but also for others and with others. Each person collaborates in the work of others and for their good.[114]

So Hauerwas sees work as the key to moral character. Work is never spiritually empty, for it enables us to serve one another and embody our relationships in goods and activities. Hauerwas feels that most modern capitalism falls a long way short of this purposive aspect of work. Moral purpose is more important than issues of distribution, which preoccupy liberals and conservatives. John Paul II reminds us that:

Economics is not just a matter of which economic systems can produce the most units to be widely distributed, but of what kind of people we become through these economic systems. How our work engenders trust in ourselves and others is surely more important than the assumption that good economics are those subject to constant growth.

It is the trust engendered by work which matters to Hauerwas.

Yet it is not only economics that Hauerwas attacks. Another issue is that of consumer demand: 'Liberalism is an attempt to defeat Marxism by its own form of materialism'[115] says Hauerwas, echoing the encyclical:

A given culture reveals its overall understanding of life through the choices it makes in production and consumption. It is there that the phenomenon of consumerism arises. In singling out new needs and new means to meet them, one must be guided by a comprehensive picture of man which respects all the dimensions of his being and which subordinates his material and instinctive dimensions to his interior and spiritual ones. If, on the contrary, a direct appeal is made to his instincts – while ignoring in various ways the reality of the person as intelligent and free – then consumer attitudes and life styles can be created which are objectively improper and often damaging to his physical and spiritual health. Of itself an economic system does not possess criteria for correctly distinguishing new and higher forms of satisfying human needs from artificial new needs which hinder the formation of a mature personality. Thus a great deal of education and cultural work is urgently needed, including the education of consumers in the responsible use of their power of choice, the formation of a strong sense of responsibility among producers and among people in the mass media in particular as well as the necessary intervention of public authorities.[116]

Hauerwas is, however, more sceptical of market forces and the ability of consumers to be educated. Market economics can subordinate everything to issue of economic rationality. Self-interest for Hauerwas is not self-evidently legitimate, nor is it obvious that greed will serve the common good through the mechanism of the market. Indeed, Hauerwas points out that liberal societies 'train us to believe' that all will be well. Yet a good that is only an aggregate of self-interest is no good at all. It is a profound question which John Paul II raises in *Centesimus Annus*, and Hauerwas is indebted to him for raising it. Yet he remains unsure what alternative there is.[117] Northcott agrees with Hauerwas. It is the Church which is an alternative to all economic or sociological models of life in society. 'The principal object of the rhetoric of *Centesimus Annus* is the incapacity of autonomous secular economics, without theology and religious community, to sustain just and sane societies, to provide a moral climate for the sustaining of family life, and to foster dignity and freedom.'[118] Northcott notes Hauerwas' criticism of the Pope. If he criticizes liberalism as no longer able to sustain a proper ordering of community, then he should have been more critical of free-market economics.

What Northcott and Hauerwas are arguing is that the statements in favour of capitalism in the encyclical are inconsistent, and should not be there. The approval of the free market is circumscribed by the 'critical reflection in the encyclical on the demise of the religious and moral foundations of democratic liberal capitalism'.[119] Northcott is critical of Preston as a traditional liberal theologian. Preston can understand why the encyclical gives priority to the social task of the Church over liberal economics, and why the theology of sin is so stressed. Sin, for Hauerwas, is a crucial theological category, since social systems that do not recognize its reality will set self-interest and social interest at odds. Politics will become a secular religion. Preston rejects an underlying dependence on theological anthropology as insufficient in a plural, secular society to bring about social coherence.

Northcott is bleak in his vision of the modern state. If states do not give recognition to a higher order, then the state and economic order will impose their own priorities such as consumerism, efficiency and controlled work. He welcomes the vision of *Centesimus Annus*: 'a theological vision of human life within a sacred order'. If this is not taken on board, then the human tasks of child-rearing, friendship, care for the weak and creative work will be marginalized. Northcott feels that *Centesimus Annus* is insufficiently aware of pluralism, and prefers the theological vision of a theologian such as the American ethicist Max Stackhouse in his book *Public Theology and Political Economy*. Yet the argument that the loss of a sacred order in a secular liberal state produces moral loss of nerve claims too much. In a colourful passage, Northcott denounces the weakness of theological liberalism:

It may be that the liberal theology has served political liberalism too well and so now at liberalism's demise its theological acolytes are unable to offer resources for resisting the secular religions of individualistic consumerism and vivacious capitalism which threaten to devour the earth, if not in a nuclear conflagration, then in the slow but inexorable destruction of the fragile resources and habitats of the planet. As these secular religions have excluded from much of western society a search for spiritual value and for truth, so the liberal theological creed has also lost touch with the source of wonder, salvation and truth, which was the miracle of the birth, life, death and resurrection of Jesus Christ.[120]

Northcott (like Hauerwas) adduces many theologians and philosophers to support his case: Stephen Clark, Max Stackhouse and Leslie Newbigin.[121] None of these, however, demonstrate how the dis-ease in the liberal state would be reversed by the readoption of a vision of a sacred order. The problem of social pluralism is also acute: which vision would one adopt? Even if one makes the nod to pluralism found in Stackhouse, the problems remain, for the renewal of public (or social) vision must be achieved through the secular, liberal societies in which we live. That is why *Centesimus Annus* in the end remains unconvincing. Stackhouse speaks of a 'constructive vision of possible forms of grace' to support 'the continued cultivation of refinement of a public theology that can give coherence to the pluralism of the core institutions of life in a way that can contain the necessarily pluralistic structure of people's lives in a great variety of societies, cultures and subcultures'.[122]

There are two problems with this approach. First, there is a strong tension between the papal teaching, with its coherent vision, and Stackhouse on the issue of pluralism. Many commentators have pointed to the hostility to pluralism in *Centesimus Annus*: it 'represents for the most part an idealist phenomenological philosophy of the person . . . In particular, its endorsement of democracy and understanding of pluralism may be seen by some to be less than full.'[123] Indeed, the rejection of pluralism is taken to the extent that there is no reference to other ecumenical traditions at all in the encyclical. The slow abandonment of a doctrine of natural law, first begun by John XXIII and Paul VI, is taken further by John Paul II. The historical, inductive method replaces the natural-law base, and there is more appeal to a doctrine of creation in *Centesimus Annus*, especially in relation to human nature.[124] The difficulty is that this anthropology shows no appreciation of the complexity of harmonizing secular anthropology in the human and social sciences with theology. The lack of complexity in the vision of the encyclical presents a 'take it or leave it' anthropology. Secondly, it still remains unclear how the emphasis desired by Hauerwas on the moral character of the person as worker will help resolve the social problems of a mature industrial democracy like Britain or the United States. A recovery of social vision can assist in deepening the sense of community, as the communitarian philosophers discussed earlier in this book suggest. So, too, will a greater sense of participation, and a reorientation of the productive powers of the economy in a post-materialist direction. This would produce less material goods, and more services, especially services which are socially beneficial to the whole community.

But it is a stipulative definition which Northcott, and others, make. It is assumed that liberal, secular democracies must treat the path of violence and competition because they have lost sight of the transcendent vision pursued by *Centesimus Annus*. The encyclical[125] begs the question as to whether economic life has been absolutized when it says that 'Economic life has been absolutized.' At the same time, western capitalism is put along-side communism in Eastern Europe: 'In the totalitarian and authoritarian regimes, the principle that force predominates over reason was carried to the extreme. Man was compelled to submit to a conception of reality imposed on him by coercion and not reached by virtue of his own reason and the exercise of his own freedom.'[126] Both capitalism and communism fail to discern the truth of Christianity, and the superiority of Christian institutions. Indeed, social solidarity is for John Paul II at the heart of the vision of what is social good – a vision approved of by Hauerwas.

There is clearly a choice between the discernment of social justice and the flourishing of human relations in and through the market (Preston's view) and a belief that society can only be cured if it returns to the Christian life and Christian institutions (Hauerwas, quoting *Rerum Novarum*).[127] Since communism was explicitly totalitarian, a move is made in the argument that capitalism is also absolutized and coercive. This ignores the way in which many social ethicists, such as Preston, have suggested modifications to the functioning of market economies which have found their way into practice through the dialogue with politicians, employers and trade unionists. Hauerwas puts in doubt the whole tradition of empirical/theological reports from western churches, and, by repudiating the method of 'middle axioms' developed by Preston, opts instead for a theological method that is only concerned with a theological vision over-arching all empirical data. This is both in tension with secular pluralism and offers no purchase on ways to improve society, or its institutions.

CHAPTER 6

Concluding reflections

Three observations come to mind at the end of this book about the speed of change, the differences in theology and the involvement of the churches. The speed of change is perhaps the most striking. Reich's book, *The Work of Nations*, read likes an epic novel, or like 'The Twilight of the Gods: *Götterdämmerung*'. In the early chapters of his book, he describes how American and European industry gradually grew out of craft industries into the mighty giants of the early twentieth century, aided by imperialism and protectionism. By the mid twentieth century, such industry employed hundreds of thousands, with corporate headquarters as grand as government buildings. They had a close relationship with government, harmonious labour relations (at least in America), a world-wide span and enormous wealth. By the end of the twentieth century, technology, world-wide competition and changing cultural tastes had reduced this mass employment to ruins. The enormous growth in unemployment in the last three decades of this century in America and Europe was not like the 1930s, for factories did not close for a while but were demolished. Those who have worked, or ministered pastorally and in Industrial Mission, in such areas in recent years know in the depths of their being what this has meant for the former industrial worker. In its place there has come the use of the service industries, global competition, new consumerism and a transformed attitude to paid employment. In a real sense, then, this book is about a revolution in paid work. Even the collapse of the command economies in Eastern Europe and China are as nothing compared to this. So, if the churches spent until the 1960s working out how they might respond to mass industrial life, then the l1960s to the 1990s speak powerfully of how the world has moved on – to a future still being shaped, still embryonic, still shaken by the collapse in the financial markets of East Asia which appeared such a threat to western industry only very recently. Perhaps it still is. The first observation, then, is that this book describes a revolution (it is not too strong a word) in the world of paid work so recent that we are still coming to terms with it. The human con-sequence is immense: Fred Robinson, in his book *Post-Industrial Tyneside* describes well the old world of the steel worker or shipbuilder, and the new era of consumer capitalism in the Metro Centre, one of the biggest shopping centres in Britain built a decade ago on the ruins of an old power station in north-east England.

The second observation is about theology. The concept which dominates this book is that of the Protestant Work Ethic. Chapter 1 describes how Habermas responds to Max Weber on the importance of the work ethic. Habermas believes that the fragmentation of culture in modernity is a more profound development than the rationalization carried into modernity by the work ethic. Nevertheless, he accepts how great a change to western culture was caused by the Protestant Work Ethic. Chapter 2 describes the transformation of this ethic into one of consumerism, while chapter 3 analyses the change in Calvin's and Luther's view of vocation. The question is what will replace it. Brunner provided an influential answer half a century ago, but Volf's criticisms are telling. In its place I appeal to the Spirit-based theology offered by Volf, with an awareness of the injustices so predominant in work, for many people. A theology of work which can be fulfilling and offer the possibility of making our society more human is about reconciliation (Ather-ton's term) and using the gifts of the Spirit.

The third observation is about the involvement of the churches. Chapter 5 describes the papal encyclicals of recent years, and the statement of the American Catholic Bishops. Elsewhere, the British document on unemployment and the German one on the social market (both ecumenical) have been warmly commended. It is clear that the churches are deeply involved, from the poverty of workers in South America to the ministry of Industrial Mission in Britain. This involvement deserves to be better known.

What, finally, can be said about the twin themes of identity and justice which run throughout this book? It is clear, as Habermas shows and the Norwegian Bishops argue, that human identity is deeply problematic in mass-consumer society with a global market-place. It is also clear that consumerism (retail therapy as it is called in humour) and paid employment provide a source of identity for many people. Theology cannot ignore this reality, but it can attempt to supplement it and deepen human identity. Equally, it can point to the importance of justice in debt, bad work and global poverty.

What should be a Christian account of identity in this world? It should be creative, recognizing the importance of fulfilment in art and design, and in employment. Creativity is one great theme which cannot be ignored. Secondly, it should be marked by restraint and an absence of compulsive desire which so marks contemporary consumerism. It needs to find its true identity in a relationship with that Spirit of love and truth which was present in the ministry of Jesus, and which raised him from the dead. That Spirit can empower human creativity, but it can also lead communities into relationships which do not simply depend on wealth, consumerism or paid employment. Finally, a Christian identity can provide a security in the fragmented world of the global economy, where all local identities are challenged and even sometimes destroyed by the power of the market.

Yet, at the same time, the opportunity of the market and the condemnation of poverty, exploitation and greed need to be held together. Holding that balance is not an easy task. It is clear that some, such as Meeks, Northcott and Hauerwas, feel that the church must stand over against this materialist culture. Such a theme can also be found in parts of *Centesimus Annus*. At the same time, theologians such as Düchrow, Gorringe and others find in the global market a threat to human well-being. This book is an appeal not to take such a clear-cut position. Alongside the poverty and exploitation there are also the great benefits provided by the next stage of global capitalism. The churches need to remain part of the debate on reforming and humanizing that world, and not abandoning it for a rhetoric of Christian identity over against that world. Such a task will appear compromised, but, as the ecumenical German document *For a Future Founded on Solidarity and Justice* shows, it can also be immensely worthwhile.

Notes

INTRODUCTION

1 J. Atherton, *Christianity and the Market*, pp. 45–6, London: SPCK, 1992.
2 R. Plant, Gore Memorial Lecture 1995 (unpublished), p. 28.
3 D. W. Hardy, *God's Ways With the World*, p. 53. Edinburgh: T. & T. Clark, 1996.
4 Ibid., p. 57.
5 Ibid., p. 57.
6 Ibid., p. 61.

I MODERNITY, THE MARKET AND HUMAN IDENTITY

1 J. Habermas, *The Theory of Communicative Action*, Volumes 1 and 2 (henceforth *TCA* 1 and *TCA* 2), pp. 145-6 and pp. 175ff., Boston: Beacon Press, 1984 and 1987.
2 Hans Gerth and C. Wright Mills (eds.), *From Max Weber*, New York: Oxford University Press, 1946.
3 Rogers Brubacker, *The Limits of Rationality: An Essay on the Social and Moral Thought of Max Weber*, pp. 69 and 82-6, London: G. Allen and Unwin, 1984.
4 *TCA* 1, pp. 61-72.
5 Stephen K. White, *The Recent Work of Jürgen Habermas*, Cambridge University Press, 1988.
6 Ibid., p. 95.
7 *TCA* 1, pp. 165 and 340.
8 *TCA* 1, p. 340.
9 *TCA* 1, p. 70.
10 *TCA* 2, p. 146.
11 *TCA* 1, p. 340.
12 Ibid.

13 Carl Gilligan, *In a Different Voice: Psychological Theory and Women's Development*, Cambridge, Mass.: Harvard University Press, 1982.

14 White, *Recent Work of Jürgen Habermas*, p. 107.

15 R. H. Preston, *Church and Society in the Late Twentieth Century*, London: SCM, 1983.

16 *TCA* 2, p. 320. White, *Recent Work of Jürgen Habermas*, p. 109.

17 J. Habermas, 'Modernity versus postmodernity', *New German Critique*, 22 (Winter 1981). D. Lage, *M. Luther's Christology and Ethics*, Lampeter: Edwin Mellen Press, 1990.

18 White, *Recent Work of Jürgen Habermas*, p. 118.

19 J. Habermas, *Legitimation Crisis*, Boston: Beacon Press, 1975.

20 J. Habermas, 'Reply to my Critics', in J. Thompson and D. Held (eds.), *Habermas: Critical Debates*, p. 279, Cambridge: MIT Press, 1982. White, *Recent Work of Jürgen Habermas*, p. 100.

21 Ibid., p. 21.

22 Max Weber, *Economics and Society*, Berkeley: University of California Press, 1978.

23 Anthony Downs, *An Economic Theory of Democracy*, New York: Harper and Row, 1957. Mancur Olsen, *The Logic of Collective Action*, Cambridge, Mass.: Harvard University Press, 1971.

24 Jon Elster, *Ulysses and the Sirens*, Cambridge University Press, 1979.

25 Brian Barry and Russel Hardin (eds.), *Rational Man and Irrational Society*, Berkeley: Sage Publications, 1982. Elster, *Ulysses and the Sirens*, p. 142; Claus Offe, 'The Two Logics of Collective Action' in *Disorganized Capitalism: Contemporary Transformations of Work and Politics*, Cambridge, Mass.: MIT Press, 1985.

26 White, *Recent Work of Jürgen Habermas*, p. 25.

27 *TCA* 1, p. 86.

28 White, *Recent Work of Jürgen Habermas*, pp. 72–3.

29 J. Habermas, 'Zur Einfuhrung', in R. Döbert and J. Habermas (eds.) *Die Entwicklung des Ichs*, Cologne: Keizenheimer, 1977.

30 White, *Recent Work of Jürgen Habermas*, p. 45.

31 J. Habermas, 'Reply to my Critics', in J. Thompson and D. Held (eds.), *Habermas: Critical Debates*, p. 279, Cambridge, Mass.: MIT Press, 1982. White, *Recent Work of Jürgen Habermas*, p. 120.

32 Ibid., p. 121.

33 *TCA* 2, pp. 365 and 317.

34 White, *Recent Work of Jürgen Habermas*, p. 115.

35 D. Held in Thompson and Held *Habermas: Critical Debates*, pp. 190-1; cf. David Ingram, *Habermas and the Dialectic of Reason*, p. 170, New Haven: Yale University Press, 1987.

36 Ibid., p. 165-6.

37 J. Habermas, *Die Neue Unubersichtlich Kert: Kleine Politische Schnften V*,

Frankfurt: Suhrkamp, 1985; cf. Ingram, *Habermas and the Dialectic of Reason*, pp. 169 and 236.

38 Daniel Hallin, 'The American News Media: A Critical Theory Perspective', in John Forester (ed.), *Critical Theory and Public Life*, Cambridge, Mass., MIT Press, 1985.

39 J. Habermas, 'Modern and Postmodern Architecture', in Forester, *Critical Theory*, p. 329.

40 Tony Smith, 'The Role of Ethics in Social Theory – Essays from a Habermasian Perspective', Albany: State University of New York Press, 1991.

41 Ibid., p. 164.

42 Rosalind Levacic and Alexander Rebmann, *Macro-economics*, pp. 362–3, London: Macmillan, 1982.

43 Charles Davies, *Religion and the Making of Society*, Cambridge University Press, 1994.

44 Al McFadyen, 'The Call to Personhood', Cambridge University Press, 1990.

45 D. S. Browning and F. S. Fiorenza (eds.), *Habermas, Modernity and Public Theology*, New York: Crossroad, 1992.

46 U. Düchrow, *Global Economy*, Geneva: WCC, 1987.

47 A. Hennelly (ed.), *Liberation Theology – A Documentary History*, Maryknoll: Orbis, 1990.

48 D. Forrester, *Christian Justice and Public Policy*, p. 230, Cambridge University Press, 1997.

49 Ibid., p. 217.

50 Ibid., p. 35.

51 Ibid., p. 200.

52 D. Bonhoeffer, *Ethics*, p. 297, London: SCM, 1978.

53 Ibid., p. 297.

54 Ibid., p. 308.

55 Ibid., p. 309.

56 Ibid., p. 180.

57 Ibid., p. 246.

58 Ibid., p. 200.

59 Ibid., p. 202.

60 Ibid., p. 202.

61 F. de Lange, 'The Christian Humanism', p. 89 in G. Carter, R. van Eyden, H. D. van Hoogstraten, J. Wiersma (eds.), *Bonhoeffer's Ethics: Old Europe and New Frontiers*, Kampen: Kok Pharos, 1991.

62 *Ethics*, p. 98. C. C. West 'Ground Under Our Feet' p. 248 in W. J. Peck (ed.), *New Studies in Bonhoeffer's Ethics*, Toronto Studies in Theology, vol 30:3, New York: Eerdmans, 1987.

63 L. Rasmussen, 'Bonhoeffer: Reality and Resistance' in Carter et al. (eds.), *Bonheffer's Ethics*, p. 3, and R. van Eyden, 'Bonhoeffer's Understanding of Male and Female', in ibid., p. 203.

64 H. Ott, *Reality and Faith*, p. 237, London: Lutterworth Press, 1971; C. Marsh, *Reclaiming Dietrich Bonhoeffer. The Promise of His Theology*, pp. 103–4. Oxford University Press, 1994.

65 P. Selby. *Grace and Mortgage*, p. 24, London: DLT Press, 1997.

66 Ibid., p. 27.

67 D. W. Hardy, *God's Way with the World*, pp. 199–200, Edinburgh: T. & T. Clark, 1996, and D. W. Hardy, 'A Magnificent Complexity', in D. F. Ford and D. Stamps (eds.) *Essentials of Christian Community*, Edinburgh: T. & T. Clark, 1996.

68 Hardy, *God's Way*, p. 201.

69 Ibid., p. 201.

70 Ibid., p. 201.

71 Ibid., p. 202 citing R. J. Siebert. *The Central Theory of Religion: The Frankfurt School*, pp. 372–3, Berlin: Mouton, 1985.

72 Hardy, *God's Way*, p. 202.

73 Ibid., p. 204.

74 Ibid., p. 177.

75 Ibid., p. 179.

76 Ibid., pp. 179–80.

77 Ibid., p. 181.

78 Ibid., p. 181.

79 Ibid., p. 183. Ibid., pp. 179–80. David Nicholls, *Deity and Domination*, London: Routledge, 1989.

80 Hardy, *God's Way*, p. 184.

81 Ibid., p. 184.

82 Ibid., p. 184.

83 Ibid., p. 185.

84 R. N. Adams, *Energy and Structure*, Austin: University of Texas Press, 1975, cited in Hardy, *God's Way*, p. 176.

85 Charles Handy, *The Age of Unreason*, London: Arrow Books, 1989.

86 Hardy, *God's Way*, p. 186.

87 Ibid., p. 186.

88 D. Tracy, 'Theology, Critical Social Theory and the Public Realm', pp. 19–43 in Browning and Fiorenza, *Habermas*.

89 Tracy, ibid., p. 33.

90 Tracy, ibid., p. 38.

91 F. S. Fiorenza, 'The Church as a Community of Interpretations', p. 71 in Browning and Fiorenza, *Habermas*.

92 J. Rawls, 'The Ideal of an Overlapping Consensus', *Oxford Journal of Legal Studies*, 7 (1987), 1–25.

93 Forrester, *Christian Justice*, p. 173.
94 Ibid., p. 173.
95 Ibid., p. 174.
96 Fiorenza, 'The Church as a Community', p. 77.
97 Ibid., p. 85. D. Ingram, *Habermas*, p. 131. Habermas, 'Transcendence from Within, Transcendence in this World', in Browning and Fiorenza, *Habermas*, pp. 226ff.
98 McFadyen, *The Call*, p. 284.
99 On covenant, J. A. Edelhert (ed.), *The Life of Covenant: The Challenge of Contemporary Judaism*, Chicago: SCJ Press, 1996; T. Deidun, *New Covenant Morality in Paul*, Rome: Biblical Institute Press, 1981; N. T. Wright, *Climax of the Covenant: Christ and the Law in Pauline Theology*, Edinburgh: T. & T. 1991; R. N. Bellah, *The Broken Covenant: American Civil Religion in the Time of Trial*, University of Chicago Press, 1992. There is an extensive literature also on the Puritan understanding of covenant.
100 N. Adams, 'Eschatology and Habermas' Ideal Speech Situation', *Modern Believing*, 37-2 (April 1996).
101 McFadyen, *The Call*, pp. 202-3.
102 Forrester, *Christian Justice*, pp. 182-3.
103 T. Rendtorff, *Ethics*, vol. 2, p. 99, Minneapolis: Fortress Press, 1989.
104 Ibid., p. 99.
105 Forrester, *Christian Justice*, pp. 244-5.

2 CONSUMERISM AND PERSONAL IDENTITY

1 Neil McKendrick, John Brewer and J. H. Plumb, *The Birth of a Consumer Society: The Commercialization of Eighteenth-Century England*, p. 13, Bloomington: Indiana University Press, 1982.
2 Colin Campbell, *The Romantic Ethic and the Spirit of Modern Consumerism*, Oxford: Blackwell, 1987.
3 J. S. Mill, *Utilitarianism*, London: J. M. Dent, 1972.
4 Campbell, *The Romantic Ethic*, p. 121. R. S. Crane, *The Idea of the Humanities and Other Essays Critical and Historical*, vol. 1, p. 211, University of Chicago Press, 1967.
5 Ibid., p. 211.
6 Max Weber, *The Protestant Ethic and the Spirit of Capitalism* (translated T. Parsons), p. 166, London: George Allen and Unwin, 1985.
7 S. Grean, *Shaftesbury's Philosophy of Religion and Ethics: A Study in Enthusiasm*, Athens, Ohio, USA: Ohio University Press, 1967.
8 T. Veblen, *The Theory of the Leisure Class: An Economic Study of Institutions*, p. 85, London: George Allan and Unwin, 1925.

9   J. P. Diggins, *The Bard of Savagery. T. Veblen and Modern Social Theory*, Brighton: Harvest Press, 1978; p. 115 on science, page 137 on technology, page 117 on his hostility to capitalism.

10 Rick Tilman, *T. Veblen and his Critics*, Princeton University Press, 1992, pages 193–6 on Adorno. Adorno's article 'Veblen's attack on culture' is reprinted in J. Cunningham (ed.), *T. Veblen Critical Assessments*, 3 vols, London 1993. Adorno's article is in vol. 3, p. 4.

11 Veblen's attitude to religion is discussed by G. Leathers in 'Veblen's Ambivalent View of Christianity' in Cunningham (ed.), vol. 3, *T. Veblen Critical Assessments*, p. 533 and A. C. Harris *'Veblen as Social Philosopher'* in ibid., vol. 1, p. 27.

12 Veblen, *Theory of the Leisure Class*, p. 70.

13 A H. Halsey, *Change in British Society*, Oxford University Press, 1995.

14 Campbell, *Romantic Ethic*, p. 209.

15 Ibid., page 188 citing Percy Bysshe Shelley *'A Defence of Poetry'*, in H. Bloom and L. Trilling (eds.), *Romantic Poetry and Prose*, p. 757, New York: Oxford University Press, 1973.

16 Ibid., p. 757.

17 Campbell, *Romantic Ethic*, p. 216.

18 Ibid., p. 185.

19 M. Weber, *The Sociology of Religion*, London: Methuen, 1965.

20 Campbell, *Romantic Ethic*, p. 183.

21 Ibid., p. 227.

22 J. K. Galbraith, *The Affluent Society*, London: Penguin, 1987.

23 Ibid., p. 143.

24 Campbell, *Romantic Ethic*, p. 43, citing McKendrick et al., *The Birth of a Consumer Society*, p. 14.

25 Halsey, *Change in British Society*, pp. 122–7. The literature on consumerism is vast but has been little explored by theologians, including social ethicists. Historical accounts include Carole Shamass, *The Pre-Industrial Consumer in England and America* Oxford: Clarendon 1990, Daniel Horowitz, *The Morality of Spending: Attitudes Towards the Consumer in America 1875-1940* Baltimore: Johns Hopkins University Press, 1985; and the wonderfully detailed account of changes in British social history full of working-class diaries and interviews, John Benson, *The Rise of Consumer Society in Britain 1880–1980*, London: Longman, 1994. Cultural studies include Gary Cross, *Time and Money: the Making of a Consumer Culture*, London: Routledge, 1993 which combines history and cultural analysis in France, America and Britain between the wars. Martyn Lee, in the same Routledge series, has written *Consumer Culture Reborn: The Cultural Politics of Consumption*, London: Routledge, 1993. Two social psychological studies are

John Willis, *Common Culture: Symbolic Work at Play in the Everyday Cultures of the Young*, Buckingham: Open University Press, 1990, and Peter Lunt and Sonia Livingstone, *Mass Consumption and Personal Identity*, Buckingham: Open University Press, 1992. This ends with a discussion of the socio-political work of Geoff Mulgan and Anthony Giddens. An excellent introduction to the theoretical debate which I have relied on is Robert Bocock, *Consumption*, London: Routledge, 1993. Two economic studies are Kevin Lancaster, *Modern Consumer Theory*, Aldershot: Elgar, 1991, and Peter Earl, *Lifestyle Economics: Consumer Behaviour in a Turbulent World*, Brighton: Wheatsheaf. John Urry has written widely on capitalism and post-modern culture. His recent book, *Consuming Places*, London: Routledge, 1994, looks at tourism and consumption. An anthropological study is given by M. Douglas and B. Isherwood in *The World of Goods: Towards an Anthropology of Consumption*, London: Allen Lane, 1979. Theological comments include the highly sophisticated report for the Norwegian Bishops' Conference 1992, *The Consumer Society as an Ethical Challenge*, Church of Norway information Service, Oslo, 1993, which is extremely well informed on French post-structuralism and the American Christopher Lasch, etc. This is by far the best place to start for a theological response to the subject. Other theological studies are the British Council of Churches, *The Consumer Goods Society*, London, 1978, J. F. Kavanagh, *Following Christ in a Consumer Society*, New York, 1981, R. Laurence Moore, *Selling God*, Oxford University Press, 1994, M. Buddle, *The (Magic) Kingdom of God: Christianity and the Global Culture Industries*, western Colorado, 1997. Andrew Morton, *Domestic Debt: Disease of Consumer Society?* Edinburgh: Centre for Theology and Public Issues, 1996, and Rodney Clapp's ecumenical study (Jewish, Roman Catholic, Orthodox, Baptist, etc.) *Consuming Passion: Christianity and the Consumer Culture*, Illinois: Inter Varsity Press, 1998. M. Douglas Meeks, *God the Economist*, Minneapolis: Fortress Press, 1989 is discussed at length later in the chapter.

26 G. Simmel, 'The Metropolis and Mental Life', p. 318 in D. Levine *On Individuality and Social Form*, Chicago, 1971.

27 D. Frisby, *Georg Simmel*, pp. 131–2, London: 1984, cited in Bocock, *Consumption*, p. 17.

28 Galbraith, *The Affluent Society*, p. 30; A. Gamble, *Britain in Decline*, London: Macmillan 1981; J. Goldthorpe et al., *The Affluent Worker in the Class Structure*, 3 vols., Cambridge University Press, 1968–9; R. Williams, *Culture and Society*, London: Hogarth 1990.

29 Harvard University Press, 1984 (French edition 1979).

30 Bocock, *Consumption*, p. 67. J. Baudrillard, *Selected Writings*, Cambridge: Polity Press, 1988.
31 Bocock, *Consumption*, p. 87. J. Lacan, *Ecrits. A Selection*, London: Tavistock Press, 1977. Norwegian Bishops, *The Consumer Society*, p. 25.
32 John Fiske, *Reading the Popular*. Boston: Unwin Hyman, 1989, cited in Bocock, *Consumption*, p. 97.
33 Bocock, *Consumption*, p. 102 citing F. Mort 'Boy's Own? Masculinity, Style and Popular Culture', in R. Chapman and J. Rutherford (eds.), *Male Order*, London: Lawrence and Wishart, 1988. See also M. Featherstone, 'The body in consumer politics', in M. Featherstone, M. Hepworth and B. Turner (eds.) *The Body: Social Process and Cultural Theory*, London: Sage, 1991.
34 A. Giddens, *Modernity and Self Identity*, Cambridge: Polity 1991.
35 Lunt and Livingstone, *Mass Consumption*, pp. 169–71.
36 Ibid., p. 92.
37 Urry, *Consuming Places*, p. 144.
38 Ibid., pp. 144–5.
39 Norwegian Bishops, *The Consumer Society*, p. 19.
40 M. Douglas Meeks. *God the Economist: The Doctrine of God and Political Economy*, Minneapolis: Fortress Press, 1989.
41 C. B. MacPherson. *The Political Theory of Possessive Individualism: Hobbes to Locke*. Oxford University Press, 1962. Ibid., 'A Political Theory of Property' in C. B. MacPherson (ed.), *Democratic Theory: Essays in Retrieval*, Oxford University Press, 1973.
42 J. Atherton, *Christianity and the Market*, London: SPCK, 1992.
43 Meeks, *God the Economist*, p. 5.
44 Ibid., p. 18.
45 Ibid., p. 10.
46 Ibid., p. 13.
47 Ibid., p. 23.
48 Ibid., p. 43.
49 Ibid., p. 52.
50 Ibid., p. 53.
51 Ibid., p. 55.
52 R. Heilbroner, *The Nature and Logic of Capitalism*, New York: Norton Press, 1985.
53 Meeks, *God the Economist*, p. 63.
54 Ibid., p. 63.
55 Ibid., p. 65.
56 Ibid., p. 67.
57 Ibid., p. 68.
58 Ibid.

59 A. Marshall. *Principles of Economics*, 8th edition, London: Macmillan, 1930. See the discussion in Atherton, *Christianity and the Market*, ch. 2, and J. K. Galbraith, *A History of Economics*, London: Penguin, 1989.

60 Meeks, *God the Economist*, p. 163. C. Lasch, *The Culture of Narcissism: American Life in an Age of Diminishing Expectations*, New York: Norton, 1978.

61 Meeks, *God the Economist*, p. 167.

62 Ibid., p. 168.

63 Karl Marx, *Capital*, vol. 1, p. 230, New York: A.P., 1977.

64 Meeks, *God the Economist*, pp. 172/173.

65 Ibid., p. 173.

66 Ibid., p. 174.

67 Ibid.

68 M. Walzer, *Spheres of Justice*, p. 7, New York: Basic Books, 1983.

69 Meeks, *God the Economist*, p. 177.

70 Ibid., p. 182.

71 Ibid., p. 44. C. McCloskey, 'The Rhetoric of Economics' in D. Hausman (ed.), *The Philosophy of Economics*, Cambridge University Press, 1995.

72 C. McCloskey, 'The Rhetoric of Economic Expertise', in R. H. Roberts and J. M. M. Good (ed.), *The Recovery of Rhetoric*, Bristol: Classical Press, 1993.

73 R. H. Roberts, 'Rhetoric and the Resurgence of Capitalism', in Roberts and Good, p. 226. For a discussion of McCloskey by an applied economist in relation to theology see R. N. Nelson, *Reaching for Heaven on Earth: The Theological Meaning of Economics*, p. 285, Maryland: Rowman and Littlefield, 1981.

74 Ibid., p. 225.

75 Ibid., p. 230. V. A. Demant. *Religion and the Decline of Capitalism*, London: Faber and Faber, 1952.

76 Ibid., p. 28.

77 Irwin Michelman, *The Moral Limitations of Capitalism*, Aldershot: Avebury, 1994.

78 Walter Owensby, *Economics for Prophets*, Michigan: Erdmans, 1988.

79 J. K. Galbraith, *The New Industrial State*, Boston: Houghton Mifflin, 1967. For an evangelical critique of Galbraith, see W. Gilbreath, 'J. K. Galbraith's Ethic of Affluence' *Crux* 14:12 (June 1988).

80 Atherton, 'Christianity and the Market', p. 59.

81 Ibid., pp. 45–6.

82 R. H. Preston, *Religion and the Ambiguities of Capitalism*, pp. 88–90, London: SCM, 1991.

83 Brian Marshall, 'Meeks and Novak on Theology and Economics', *MC*, 34:2 (1992), 27–31.
84 C. Schwöbel, *God: Action and Revelation*, p. 60, Kampen, The Netherlands: Kok Pharos 1992.
85 Ibid., p. 75.
86 Ibid., p. 58.
87 Preston, *Religion and the Ambiguities*, ch. 7, 'The Bible, Doctrine, and Economic Issues'.
88 P. Oppenheimer, *An Intelligent Person's Guide to Modern Guilt*, London: Duckworth, 1997.
89 Ibid., p. 93.
90 Ibid., p. 108.
91 Ibid., p. 112.
92 Ibid., pp. 92–3.
93 Ibid., p. 112.
94 Ibid., p. 110.
95 Ibid.
96 Ibid., p. 111.
97 Ibid., p. 118.
98 Ibid.
99 Ibid., p. 41.
100 J. Gray, *Enlightenment's Wake*, London: Routledge, 1996. (See especially pp. 93–100 on 'the self-destruction of traditional conservatism' at the hands of the market, ch. 2 on 'Toleration: a post-liberal perspective', p. 145 on disenchantment with the enlightenment project, p. 184 on the possibility of cultural recovery through piety and mysticism.)
101 Preston, *Religion and the Ambiguities*, pp. 89–91, 105.
102 A. Morton (ed.), *Domestic Debt: Disease of Consumer Society?* Edinburgh: Centre for Theology and Public Issues, 1996.
103 See the discussion in *The Independent*, 21 July 1998 on the ambiguity of celebrities in promoting ethical consumerism. The outstanding examples are Pamela Anderson and Naomi Campbell, who starred in a campaign against furs for PETA (People for the Ethical Treatment of Animals). Campbell later appeared wearing furs at a fashion display.
104 The magazine *New Consumer* has an explicitly ethical focus. *Which*, the journal of the Consumers' Association which began the consumer movement in the 1960s, does not.
105 See *Cracking the Code: Monitoring the International Edge of Marketing Breast-Milk Substitutes*, 'The Interagency Group on Breastfeeding Monitoring', London, 1997.

106 *Something to Celebrate*, 238 pages, London: Church House Publishing, 1995.

107 Daniel Cohen, *The Wealth of the World and the Poverty of Nations*, Boston: MIT Press, 1998. See also Peter Stubley, 'Globalization and the Social Elite', *Crucible* (October 1998).

108 Diane Coyle, 'On the Force Behind Rising Inequality', *The Independent*, 21 May 1998.

109 R. Clapp. *The Consuming Passion: Christianity and the Consumer Culture*, Illinois: Inter Varsity Press: 1998. The collection has essays by Roman Catholics, Jews, Orthodox and Evangelicals of the main Protestant denominations.

110 Ronald Ingelhart, *Culture Shift in Advanced Industrial Society*, Princeton University Press, 1990.

111 D. Coyle, 'On the Force behind Rising Inequality'.

112 P. Selby, *Grace and Mortgage: The Language of Faith and the Debt of the World*, London: Darton, Longman & Todd, 1998.

113 G. Blount, 'Sketching the Problem and Assessing Responses', in Morton, *Domestic Debt*, p. 7. The literature on debt is enormous. R. Berthoud and E. Kempson, *Credit and Debt (the P.S.I. Report)* is the result of a long-term study by the Policy Studies Institute, London 1992. J. Ford, *The Indebted Society*, London: 1988; *The Joseph Rowntree Foundation into Income and Wealth*, 2 vols., York: 1995; NCH, *Deep in Debt*, London: 1992, NCC, *Credit and Debt (The Consumer Interest)*, London: HMSO, 1990; H. Barty-King, *The Worst Poverty*, London 1991.

114 J. K. Galbraith, *Money – Whence it Came, Where it Went*, p. 79, London: n.p., 1975, cited by Blount, 'Sketching the Problem', p. 8.

115 Selby, *Grace and Mortgage*, p. 31.

116 Blount, 'Sketching the Problem', p. 111 and Selby, *Grace and Mortgage*, p. 56. For stories of families struggling to cope, see the articles by Margaret Walsh in P. H. Sedgwick (ed.), *God in the City*, London: Mowbrays, 1995.

117 Michael Adler, pp. 29–32 in the Centre for Theology and Public Issues report, quoting the Rowntree report 1995, Figure 16.

118 Blount, 'Sketching the Problem', p. 14.

119 Selby, *Grace and Mortgage*, p. 52, quoting the research of Berthoud and Hinton.

120 *Religion and Economic Ethics* (ed.) J. Gower, College Theological Society, vol. 31, Lauham, USA, 1988. See especially three articles in section II, Theological Resources: Andrew Tallon, 'Affectivity and Praxis in Lonergan, Rahner and Others in the Heart Tradition', pp. 87–123, Ronald Modras, 'Karl Rahner and John

Paul II: Anthropological Implications for Economics and the Social Order', pp. 123–151, Joseph La Burge, 'Economic Systems and the Sacramental Imagination', pp. 151–73. Of central importance are the essays of Karl Rahner and David Hollenbach. Rahner, 'Theology of Poverty' *Theological Investigations*, 8, pp. 168–214. Hollenbach, 'A Prophetic Church and the Catholic Sacramental Imagination', in J. C. Haughey (ed.), *The Faith that does Justice*, New York: n.p., 1977. These essays have shaped an entire Catholic social tradition.

121 Modras in Gower, *Religion and Economic Ethics*, p. 130.
122 D. W. Hardy, 'A Magnificent Complexity', commenting on John Hull's article 'Christian Education in a Capitalist Society: Money and God', in D. Ford and D. Stamps (eds.), *Essentials of Christian Community*, Edinburgh: T. & T. Clark, 1996.
123 Norwegian Bishops, *The Consumer Society*, pp. 33 and 120, citing C. Lasch, *The True and Only Heaven*, New York: Norton, 1991, and *The Minimal Self*, London: Pan, 1984.
124 D. Ford, *The Shape of Living*, London: Collins, 1998. See also B. Brecher, *Getting What You Want?* London: Routledge, 1998, and D. Levine, *Wealth and Freedom: An Introduction to Political Economy*, Cambridge University Press, 1995.

3 THE WORK ETHIC

1 A. Richardson, *The Biblical Doctrine of Work*, London: SCM, 1952.
2 *Laborens Exercens*, Catholic Trust Society, 1981.
3 Max Weber, *The Protestant Ethic and the Spirit of Capitalism*, London: George Allen and Unwin, 1930.
4 Werner Sombart, *Der Moderne Kapitalismus*, 2 vols., Leipzig: Duncker and Humblot, 1902.
5 Justo Gonzalez, *Faith and Wealth*, London: Harper and Row, 1990.
6 G. Marshall, *In Search of the Spirit of Capitalism*, p. 54. Aldershot: Gregg Revivals, 1993.
7 M. Lessnoff, *The Spirit of Capitalism and the Protestant Ethic*, p. 85. Aldershot: Edward Elgar, 1994.
8 Marshall, *In Search of the Spirit*, p. 125.
9 Lessnoff, *The Spirit of Capitalism*, p. 116. Brian Griffith, *Morality and the Market Place*, London: Hodder and Stoughton 1982, and *The Creation of Wealth*, London: Hodder and Stoughton, 1984.
10 Peter Stubley, *A House Divided*, p. 10. University of Hull Press, 1995.
11 Ibid., p.10. W. Richardson (ed.), *Milner's Sermons*, vol. 2, York: 1808.
12 For another general study of this point, see Boyd Hilton, *The Age of Atonement*, Oxford: Clarendon Press, 1988, and A. M. C.

Waterman, *Revolution, Economics and Religion: Christian Political Economy 1798-1833*, Cambridge University Press, 1991.

13 A. Furnham, *The Protestant Work Ethic. The Psychology of Work-Related Beliefs and Behaviours*, p. 13, London: Routledge, 1990. D. Cherrington, *The Work Ethic: Working Values and Values that Work*, p. 20, New York: Amacom, 1980.

14 W. Oates, *Confessions of a Workaholic: The Facts about Work Addiction*, p. 84, New York: World Publishing Company, 1971. Furnham, *The Protestant Work Ethic*, p. 13.

15 M. Maccoby, and R. Terzi, 'What happened to the Work Ethic?', in W. Hoffman and T. Wyly (eds.) *The Work Ethic in Business*, Cambridge, Mass.: OGH Publishers, 1979. Furnham, *The Protestant Work Ethic*, p. 15.

16 Ibid., p. 34.

17 Ibid., p. 42.

18 Ibid., p. 62.

19 Ibid., p. 56.

20 J. McGrath and J. Kelly, *Time and Human Interaction: Towards a Social Psychology of Time*, p. 108, New York: Guildford Press, 1986. Furnham, *The Protestant Work Ethic*, p. 63.

21 M. Jahoda, *Employment and Unemployment: A Social-Psychological Analysis*, p. 313, Cambridge University Press, 1982.

22 D. Fryer, 'Employment, Deprivation and Personal Agency During Unemployment', *Social Behaviour*, 1, (1986), 3-23.

23 R. Lane, *The Market Experience*, Cambridge University Press, 1991.

24 Theodore W. Schultz, *Investment in Human Capital*, New York: Free Press, 1971 and (ed.), *Economics of the Family*, University of Chicago Press, 1974.

25 The classic book which restated Marxist theory of deskilling at work is Harry Braverman, *Labor and Monopoly Capital*, New York: Monthly Review Press, 1971. Cf., Lane, *The Market Experience*, p. 20.

26 Alfred Marshall, *Principles of Economics*, 8th edition, London: Macmillan, 1930.

27 R. Reich, *The Work of Nations*, New York: Alfred Knopf, 1991. For a discussion, P. Stubley, 'Globalization and the Social Elite', *Crucible* (Oct.–Dec. 1998).

28 P. Ballard, *In and Out of Work: A Pastoral Perspective*, p. 131. Edinburgh: The Saint Andrew Press, 1987. John Horne, *Work and Unemployment*, London: Longman, 1967. Charles Leadbeater and John Lloyd, *In Search of Work*, London: Penguin, 1987.

29 Lane, *The Market Experience*, p. 242.

30 Ibid., p. 246, citing, G. and C. Vaillant, 'Work as a Predictor of Positive Mental Health', *American Journal of Psychiatry*, 138 (1981).

31 Lane, *The Market Experience*, p. 247.

32 Ibid., p. 259. J. S. Mill, *Utilitarianism, Liberty and Representative Government*, p. 216, London: J. M. Dent, 1974.

33 Adam Smith, *The Wealth of Nations*, p. 734, New York: Random House, 1937 (originally printed 1776). Lane, *The Market Experience*, p. 253.

34 Smith, *The Wealth of Nations*, pp. 734-5, cited Lane, *The Market Experience*, p. 323.

35 Ibid., p. 265. R. H. Tawney, *The Acquisitive Society*, p. 35, New York: Harcourt Brace, 1920. Chapter 16 of Lane, *The Market Experience*, (pp. 314-36) is headed 'Giving Work Priority Over Consumption'.

36 C. Kerr and J. Rosow (eds.), *Work in America: The Decade Ahead*, New York: Van Nostrand, 1979. Cited in Furnham, *The Protestant Work Ethic*, p. 246.

37 D. Yankevolich, 'Work, Values and the New Breed', pp. 2–26 in Kerr and Rosow (eds.), *Work in America*.

38 R. Katzell, 'Changing attitudes to work', pp. 35–7 in Kerr and Rosow, *Work in America*.

39 S. Parker, *Leisure and Work*, p. 106, London: George Allen, 1983. Cited in Furnham, *The Protestant Work Ethic*, p. 244.

40 C. Handy, *The Future of Work*, p. 180, Worcester: Belling and Sons, 1985.

41 D. Yankevolich and J. Immerwahr, 'Putting the work ethic to work', *Society*, (January 1984), 58–76, cited in Furnham, *The Protestant Work Ethic*, p. 208.

42 M. Csikszentmihaly, 'The Americanization of Rock-Climbing', in J. Bruner, A. Jolly and K. Sylva (eds.), *Play: Its Role in Development and Evolution*, pp. 487–8, New York: Basic Books, 1976 cited in Furnham, *The Protestant Work Ethic*, p. 210.

43 Lane, *The Market Experience*, p. 255. Yankelovitch, 'Putting the Work Ethic to Work', p. 58.

44 Lane, *The Market Experience*, p. 257. A. Furnham, 'The Protestant Work Ethic and Attitudes to Unemployment', *Journal of Occupational Psychology*, 55 (1982), 277-85.

45 Reich, *The Work of Nations*, p. 51.

46 Ibid., p. 83.

47 Ibid., p. 176.

48 D. Halpern, S. Wood, S. White and G. Cameron (eds.), *Options for Britain*, Aldershot: Dartmouth, 1996, and R. Dahrendorf, 'Changing Social Values under Mrs Thatcher', in R. Skidelsky (ed.), *Thatcherism*, Oxford: Blackwell, 1988.

49 A. Adonis, 'Tomorrow's Money Today', in 'The State We're In', Basingstoke, 1996.

50 Reich, *The Work of Nations*, p. 322.

51 Thomas Aquinas, *Summa Theologica* II-II q. 182 a 1. See also Peter Sedgwick, 'The Compulsion to be Good: Aquinas on the Formation of Human Character', *Theology*, 91:741 (May 1988). Carl-Henne Grenholm, *Protestant Work Ethics*, p. 40, Uppsala Studies in Social Ethics 15: Uppsala, 1993.

52 Sedgwick, 'The Compulsion to be Good', citing *ST* II-II q. 182 a 2.

53 Peter Sedgwick, 'Wealth Creation and the Early Church', *Epworth Review*, 20-1 (1993), 65-74 discusses Augustine's views in detail.

54 *ST* II-II q. 187 a 3.

55 *ST* II-II q. 182 a 2.

56 Martin Luther, The *German Cathecism* (1529), WA 30:1, 183:30–184:33. Grenholm, *Protestant Work Ethics*, p. 44.

57 *Commentary on St Paul's Epistle to the Galatians* (1535), WA 40:1, 174:12–175:24.

58 *German Catechism*, WA 30:1, 178:33.

59 *On Good Works* (1520), WA 6, 270:27-271:9.

60 Grenholm, *Protestant Work Ethics*, pp. 41-7. Paul Marshall, *A Kind of Life Imposed on Man: Vocation and Social order from Tyndale to Locke*, University of Toronto Press, 1996. See also the review by J. C. D. Clark in *Studies in Christian Ethics*, 11:1 (1998).

61 K. Barth, *Church Dogmatics*, III/4, Edinburgh: T. & T. Clark, 1968; D. Jenkins, *God, Politics and the Future*, especially Part One 'Politics, Economics and Industry', London: SCM Press, 1988; Margaret Kane, *Theology in an Industrial Society*, London: SCM Press, 1982; Margaret Kane, *Gospel in an Industrial Society*, London: SCM Press, 1980; Margaret Kane, *What Kind of God?*, London: SCM Press, 1986; Andrew Stokes, *Working with God*, London: Mowbrays, 1992; Ronald Preston (ed.), *Perspective on Strikes*, London: SCM, 1975; John Atherton, *Faith in the Nation: A Christian Vision for Britain*, London: SPCK, 1988; John Atherton, *Christianity in the Market*, London: SPCK, 1992; Jack Keiser, *Men at Work*, London: Epworth Press, 1978; Howard Davis and David Gosling, *Will the Future Work*, Geneva: WCC, 1986; Brian Jenner, *The Coal Strike*, Sheffield: New City, 1986.

62 Paul Ballard, *In and Out of Work: A Pastoral Perspective*, Edinburgh: St Andrews Press, 1987; Elaine Graham and Margaret Halsey, *Life Cycles*, London: SPCK, 1993; Margaret Halsey, *Invisible Hands*, Manchester: William Temple Foundation, 1996; Alan Suggate 'Towards a WEN. Theology of the Future of Work', in *Theology and the Future of Work*, Manchester: William Temple Foundation, 1998; Hugh Ormiston and Donald Ross (eds.), *New Patterns of Work*, Edinburgh: St Andrews Press, 1990; W. Rogerson (ed.), *Industrial*

Mission in a Changing World, Sheffield Academic Press, 1996; Nigel Biggar, *Good Life* (ch. 4 'Work'), London: SPCK, 1997; Miroslav Volf, *Work in the Spirit*, Oxford University Press, 1991; Stephen Pattison, *The Faith in the Managers*, London: Cassell, 1997; Ann Borrowdale, *A Woman's Work*, London: SPCK, 1989; P. Sedgwick, *The Enterprise Culture*, London: SPCK, 1992; P. Sedgwick and M. Brown (eds.), *Putting Theology to Work*, London: Council of Churches for Britain and Ireland, 1998.

63 There is an extensive Bibliography on work, unemployment and theology in *Unemployment and the Future of Work*, London: Council of Churches for Britain and Ireland, 1997; Ken Leech, *Struggle in Babylon*, London: SCM, 1988; Ken Leech, *The Sky is Red*, London: DLT, 1997.

64 Emil Brunner, *Das Gebot und die Ordnungen* Tubingen: Verlag van J. C. B. Mohr, 1932; Emil Brunner *Der Kapitalismus als Problem der Kirche* Zurich: Zwingly-Verlag, 1945; Grenholm, *Protestant Work Ethics*.

65 Ibid., p. 90. Brunner, *Das Gebot*, pp. 112ff.

66 Grenholm, *Protestant Work Ethics*, p. 124. Brunner, *Das Gebot*, p. 452.

67 Atherton, *Faith in the Nation*, pp. 95-9.

68 Ibid., p. 92.

69 Ibid., p. 10.

70 Ballard, *In and Out of Work*, p. 109.

71 Ibid., p. 108.

72 Will Hutton, *The State We're In*, p. 95, London: Vintage, 1996.

73 Ballard, *In and Out of Work*, p. 82.

74 Halsey, *Invisible Hands*. See also Ann Loades 'A Feminist Perspective on the Morality of the New Right', in Michael Northcott (ed.), *Vision and Prophecy: The Tasks of Social Theology Today*, Edinburgh: Centre for Theology and Public Issues, 1991. Paul Ballard, *In and Out of Work*, has a chapter on women and employment, and there are essays by Sue Havens and Caroline Barker Bennett in Rogerson, *Industrial Mission. Foundations*, 1–3 (July 1998) has articles on marginal work and trade unions from a Christian perspective.

75 Michael Northcott charts the changes in a theology of work and industrial mission in chs. 8 (Work) and 10 (Industry) of his *Urban Theology: A Reader*, London: Cassell, 1998. The period covered is from 1940 to the present day. Volf, pp. 107-8.

76 Ibid., p. 116.

77 Ibid., p. 118.

78 Ibid., pp. 130-1.

79 Ibid., p. 178.
80 Ibid., p. 193.
81 C. Schumacher, *To Live and Work*, p. 153, London: Marc Europe, 1987.
82 Ibid., p. 40.
83 Pattison, *Faith of the Managers*, p. 161. See the review of Pattison in *The Independent*, 7 May 1998.
84 Pattison, *Faith of the Managers*, p. 91.
85 Ibid., p. 72.
86 J. Atherton, 'Contracting and Covenanting in an Age of Partnership and Reconciliation?' *IMA Agenda*, p. 6, March 1997.
87 Ibid., pp. 6-7.
88 Ibid., p. 7.
89 Brown, p. 27 in Brown and Sedgwick, *Putting Theology to Work*.
90 P. Bagshaw, 'The Politics of Holiness', p. 30 in Rogerson *Industrial Mission*. See also P. Bagshaw, *The Church Beyond the Church: Sheffield Industrial Mission 1944-1994*, Sheffield: Industrial Mission in South Yorkshire, 1994.

4 GLOBALIZATION

1 Michael Walzer, *Spheres of Justice*, p. 31, New York: Basic Books, 1983.
2 Ibid., p. 32.
3 Henry Sidgwick, *Elements of Politics*, p. 296, Bristol: Thoemmes, 1996 (first printed 1881).
4 Walzer, *Spheres of Justice*, p. 39.
5 Ibid., p. 39.
6 Ibid., p. 58.
7 Ibid., p. 61.
8 Ibid., p. 62.
9 Ibid., p. 106.
10 Ibid., p. 313.
11 Ibid., p. xv.
12 Ibid., p. 316.
13 J. Gray, *False Dawn: The Delusions of Global Capitalism*, p. 206, London: Granta, 206.
14 Ibid., p. 113.
15 Ibid., p. 99.
16 N. Boyle, *Who Are We Now? Christian Humanism and the Global Market from Hegel to Heaney*, p. 123, Edinburgh: T. & T. Clark, 1998.
17 Ibid., p. 78.
18 Ibid., p. 79.

19 Ibid., p. 81.

20 Ibid., p. 120.

21 *For a Future Founded on Solidarity and Justice. A Statement of the Evangelical Church in Germany and the German Bishops' Conference on the Economic and Social Situation in Germany,* p. 32, Hannover: Evangelical Church in Germany, 1997.

22 Ibid., p. 34.

23 Ibid., p. 41.

24 Ibid., p. 55.

25 Ibid., p. 57.

26 J. Sachs, 'The Limits of Convergence: Nature, Nurture and Growth' p. 21, *The Economist,* June 14 1997.

27 Ibid., p. 22.

28 Charles Elliott, *Let Justice Flow,* p. 5, London: Church House Publishing 1986.

29 Sachs, 'The Limits of Convergence', p. 24.

30 Ibid., p. 24. On the environment and global capitalism see J. Elkington, *The Green Capitalists,* London: Gollancz, 1989. See also J. Davis, *Greenery Business,* Oxford: Blackwell, 1991.

31 The wcc has published extensively on the subject of the global economy. Rob van Drimmelen, *Faith in a Global Economy,* Geneva: Risk Book Series WCC, 1998; Bas de Gaay Fortman, *God and the Goods. Global Economy in a Civilizational Perspective,* Geneva: WCC, 1998; Ulnch Duchrow, *Europe in the World System 1492–1992* Geneva: WCC, 1992; *Christian Faith and the World Economy Today,* Geneva: WCC, 1992; Christian Aid, *Who Runs the World?,* London, 1994; Michael Taylor, *Good for the Poor,* London: Mowbray, 1990; Richard Adams, *Who Profits?* Oxford: Lion, 1989. T. Gorringe, *Capital and the Kingdom,* London: Orbis/SPCK, 1994. From a different perspective, Deepak Lal, *The Poverty of Development Economics,* 2nd edition, London: Institute of Economic Affairs, 1997; Susan Strange, *The Retreat of the State: The Diffusion of Power in the World Economy,* Cambridge University Press, 1997; OECD, *Towards a New Global Age,* Pans, 1997; OECD Proceedings, *Globalization and Linkages to 2020,* Pans, 1996; Hans Küng (ed.), *Yes to a Global Ethic,* London: SCM, 1996; Hans Küng, *A Global Ethic for Global Politics and Economics,* London: SCM, 1997; J. Boswell, *Community and the Economy,* London: Routledge, 1990; Hamish McRae, *The World in 2020,* London: HarperCollins, 1995.

32 Strange, *The Retreat of the State,* p. 53.

33 Ibid., p. 65.

34 Ibid., p. 194. See also Edward Luce, 'The Age of Uncertainty' (on the global capital market), *Prospect* (July 1998); *The Retreat of*

the State, p. 58. McRae, *The World in 2020*, ch. 1 'What Makes Countries Grow'; OECD, *Globalisation and Linkages*, p. 55 on the environment. *Towards a New Global Age*, p. 31 on sustainable development.

35 Lal, *Poverty of Development Economics*, p. 95.

36 Ibid., p. 98.

37 Ibid., p. 105.

38 Van Drimmelen, *Faith in a Global Economy*, p. 17.

39 Selby, *Grace and Mortgage*, p. 85.

40 Van Drimmelen, *Faith in a Global Economy*, p. 73.

41 Selby, *Grace and Mortgage*, p. 167.

42 Van Drimmelen, *Faith in a Global Economy*, p. 115.

43 McRae, *The World in 2020*, p. 139.

44 Hans Küng, *A Global Ethic for Global Politics and Economics*, p. 231, London: SCM, 1997.

45 Ian Linden, *Liberation Theology – Coming of Age*, pp. 38–40: London: Catholic Institute for International Relations, 1997.

46 Ibid., pp. 27 and 37.

47 Reich, *Liberation Theology*, p. 307.

48 Paul Valley and Ian Linden, 'Globalization in Question', 9 and 16 August 1997, *The Tablet*. Van Drimmelen, *Faith in a Global Economy*, p. 41 on the monitoring of TNCs, London: Board for Social Responsibility, Church House Publishing 1998.

49 Work and Economy Network, *From Exclusion to Participation*, Manchester: William Temple Foundation, 1997; Christian Aid / Church Action on Poverty, *Manila to Manchester: Globalization and Local Poverty*, National Poverty Consultation, 3–4 November 1997, especially Michael Jacobs, 'Globalization Overview', London: Christian Aid, 1998; U. Düchrow, *Global Economy*, Geneva: WCC, 1987; R. Preston, 'Christian Faith and Capitalism', *Ecumenical Review* (1988), and *Religion and the Ambiguities of Capitalism*, London: SCM, 1991; P. H. Sedgwick, 'Christianity and Capitalism', *Crucible* (1991) surveys the debate.

50 C. Hird, 'The Capable State', in IDOC, vol. 29:1 January 1998 *Nation States in the Global Village*, Rome: International Documentation and Communication Centre (IDOC), 1998.

5 THE RESPONSE OF THE CHURCHES

1 Peter Sedgwick, 'Capitalism and Christianity: Responses to the US. Roman Catholic Bishops' Letter on the Economy'. *MC*, 33:3 (1991).

2 Kenneth Leech (ed.), *The Bishops and the Economy*, London: Jubilee Group, 1985.

3 *Economic Justice for All (EJFA)*, Washington DC, USA, 1986, p. ix. R. L. Stivens (ed.), *Reformed Faith and Economics*, Lanham, Maryland: University Press of America, 1989, has a chapter on *EJFA* by Carol Johnston, and its implications for reformed theology.

4 T. Sedgwick and P. Turner (eds.), *The Crisis in Moral Teaching in the Episcopal Church*, Hamsburg, USA: Morehouse Publishing, 1992, p. 152.

5 Ibid., p. 152.

6 Ibid., p. 153.

7 *EJFA*, p. IX, paragraph 13.

8 Ibid., p. IX, paragraph 14.

9 Ibid., p. X, paragraph 15.

10 Ibid., p. X, paragraph 16.

11 Ibid., p. XI, paragraph 17.

12 Ibid., p. XI, paragraph 18.

13 Ibid., p. 4, paragraph 6.

14 *Familiaris Consortio*, paragraph 46, Catholic Truth Society, London, 1981.

15 Ibid., p. 9, paragraph 18.

16 *EJFA*, p. 66, paragraph 131.

17 Ibid., p. 67, paragraph 132.

18 D. Hollenbach, 'Modern Catholic Teachings Concerning Justice', in J. C. Haughey (ed.), *The Faith that does Justice*, pp. 207–31, New York: n.p., 1977.

19 *EJFA*, p. 50, paragraph 97. *On Human Work*, 5, 6.

20 *EJFA*, p. 54, paragraph 106. *On Human Work*, 20.

21 Ibid., p. 55, paragraph 108.

22 Ibid., p. 71, paragraph 141.

23 Ibid., pp. vii–viii, paragraph 8 and 11.

24 *Gaudium et Spes (The Church in the World of Today)*, p. 71, paragraph 69, Catholic Truth Society, London 1966.

25 *EJFA*, p. 29, paragraph 52.

26 Ibid., p. 92, paragraph 185.

27 Ibid., p. 98, paragraph 200.

28 Ibid., p. 101, paragraph 207. *On Human Work* 19. *Familiaris Consortio* 23, 81.

29 Ibid., p. 88, paragraph 179.

30 A. Etzioni, *An Immodest Agenda*, New York: n.p., 1983. C. Lindblom, *Politics and Markets*, New York, 1977. D. Sturm, 'Corporations, Constitutions and Covenants', Journal of the American Academy

of Religion 41 (1973). L. Thurow, *The Zero-Sum Society*, New York: n.p., 1980.

31 *EJFA*, p. 146, paragraph 297.

32 Ibid., p. 149, paragraph 300, citing D. Byer (ed.), *Justice in the Marketplace: Collected Statements of the Vatican and the U.S. Catholic Bishops on Economic Policy 1891–1984*, Washington, DC, 1985.

33 *EJFA*, p. 151, paragraph 303. *On Human Work*, 12.

34 John F. Cronin, *Catholic Social Principles*, p. 418, Milwaukee, USA, 1950, cited in *EJFA*, p. 151, footnote 13.

35 *EJFA*, p. 152, paragraph 305.

36 Ibid., p. 153, paragraph 309.

37 Ibid., p. 157, paragraph 316.

38 Ibid., p. 159, paragraph 320. The US Catholic Bishops' Pastoral Letter, *The Challenge of Peace*, Catholic Truth Society/SPCK, 1983, p. 270.

39 *EJFA*, p. 161, paragraph 324.

40 *Libertatis Nuntius*, ch. 1, paragraph 6, Catholic Truth Society, 1984.

41 *EJFA*, pp. 121–2, paragraph 251.

42 Ibid., p. 137, paragraph 280.

43 Ibid., p. 13, paragraph 26.

44 R. Preston, 'Theology and the Economy. The Roman Catholic Bishops in the USA', *Crucible* (July 1987).

45 Published in *Crisis* (Dec., 1986). It was discussed by J. Langan, SJ, 'The Pastoral on the Economy: From Drafts to Policy', *Theological Studies*, 48:1 (March 1987), 135ff.

46 Institute of Economic Affairs, Health and Welfare Unit, London, 1991.

47 R. Niebuhr, 'Pacem in Terris', *Christianity and Crisis* (May 13 1963). Paul Ramsey, *The Just War*, p. 85, New York: Charles Scribner's Sons, 1968. See also the discussion by G. Weigel 'Pacem in Terris', in G. Weigel and R. Royal (eds.), *A Century of Catholic Social Thought*, Washington DC: Ethics and Public Policy Center, 1991.

48 Lisa S. Cahill. 'The Catholic Tradition: Religion, Morality and the Common Good', *Journal of Law and Religion*, 5 (1987), 75.

49 H. Briefs, 'The Limits of Scripture: Theological Imperatives and Economic Realities', in R. Bruce Douglas (ed.), *The Deeper Meaning of Economic Life*, p. 71, Washington DC: Georgetown University Press, 1986.

50 Langan, 'The Pastoral on the Economy', p. 153.

51 *Populorum Progressio*, Catholic Truth Society. 1967 (hereafter PP) 57.

52 Ibid., p. 52.

53 Ibid., pp. 23–34.

54 Ibid., p. 70.

55 Ibid., p. 29.
56 Ibid., p. 55.
57 Ibid., p. 59.
58 Ibid., p. 59.
59 Ibid., p. 26.
60 Ibid., p. 24.
61 Ibid., p. 47.
62 Ibid., p. 61.
63 *Sollicitudo Rei Socialis* (*SRS*) Catholic Truth Society, 1988 paragraph 12. See Paul Lakeland, 'Development and Catholic Social Teaching: Pope John Paul's New Encyclical', *The Month* 21 (June 1988), and Matthew Killimor, 'Social Doctrine', in 'Sollicitudo Rei Socialis', *The Month*, 21 (June 1988).
64 *SRS*, 14.
65 Ibid., 15.
66 Ibid., 16.
67 Ibid., 17 and 18.
68 Ibid., 19.
69 Ibid., 28.
70 Ibid., 36.
71 Ibid., 37.
72 Ibid., 38
73 Ibid., 39.
74 Ibid., 40.
75 Ibid., 41.
76 Ibid., 43.
77 Ibid., 44.
78 There is an extensive discussion of this whole body of teaching in Judith A. Dwyer (ed.), *The New Dictionary of Catholic Social Thought*, Collegeville, Minn.: Michael Glazier Book/Liturgical Press, 1994. See especially the articles on *Populorum Progressio* by Alfred Hennelly, SJ, *Sollicitudo Rei Socialis* by Jean-Yves Calvez SJ, *Signs of the Times* by Dennis McCann, *Economic Planning* by Barbara Hogan, *Capitalism* by Oliver Williams, *Economic Order* by Daniel Finn, and many others. See also P. B. Clarke and A. Linzey (ed.), *Dictionary of Ethics, Theology and Society*, London: Routledge, 1996, especially T. S. Torrance on *Capitalism*.
79 Hogan in Dwyer, *New Dictionary*, quoting G. Baum, 'Towards a Canadian Catholic Social Theory', *Cross Currents*, 35:2–3 (Summer/Fall 1985), 242–56.
80 *SRS*, 22.
81 Ibid., 22.
82 Ibid., 31.

83 G. Baum, 'Liberal Capitalism: Has John Paul II Changed His Mind?' in *Essays in Critical Theology*, Kansas City: Sheed and Ward, 1994.

84 *SRS*, 20.

85 *Centesimus Annus (CA)* paragraph 34, Catholic Truth Society, 1991.

86 Ibid., paragraph 24.

87 Ibid., paragraph 30.

88 Ibid., paragraph 33.

89 *Gaudium et Spes*, 69.

90 Ibid., 71. Quoted in *CA*, paragraph 31.

91 *CA*, paragraph 31.

92 Ibid.

93 Ibid., paragraph 32. See *SRS*, 15.

94 *CA*, paragraph 32.

95 Ibid., paragraph 31.

96 Ibid., paragraph 33.

97 Ibid., paragraph 33.

98 Ibid., paragraph 33.

99 Ibid., paragraph 35.

100 Ibid., paragraph 35.

101 The debate is found in *Theology*, 95:768 (November/December 1992) and 96:769 (January/February 1993); R. H. Preston 'Centesimus Annus: An Appraisal', (November/December 1992), 405–16; Stanley Hauerwas, 'In Praise of Centesimus Annus', (November/December 1992) 416–32 (and the Editorial by Ann Loades on pp. 403–4); Michael Northcott, 'Preston and Hauerwas on Centesimus Annus: Reflections on the Incommensurability of the Liberal and Post-Liberal Mind', (January/February 1993), 27–36. See also John Morgan, 'Centesimus Annus', *Crucible* (October/December 1991).

102 Preston, 'Centesimus Annus', p. 412.

103 *CA*, paragraph 48 (Preston lists it as paragraph 46).

104 Preston, 'Centesimus Annus', p. 413.

105 *CA*, paragraph 47.

106 Ibid., paragraph 59.

107 There is a brief reference to sin in paragraph 25, and to structural sin on paragraph 38.

108 Hauerwas, 'In Praise of Centesimus Annus', p. 417. *CA*, paragraph 43.

109 Hauerwas, 'In Praise of Centesimus Annus', p. 429. *CA*, paragraph 54.

110 Hauerwas,'In Praise of Centesimus Annus', p. 427. J. Milbank,

Theology and Social Theory: Beyond Secular Reason, London: Black-wells, 1990.

111 Hauerwas, 'In Praise of Centesimus Annus', p. 417.
112 *CA*, paragraph 39.
113 Ibid., paragraph 31.
114 Ibid., paragraph 43.
115 Hauerwas, 'In Praise of Centesimus Annus', p. 425.
116 *CA*, paragraph 36.
117 Hauerwas, 'In Praise of Centesimus Annus', p. 426.
118 Northcott, 'Preston and Hauerwas on Centesimus Annus', p. 29.
119 Ibid.
120 Ibid., p. 32.
121 Max Stackhouse, *Public Theology and Political Economy*, Michigan: Eerdmans, 1987. Stephen Clark, *Civil Peace and Sacred Order: Limits and Renewals*, Oxford University Press, 1989. Leslie Newbigin, *Foolishness to the Greeks*, London: British Council of Churches, 1986.
122 Stackhouse, *Public Theology*, p. 166 quoted in Northcott, 'Preston and Hauerwas on Centesimus Annus', p. 33.
123 Morgan, 'Centesimus Annus', p. 197.
124 Ibid., p. 198.
125 *CA*, paragraph 39.
126 Ibid., paragraph 29.
127 *Rerum Novarum*, paragraph 29. Hauerwas quotes it with approval in 'In Praise of Centesimus Annus', p. 422.

Select bibliography

Adams, R. *Who Profits?*, Oxford: Lion, 1989.

Adams, R. N., *Energy and Structure*, Austin: University of Texas, 1975.

Adams, N., 'Eschatology and Habermas' Ideal Speech Situation' *Modern Believing*, 37:2 (April 1996).

Adonis, A., "Tomorrow's Money Today', in *The State We're In. The Shape We Could Become*, Banhim Seminars 1995–6, Basingstoke, 1996.

Adorno, T., 'Veblen's Attack on Culture', in J. Cunningham (ed.), *T. Veblen: Critical Assessments*, 3 vols., London: n.p., 1993.

Aquinas, Thomas, *Summa Theologica*, II–II q. 182 a 1.

Atherton, J., *Faith in the Nation*, London: SPCK, 1988.

Christianity and the Market, London: SPCK, 1992.

Social Christianity, London: SPCK, 1995.

'Contracting and Covenanting in an Age of Partnership and Reconciliation', *IMA Agenda*, March 1997.

Bagshaw, P., 'The Politics of Holiness,' in J. W. Rogerson (ed.), *The Church Beyond the Church: Sheffield Industrial Mission 1944–1994*, Sheffield: Industrial Mission in South Yorkshire, 1994.

Ballard, P., *In and Out of Work: A Pastoral Perspective*, Edinburgh: St Andrews Press, 1987.

Barry, B. and Hardin, R. (eds.) *Rational Man and Irrational Society*, Berkeley: Sage Publications, 1982.

Barth, K. *Church Dogmatics III/4*, Edinburgh: T. & T. Clark, 1961.

Baudrillard, J. *Selected Writings*, Cambridge: Polity Press, 1988.

Baum, G., *Essays in Critical Theology*, Kansas City: Sheed and Ward, 1994.

Bellah, R. N., *The Broken Covenant: American Civil Religion in the Time of Trial*, University of Chicago Press, 1992.

Benson, J., *The Rise of Consumer Society in Britain 1880–1980*, London: Longman, 1994.

Berthoud, R. and Kempson, E., *Credit and Debt: The P. S. I. Report*, London: Policy Studies Institutes 1992.

Biggar, N., *Good Life*, London: SPCK, 1997.

Bloom, H. and Trilling, L. (eds.), *Romantic Poetry and Prose*, New York: Oxford University Press, 1973.

Blount, G., 'Sketching the Problem and Assessing Responses', in A. Morton, (ed.), *Domestic Debt*, Edinburgh: Centre for Theology and Public Issues, 1996.

Bocock, R., *Consumption*, London: Routledge, 1993.

Bonhoeffer, D., *Ethics*, London: SMC, 1978.

Borrowdale, A., *A Woman's Work*, London: SCPK, 1989.

Boswell, J., *Community and the Economy*, London: Routledge, 1990.

Boyle, N., *Who Are We Now? Christian Humanism and the Global Market from Hegel to Heaney*, Edinburgh: T. & T. Clark, 1998.

Braverman, H., *Labour and Monopoly Capital*, New York: Monthly Review Press, 1971.

Brecher, B., *Getting What You Want?*, London: Routledge, 1998.

Briefs, H., 'The Limits of Scripture: Theological Imperatives and Economic Realities', in B. Douglas (ed.), *The Deeper Meaning of Economic Life*, Washington: Georgetown University Press, 1986.

British Council of Churches, *The Consumer Goods Society*, London: 1978.

Brown, M. and Sedgwick, P. (eds.), *Putting Theology to Work*, London: Council of Churches for Britain and Ireland, 1998.

Browning, D. S. and Fiorenza, F. (eds.), *Habermas, Modernity and Public Theology*, New York: Crossroads, 1992.

Brubacker, R., *The Limits of Rationality: An Essay on the Social and Moral Thought of Max Weber*, London: George Allen and Unwin, 1984.

Brunner, E., *Das Gebot und die Ordnungen*, Tubingen: Verlag van J. C. B. Mohr, 1932.

Der Kapitalismus als Problem der Kirche, Zurich: Zwingli-Verlag, 1945.

Brunner, J., Jolly, A. and Sylva, K. (eds.), *Play: Its Role in Development and Evolution*, New York: Basic Books, 1976.

Buddle, M., *The (Magic) Kingdom of God*, Boulder, Colo.: Westview, 1997.

Byer, D. (ed.), *Justice in the Marketplace: Collected Statements of the Vatican and US. Catholic Bishops on Economic Policy 1891–1984*, Washington DC: n.p., 1985.

Campbell, C., *The Romantic Ethic and the Spirit of Modern Consumerism*, Oxford: Blackwell, 1987.

Carter, G., van Eyden, R., van Hoogstraten, H. D. and Wiersma, J. (eds.), *Bonhoeffers' Ethics: Old Europe and New Frontiers*, Kampen, The Netherlands: Kok Pharos, 1991.

Chapman, R. and Rutherford, T. (eds.), *Male Order*, London: Lawrence and Wishart, 1988.

Cherrington, D., *The Work Ethics: Working Values and Values that Work*, New York: Amacom, 1980.

Christian Aid, *Who Runs the World?*, London, 1994.

Clapp, R., *The Consuming Passion: Christianity and the Consumer Culture*, Illinois: Inter Varsity Press, 1998.

Clark, J. C. D., Review of Paul Marshall, *Studies in Christian Ethics*, vol. II:1, 1998.

Cohen, D., *The Wealth of the World and the Poverty of Nations*, Boston: MIT Press, 1998.

Coyle, D., 'On the Force Behind Rising Inequality', *The Independent*, 21 May 1998.

Crane, R. S., *The Idea of the Humanities and Other Essays Critical and Historical*, University of Chicago Press, 1967.

Cronin, J., *Catholic Social Principles*, Milwaukee: n.p., 1950.

Csikzsentmihaly, M., 'The Americanization of Rock-Climbing', in J. Bruner, A. Jolly and K. Sylva (eds.), *Play: Its Role in Development and Evolution*, New York: Basic Books, 1976.

Cunningham, J. (ed.), *T. Veblen: Critical Assessments*, 3 vols., London: n.p., 1993.

Dahrendorf, R., 'Changing Social Values under Mrs Thatcher', in R. Skidelsky (ed.), *Thatcherism*, Oxford: Blackwell, 1988.

Davies, C., *Religion and the Making of Society*, Cambridge University Press, 1994.

Davies, H. and Gosling, D., *Will the Future Work?*, Geneva: World Council of Churches, 1986.

Davis, J., *Greening Business*, Oxford: Blackwell, 1991.

Deidun, T., *New Covenant Morality in Paul*, Rome: Biblical Institute Press, 1981.

Demant, V. A., *Religion and the Decline of Capitalism*, London: Faber and Faber, 1952.

Diggins, J. P., *The Bard of Savagery. T. Veblen and Modern Social Theory*, Brighton: Harvester Press, 1978.

Douglas, B. (ed.), *The Deeper Meaning of Economic Life*, Washington: Georgetown University Press, 1986.

Douglas, M. and Isherwood, B., *The World of Goods: Towards an Anthropology of Consumption*, London: Allen Lane, 1979.

Downs, Anthony, *An Economic Theory of Democracy*, New York: Harper and Row, 1957.

Düchrow, U., *Global Economy*, Geneva: World Council of Churches, 1987.

Dwyer, Judith, *The New Dictionary of Catholic Social Thought*, Collegeville, Minn.: Michael Glazier Book / Liturgical Press, 1994.

Earl, P., *Lifestyle Economics: Consumer Behavior in a Turbulent World*, Brighton: Wheatsheaf, 1986.

Economic Justice for All, Washington DC: US. Catholic Bishops' Conference, 1986.

Edelheit, J. A., *The Life of Covenant: The Challenge of Contemporary Judaism*, Chicago: SCJ. Press, 1996.

Elkington, J., *The Green Capitalists*, London: Gollancz, 1989.

Elliott, C., *Let Justice Flow*, London: Church House Publishing, 1986.

Elster, J., *Ulysses and the Sirens*, Cambridge University Press, 1979.

Faith in a Global Economy, London: Church House, Board for Social Responsibility, 1998.

Featherstone, M., 'The body in consumer politics', in M. Featherstone, M. Hepworth and B. Turner (eds.), *The Body: Social Process and Cultural Identity*, London: Sage, 1991.

Fiorenza, F. S., 'The Church as a Community of Interpretation', in D. S. Browning and F. Fiorenza (eds.), *Familiaris Consortio*, London: Catholic Truth Society, 1981.

Fiske, J., *Reading the Popular*, Boston: Unwin Hyman, 1989.

For a Future Founded on Solidarity and Justice: A Statement of the Evangelical Church in Germany and The German Bishops' Conference on the Economic and Social Situation in Germany, Hannover: Evangelical Church in Germany, 1997.

Ford, D. F., *The Shape of Living*, London: Collins, 1997.

Ford, D. F. and Stamps, D., *The Essentials of Christian Community*, Edinburgh: T. & T. Clark, 1996.

Forester, J. (ed.), *Critical Theory and Public Life*, Cambridge, Mass.: MIT Press, 1985.

Forrester, D., *Christian Justice and Public Policy*, Cambridge University Press, 1997.

Foundations, 1:3 (July 1998).

Frisby, D., *Georg Simmel*, London: n.p., 1984.

Fryer, D., 'Employment, Deprivation and Personal Agency During Unemployment', *Social Behaviour* (1986).

Furnham, A., 'The Protestant Work Ethic and Attitudes to Unemployment', *Journal of Occupational Psychology*, 55 (1982).
    The Protestant Work Ethic: the Psychology of Work-Related Beliefs and Behaviours, London: Routledge, 1990.

Galbraith, J. K., *The New Industrial State*, New York: Houghton Mifflin, 1967.
    Money – Whence it Came, Where it Went, London: n.p., 1975.
    The Affluent Society, London: Penguin, 1987.

Gamble, B., *Britain in Decline*, London: Macmillan, 1994.

Gaudium et Spes, London: Catholic Truth Society, 1963.

Gerth, H. and Wright Mills, C. (ed.), *From Max Weber*, New York: Oxford University Press, 1962.

Giddens, A., *Modernity and Self Identity; Self and Society in the Late Modern Age*, Cambridge: Polity Press, 1991.

Gilbreath, W., 'J. K. Galbraith's Ethic of Affluence', *Crux*, 24:2 (June 1988).

Gilligan, C., *In a Different Voice: Psychological Theory and Women's Development*, Cambridge, Mass.: Harvard University Press, 1982.

Goldthorpe, J., *The Affluent Worker in the Class Structure*, 3 vols., Cambridge University Press, 1968–9.

Gonzalez, J., *Faith and Wealth*, London: Harper and Row, 1990.

Gorringe, T., *Capital and the Kingdom*, London: Orbis / SPCK, 1994.

Gower, J. (ed.), *Religion and Economic Ethics*, vol. 31, Lanham, USA: College Theological Society, 1988.

Gray, J., *Enlightenment's Wake*, London: Routledge, 1996.
  False Dawn. The Delusions of Global Capitalism, London: Granta, 1998.
  Endgames: Questions in Late Modern Political Thought, Cambridge: Polity Press, 1996.

Grean, S., *Shaftesbury's Philosophy of Religion and Ethics: A Study in Enthusiasm*, Athens, Ohio: Ohio University Press, 1967.

Grenholm, C.-H., *Protestant Work Ethics*, Uppsala: Uppsala Studies in Social Ethics 15, 1993.

Griffiths, B., *Morality and the Market Place*, London: Hodder and Stoughton, 1982.
  The Creation of Wealth, London: Hodder and Stoughton, 1984.

Habermas, J., *Legitimation Crisis*, Boston: Beacon Press, 1975.
  The Theory of Communicative Action, 2 vols.; Boston: Beacon Press, 1984 and 1987.
  Die Neue Unubersichtlich Kert: Kleine Politisch Schiften V, Frankfurt: Suhrkamp, 1985.
  'Modernity versus Postmodernity', *New German Critique*, 22 (Winter 1981).
  'Reply to My Critics', in J. Thompson and D. Held (eds.), *Habermas: Critical Debates*, Cambridge, Mass.: MIT Press, 1982.
  'Modern and Postmodern Architecture', in J.n Forester (ed.), *Critical Theory and Public Life*, Cambridge, Mass.: MIT Press, 1985.
  'Transcendence from Within, Transcendence in this World', in D. S. Browning and F. Fiorenza (eds.), *Habermas, Modernity and Public Theology,* New York.

Habermas, J. and Döbert, D. R. (eds.), *Die Entwicklung des Ichs*, Cologne: Keizenheimer, 1977.

Hallin, D., 'The American News Media: A Critical Theory Perspective', in J. Forester (ed.), *Critical Theory and Public Life*, Cambridge, Mass.: MIT Press, 1985.

Halpern, D., Wood, S., White, S. and Cameron, G. (eds.), *Options for Britain*, Aldershot: Dartmouth, 1996.

Halsey, A., *Change in British Society*, Oxford University Press, 1995.

Halsey, M., *Invisible Hands*, Manchester: William Temple Foundation, 1996; occasional Paper no. 22.

Halsey, M. and Graham, E., *Life Cycles*, London: SPCK, 1993.

Handy, C., *The Future of Work*, Worcester: Belling and Sons, 1985.

Hardy, D. W., *God's Way with the World*, Edinburgh: T. & T. Clark, 1996.

'A Magnificent Complexity', in D. F. Ford and D. Stamps (eds.), *The Essentials of Christian Community*, Edinburgh: T. & T. Clark, 1996.

Harrns, A. C., 'Veblen as Social Philosopher' in J. Cunningham (ed.), *T. Veblen: Critical Assessment*, 3 vols., London: n.p., 1993.

Hauerwas, S., 'In Praise of Centesimus Annus', *Theology* (November 1992).

Heilbroner, R., *The Nature and Logic of Capitalism*, New York: Norton Press, 1985.

Hennelly, A. (ed.), *Liberation Theology: A Documentary History*, Maryknoll: Orbis, 1990.

Hilton, B., *The Age of Atonement*, Oxford: Clarendon Press, 1988.

Hird, C., 'The Capable State', in *Nation States in The Global Village*, 29:1, Rome: IDOC, January 1998.

Hoffman, W. and Wyly, T. (ed.), *The Work Ethic in Business*, Cambridge, Mass.: OGH Publishers, 1979.

Hollenbach, D., 'Modern Catholic Teachings Concerning Justice', in J. C. Haughey (ed.), *The Faith That Does Justice*, New York: n.p., 1977.

Horne, J., *Work and Unemployment*, London: Longman, 1987.

Horowitz, D., *The Morality of Spending: Attitudes Towards the Consumer in America 1875–1940*, Baltimore: Johns Hopkins University Press, 1985.

Hull, J., 'Christian Education in a Capitalist Society: Money and God', in D. F. Ford and D. Stamps (ed.), *The Essentials of Christian Community*, Edinburgh: T. & T. Clark, 1996.

Hutton, W., *The State We're In*, London: Vintage, 1996.

Ingelhart, R., *Culture Shift in Advanced Industrial Society*, Princeton University Press, 1990.

Ingram, D., *Habermas and the Dialectic of Reason*, New Haven: Yale University Press, 1987.

Jacobs, M., 'Globalization Overview', in Christian Aid / Church

Action on Poverty *Manila to Manchester: Globalization and Local Poverty*, London: Christian Aid, 1998.

Jahoda, M., *Employment and Unemployment: A Social – Psychological Analysis*, Cambridge University Press, 1982.

Jenkins, D., *God, Politics and the Future*, London: SCM, 1988.

Jenner, B., *The Coal Strike*, Sheffield: New City, 1986.

Joyce, P., (ed.), *The Historical Meanings of Work*, Cambridge University Press, 1987.

Kane, Margaret, *Theology in an Industrial Society*, London: SCM, 1975.
   Gospel in an Industrial Society, London: SCM, 1980.
   What Kind of God?, London: SCM, 1986.

Katzell, R., 'Changing Attitudes to Work', in C. Kerr and J. Rosow (eds.), *Work in America*, New York: Van Nostrand, 1979.

Kavanagh, J. F., *Following Christ in a Consumer Society*, New York: n.p., 1981.

Keiser, J., *Men at Work*, London: Epworth Press, 1978.

Kerr, C. and Rosow, J. (eds.), *Work in America: The Decade Ahead*, New York: Van Nostrand, 1979.

Killimor, M., 'Social Doctrine', in 'Sollicitudo Rei Socialis', *The Month*, 21 (June 1988).

Küng, H., *A Global Ethic for Global Politics and Economics*, London: SCM, 1997.

Küng, H. (ed.), *Yes to a Gobal Ethic*, London: SCM, 1996.

La Burge, J., 'Economic Systems and the Sacramental Imagination', in J. Gower (ed.), *Religion and Economic Ethics*, vol. 31, Lanham USA: College Theological Society, 1988.

Laborens Exercens (On Human Work), London: Catholic Truth Society, 1982.

Lacan, J., *Ecrits: A Selection*, London: Tavistock Press, 1977.

Lage, D., *Martin Luther's Christology and Ethics*, Lampeter: Edwin Mellen Press, 1990.

Lakeland, P., 'Development and Catholic Social Teaching: Pope John Paul's New Encyclical', *The Month*, 21 (June 1988).

Lange, F. de, 'The Christian Humanism', in G. Carter, R. van Eyden, H. D. van Huogstraten and J. Wiersma (eds.), *Bonhoeffers' Ethics: Old Europe and New Frontiers*, Kampen, The Netherlands: Kok Pharos, 1991.

Lal, D., *The Poverty of Development Economics*, 2nd edition, London: Institute of Economic Affairs, 1997.

Lancaster, K., *Modern Consumer Theory*, Aldershot: Edward Elgar, 1991.

Lane, R., *The Market Experience*, Cambridge University Press, 1991.

Langan, J., 'The Pastoral on the Economy', from 'Drafts to Policy', *Theological Studies*, 48:1 (March 1987).

Langholm, O., *Economics in the Medieval Schools*, Leiden: E. Brill, 1992.

Lasch, C., *The Culture of Narcissism: American Life in an Age of Diminishing Expectations*, New York: Norton, 1978.

The Minimal Self, London: Pan, 1984.

The True and Only Heaven, New York: Norton, 1991.

Laurence Moore, R., *Selling God*, Oxford University Press, 1994.

Leadbeater, C. and Lloyd, J., *In Search of Work*, London: Penguin, 1987.

Leathers, G., 'Veblen's Ambivalent View of Christianity', in J. Cunningham (ed.), *T. Veblen: Critical Assessment*, 3 vols., London: n.p., 1993.

Lee, M., *Consumer Culture Reborn: The Cultural Politics of Consumption*, London: Routledge, 1993.

Leech, K., *Struggle in Babylon*, London: SCM, 1988.

Leech, K., *The Sky is Red*, London: DLT, 1997.

Leech, K. (ed.), *The Bishops and the Economy*, London: Jubilee Group, 1985.

Lessnoff, M., *The Spirit of Capitalism and the Protestant Ethic*, Aldershot: Edward Elgar, 1994.

Levacic, R. and Rebmann, A., *Macroeconomics*, London: Macmillan, 1982.

Levine, D. (ed.), *On Individuality and Social Form*, University of Chicago Press, 1971.

Levine, E., *Wealth and Freedom: An Introduction to Political Economy*, Cambridge University Press, 1995.

Libertatis Nuntius, London: Catholic Truth Society, 1984.

'Liberty and Justice for All', Lay Commission on Catholic Social Teachery and the US. Economy, *Crisis* (December 1986).

Linden, I., *Liberation Theology – Coming of Age?*, London: Catholic Institute for International Relations, 1997.

Linden, I. and Vallely, P., 'Globalization in Question', *The Tablet*, (9/16 August 1997).

Loades, A., 'A Feminist Perspective on the Morality of the New Right', in M. Northcott (ed.), *Vision and Prophecy*, Edinburgh: Centre for Theology and Public Issues, 1991.

Luce, E., 'The Age of Uncertainty', *Prospect*, (July 1998).

Lunt, P. and Livingstone, S., *Mass Consumption and Personal Identity*, Buckingham: Open University Press, 1992.

Luther, M., *The German Catechism*, (1529) WA 30:1, 183.

Commentary on Galatians, (1535) WA 40:1, 174.

On Good Works, (1520) WA 6, 270.

Maccoby, M. and Terzi, R., 'What Happened to the Work Ethic?', W. Hoffman and T. Wyly (eds.), *The Work Ethic in Business*, Cambridge, Mass.: OGH Publishers, 1979.

MacPherson, C. B., *The Political Theory of Possessive Individualism: Hobbes to Locke*, Oxford University Press, 1962.

MacPherson, C. B. (ed.), *Democratic Theory: Essays in Retrieval*, Oxford University Press, 1973.

Marsh, B., *Reclaiming Dietrich Bonhoeffer: The Promise of His Theology*, Oxford University Press, 1994.

Marshal, A., *Principles of Economics*, London: Macmillan, 1930.

Marshall, B., 'Meeks and Novak on Theology and Economics', *MC*, 34:2 (1992).

Marshall, G., *In Search of the Spirit of Capitalism*, Aldershot: Gregg Revivals, 1993.

Marshall, P., *A Kind of Life Imposed on Man: Vocation and Social Order from Tyndale to Locke*, University of Toronto Press, 1996.

Marx, K., *Capital*, in L. S. Feuer (ed.), *Marx and Engels: Basic Writing on Politics and Philosophy*, London: Fontana Library, 1969 (first printed New York: Anchor Books, Doubleday and Company, 1959).

McCloskey, C., 'The Rhetoric of Economic Expertise', in R. H. Roberts and J. M. M. Good (ed.), *The Recovery of Rhetoric*, Bristol: Bristol Classical Press, 1993.

'The Rhetoric of Economics', in D. Hausman (ed.), *The Philosophy of Economics*, Cambridge University Press, 1995.

McFadyen, A., *The Call to Personhood*, Cambridge University Press, 1990.

McGrath, J. and Kelly, J., *Time and Human Interaction: Towards a Social Psychology of Time*, New York: Guildford Press, 1986.

McKendrick, N. Brewer, J. and Plumb, J. H., *The Birth of a Consumer Society: The Commercialisation of Eighteenth-Century England*, Bloomington, Indiana University Press, 1982.

McRae, H., *The World in 2020*, London: HarperCollins, 1995.

Meeks, D., *God the Economist: The Doctrine of God and Political Economy*, Minneapolis: Fortress Press, 1989.

Michelman, I., *The Moral Limitations of Capitalism*, Aldershot: Avebury, 1994.

Mill, J. S., *Utilitarianism*, London: J. M. Dent, 1972.

Modras, R., 'Karl Rahner and John Paul II: Anthropological Implications for Economics and the Social Order', in J. Gower (ed.), *Religion and Economic Ethics*, vol. 31, Lanham, USA: College Theological Society, 1988.

Morgan, J., 'Centesimus Annus', *Crucible* (October 1997).

Mort, F., 'Boy's Own? Masculinity, Style and Popular Culture', in R. Chapman and J. Rutherford (eds.), *Male Order*, London: Lawrence and Wishart, 1988.

Morton, A. (ed.), *Domestic Debt: Disease of Consumer Society?*, Edinburgh: Centre for Theology and Public Issues, 1996.

Nelson, R. H., *Reaching for Heaven on Earth: The Theological Meaning of Economics*, Maryland: Rowman and Littlefield, 1981.

Nicholls, D., *Deity and Domination*, London: Routledge, 1989.

Niebuhr, R., 'Pacem in Terris', *Christianity and Crisis* (13 May 1963).

Northcott, M., 'Preston and Hauerwas on Centesimus Annus: Reflections on the Incommensurability of the Liberal and Post-Liberal Mind', *Theology* (January 1993).

Northcott, M. (ed.), *Vision and Prophecy: The Tasks of Social Theology Today*, Edinburgh: Centre for Theology and Public Issues, 1991.

Urban Theology: A Reader, London: Cassell, 1998.

Norwegian Bishops' Conference, *The Consumer Society As An Ethical Challenge*, Oslo: Church of Norway Information Service, 1993.

Novak, M., *The Spirit of Democratic Capitalism*, London: Institute of Economic Affairs, Health and Welfare Unit, 1991.

Oates, W., *Confessions of a Workaholic*, New York: World Publishing Company, 1971.

OECD, *Globalization and Linkages to 2020*, Paris:, 1996.

Towards a New Global Age, Paris: 1997.

Offe, C., *Disorganized Capitalism: Contemporary Transformation of Work and Politics*, Cambridge, Mass.: MIT Press, 1985.

Olsen, M., *The Logic of Collective Action*, Cambridge, Mass.: Harvard University Press, 1971.

Oppenheimer, P., *An Intelligent Person's Guide to Modern Guilt*, London: Duckworth, 1997.

Ormiston, H. and Ross, D. (eds.), *New Patterns of Work*, Edinburgh: St Andrews Press, 1990.

Ott, H., *Reality and Faith*, London: Lutterworth Press, 1971.

Owensby, W., *Economics for Prophets*, Michigan: Eerdmans, 1988.

Parker, S., *Leisure and Work*, London: George Allen and Unwin, 1983.

Pattison, S., *The Faith of the Managers*, London: Cassell, 1997.

Peck, W. J. (ed.), *New Studies in Bonhoeffer's Ethics*, Toronto Studies in Theology, vol. 30:3, New York: Eerdmans, 1987.

Populorum Progressio, London: Catholic Truth Society, 1987.

Preston, R. H., *Perspective on Strikes*, London: SCM, 1975.

Church and Society in the Late Twentieth Century, London: SCM, 1981.

Religion and the Ambiguities of Capitalism, London: SCM, 1991.

'Theology and the Economy – The Roman Catholic Bishops in the USA', *Crucible* (July 1987).

'Centesimus Annus: An Appraisal', *Theology* (November 1988).

'Christian Faith and Capitalism', *Ecumenical Review*, 1988.

Ramsey, P., *The Just War*, New York: Charles Scribner's Sons, 1968.

Rasmussen, L., 'Bonhoeffer: Reality and Resistance', in G. Carter, R. van Eyden, H. D. Hoogstraten and J. Wiersma (eds.),

Bonhoeffer's Ethics: Old Europe and New Frontiers, Kampen, The Netherlands: Kok Pharos, 1991.

Rawls, J., 'The Ideal of an Overlapping Consensus', *Oxford Journal of Legal Studies*, 7, 1987.

Reich, R., *The Work of Nations*, New York: A. Knopf, 1991.

Rendtorff, T., *Ethics*, 2 vols., Minneapolis: Fortress Press, 1989.

Richardson, A., *The Biblical Doctrine of Work*, London: SCM, 1952.

Roberts, R. H., 'Rhetoric and the Resurgence of Capitalism', in R. H. Roberts and J. M. M. Good (eds.), *The Recovery of Rhetoric*, Bristol: Bristol Classical Press, 1993.

Robinson, F. (ed.), *Post-Industrial Tyneside*, Newcastle, UK: University of Newcastle, 1990.

Rogerson, J. W. (ed.), *Industrial Mission in a Changing World*, Sheffield Academic Press, 1996.

Sachs, J., 'The Limits of Convergence: Nature, Nurture and Growth', *The Economist*, 14 June 1997.

Schultz, T. W., *Investment in Human Capital*, New York: Free Press, 1971.

Schultz, T. W. (ed.), *Economics of the Family*, University of Chicago Press, 1974.

Schumacher, C., *To Love and Work*, London: Marc Europe, 1987.

Schwöbel, C., *God: Action and Revelation*, Kampen, The Netherlands: Kok Pharos, 1992.

Sedgwick, P. H., *The Enterprise Culture*, London: SPCK, 1992.

Sedgwick, P. H. (ed.), *God in the City*, London: Mowbrays, 1995.

Sedgwick, P. H., 'The Compulsion to be Good: Aquinas on the Formation of Human Character', *Theology*, 91:741 (May 1988).

'Christianity and Capitalism', *Crucible* (1991).

'Capitalism and Christianity: Responses to the US. Roman Catholic Bishops' Letter on the Economy', *MC*, 33:3 (1991).

'Wealth Creation in the Early Church', *Epworth Review*, 20:1 (1993).

'Review of Odd Langholm "Economics in the Medieval Schools"', *Studies in Christian Ethics*, 9:1 (1996).

Christian Teaching on Work and the Economy', in *Unemployment and the Future of Work*, London: Council of Churches for Britain and Ireland,, 1997, pp. 219–29.

Selby, P., *Grace and Mortgage*, London: DLT, 1997.

Shamass, C., *The Pre-Industrial Consumer in England and America*, Oxford: Clarendon Press, 1990.

Sidgwick, H., *Elements of Politics*, Bristol: Thoemmes 1996 (first printed 1881).

Siebert, R. J., *The Central Theory of Religion: The Frankfurt School*, Berlin: Mouton, 1985.

Simmel, G., 'The Metropolis and Mental Life', in D. Levine (ed.), *On Individualtity and Social Form*, University of Chicago Press, 1971.

Skidelsky, R. (ed.), *Thatcherism*, Oxford: Blackwell, 1988.

Smith, A., *The Wealth of Nations*, New York: Random House, 1937 (originally printed 1776).

Smith, T., *The Role of Ethics in Social Theory – Essays from a Habermasian Perspective*, Albany: State University of New York Press, 1991.

Sollicitudo Rei Socialis, London: Catholic Truth Society, 1988.

Sombart, W., *Der Moderne Kapitalismus*, 2 vols., Leipzig: Duncker und Humblot, 1902.

Something to Celebrate, London: Church House Publishing, 1995.

Stivens, R. L. (ed.), *Reformed Faith and Economics*, Lanham, Md.: University Press of America, 1989.

Stokes, A., *Working with God*, London: Mowbrays, 1992.

Strain, C. R. (ed.), *Prophetic Visions and Economic Realities*, Michigan: Eerdmans, 1989.

Strange, S., *The Retreat of the State: The Diffusion of Power in the World Economy*, Cambridge University Press, 1997.

Stubley, P. D., *A House Divided: Evangelicals and the Establishment in Hull*, University of Hull Press, 1995.

'Globalization and the Social Elite', *Crucible* (October 1998).

Tallon, A., 'Affectivity and Praxis in Lonergan Rahner and Others in the Heart Tradition', in J. Gower (ed.), *Religion and Economic Ethics*, vol. 31, Lanham, USA: College Theological Society, 1988.

Tawney, R., *The Acquisitive Society*, New York: Harcourt Brace, 1920.

Tilman, R., *T. Veblen and His Critics*, Princeton University Press, 1992.

Tracy, D., 'Theology, Critical Social Theory and the Public Realm', in D. S. Browning and F. Fiorenza (eds.), *Habermas, Modernity and Public Theology*, New York: Crossroads, 1992.

Unemployment and the Future of Work, London: Council of Churches for Britain and Ireland, 1997.

Urry, J., *Consuming Places*, London: Routledge, 1994.

Van Drimmelen, R., *Faith in a Global Economy*, Geneva: Risk WCC, 1998.

Veblen, T., *The Theory of the Leisure Class: An Economic Study of Institutions*, London: Allen and Unwin, 1925.

Volf, M., *Work in the Spirit*, Oxford University Press, 1991.

Walzer, M., *Spheres of Justice*, New York: Basic Books, 1983.

Waterman, A. M. C., *Revolution, Economics and Religion: Christian Political Economy 1798–1833*, Cambridge University Press, 1991.

Weber, M., *The Sociology of Religion*, London: Methuen, 1965.

Economics and Society, Berkeley: University of California Press, 1978.

The Protestant Ethic and the Spirit of Capitalism, London: Allen and Unwin, 1985.

Weigel, G., 'Pacem in Terris', in G. Weigel and R. Royal (eds.), *A Century of Catholic Social Thought*, Washington DC: n.p., 1991.

West, C. C., 'Ground Under Our Feet', in W. J. Peck (ed.), *New Studies in Bonhoeffer's Ethics*, Toronto Studies in Theology, vol. 30:3, New York: Eerdmans, 1987.

White, S. K., *The Recent Work of Jürgen Habermas*, Cambridge University Press, 1988.

Williams, R., *Culture and Society*, London: Hogarth Press, 1990.

Willis, J., *Common Culture: Symbolic Work at Play in the Everyday Cultures of the Young*, Buckingham: Open University Press, 1990.

Work and Economy Network, *From Exclusion to Participation*, Manchester: William Temple Foundation, 1997.

Wright, N. T., *Climax of the Covenant: Christ and the Law in Pauline Theology*, Edinburgh: T. & T. Clark, 1991.

Yankevolich, D. and Immerwahr, J., 'Putting the Work Ethic to Work', *Society* (January 1984).

Index of names and subjects

Index of biblical references